AUDIO PRODUCTION
AND
POSTPRODUCTION

Woody Woodhall, CAS

JONES & BARTLETT
LEARNING

World Headquarters

Jones & Bartlett Learning
40 Tall Pine Drive
Sudbury, MA 01776
978-443-5000
info@jblearning.com
www.jblearning.com

Jones & Bartlett Learning Canada
6339 Ormindale Way
Mississauga, Ontario L5V 1J2
Canada

Jones & Bartlett Learning International
Barb House, Barb Mews
London W6 7PA
United Kingdom

Jones & Bartlett Learning books and products are available through most bookstores and online booksellers. To contact Jones & Bartlett Learning directly, call 800-832-0034, fax 978-443-8000, or visit our website, www.jblearning.com.

Substantial discounts on bulk quantities of Jones & Bartlett Learning publications are available to corporations, professional associations, and other qualified organizations. For details and specific discount information, contact the special sales department at Jones & Bartlett Learning via the above contact information or send an email to specialsales@jblearning.com.

Production Credits

Publisher: David Pallai
Acquisitions Editor: Timothy McEvoy
Editorial Assistant: Molly Whitman
Production Director: Amy Rose
Senior Production Editor: Katherine Crighton
Senior Marketing Manager: Andrea DeFronzo
Associate Marketing Manager: Lindsay Ruggiero
V.P., Manufacturing and Inventory Control: Therese Connell
Composition: diacriTech
Cover Design: Scott Moden
Cover and Title Page Image: © Gangster/ShutterStock, Inc.
Printing and Binding: Malloy, Inc.
Cover Printing: Malloy, Inc.

Library of Congress Cataloging-in-Publication Data
Woodhall, Woody.
    Audio production and postproduction / Woody Woodhall.
      p. cm.
    ISBN-13: 978-0-7637-9071-4 (pbk.)
    ISBN-10: 0-7637-9071-0 (ibid.)
    1. Sound—Recording and reproducing.   2. Motion pictures—Sound effects.   3. Sound in motion pictures.   I. Title.
    TK7881.4.W66 2010
    778.5'344—dc22
                                                                    2010019454

6048

Printed in the United States of America
14 13   10 9 8 7 6 5 4 3

UniversityCampus
Oldham

A partnership between
the University of Huddersfield & Oldham College

Library & Computing Centre: 0161 344 8888
UCO Main Reception: 0161 344 8800
Cromwell Street, Oldham, OL1 1BB

**Text renewals: text `renew' and your UCO ID number to
07950 081389.**

This book is to be returned by the date on the self-service receipt.
Your library account can be accessed online at:
http://www.uco.oldham.ac.uk/library/catalogue.aspx
Follow UCO Library on Twitter: www.twitter.com/ucolcc

CONTENTS

Chapter 8 The Dialogue Edit   143

Chapter 9 Voice-Over Recording   161

Chapter 10 Recording and Editing Dialogue Replacement   177

Chapter 14   Mixing, Filters, and Effects   255

PREFACE

Sound for film and television is a complex and exacting craft. There are numerous skills involved in recording sound well, editing those recordings properly, and then mixing them into a seamless soundtrack. Despite the amazing capability that digital technology provides today's filmmaker, the ultimate craft of movie-making remains the same. The shots need to be in focus, the lighting needs to be defined, and the sound recordings need to be free from distortion and noise.

The advances in computer and digital filmmaking equipment make the ability to create high-quality, professional movies available to just about anyone. But owning a top-of-the-line camera and a computer editing system does not guarantee that your movies will be premiering at the local Cineplex. Making movies is a task that requires a number of demanding skill sets.

This book is meant for anyone—from beginning digital filmmakers to seasoned producers—seeking a greater understanding of how to create sound for film. The field of sound changes constantly with the introduction of new technology, but its foundation remains as old as filmmaking itself. Everyone involved in the filmmaking process can benefit from a better knowledge of the techniques, concepts, and practices outlined here. This text has two essential parts: The first focuses on the tools and techniques for excellent recordings, and the second discusses the tools, concepts, and techniques necessary to edit and mix those sounds into a cohesive whole.

I wrote this book using knowledge gained from years of working in the film and television industry in Hollywood, California. A trained musician, I gravitated toward sound as I moved from film to film and show to show. In time I began using my mixing skills from music to mix live television programs. I started by mixing news programming and then moved on to mixing live game shows and talk shows. Finally, I embraced postproduction audio as a career path. One thing I learned is that few professionals working in the business have a strong understanding of the sound side of production and postproduction.

I have addressed the major points of the sound process, from the tools, to recording, to the techniques for editing and mixing. I have also created an extensive glossary for sound-specific terms. Use the glossary often to familiarize yourself with the definitions and explanations of sound for filmmaking. It is a valuable resource to learn the language used in creating soundtracks for film and television. The accompanying CD provides numerous audio examples of the concepts.

Through the ideas expressed in this book, I hope to convey the best practices to elevate the sound in your digital filmmaking projects. Sound is a fascinating and important art, and the contribution of sound for film is immeasurable to the final project. I invite you to read the chapters, complete the exercises, and apply these concepts to your own movies. Learn to hear the world around you, and take the same care with the sound that you do with the picture. Tell stories that sound as good as they look. I'll see you at the movies.

ACKNOWLEDGMENTS

A note of heartfelt thanks to the many individuals whose generous contributions of time, knowledge, resources, and energy have made this book possible.

To Kathy Lee for help with the chapter templates;

Colleen Dooley for assistance with the graphics;

Iryna Kucherenko, of Prime Sound Productions, for help with many of the graphics, photos, and accompanying disk;

David Panfili, president of Location Sound Corporation, for the use of production gear for several of the figures in this book;

James Eccles, general manager of Chace Audio by Deluxe, for the use of the Foley stage;

Jay Miracle for the use of wireless location recording gear;

Dr. Fred Ginsburg, CAS, PhD, MBKS, for your vast production knowledge and invaluable tips;

Eric Pierce, CAS, for location recording insights;

Jackie Johnson for insights and assistance on the dialogue editing chapter;

Monique Reymond for invaluable input and photographs for the Foley chapter;

Roxanna Sandoval for the dedicated and tireless work on the figures, documentation, disk, and the glossary;

Gerald Jones for making the connection, Pete Shaner for all the insightful notes and motivation, and Tim McEvoy for the patience;

the staff of Allied Post Audio in Santa Monica, CA;

the membership and support of The Los Angeles Post Production Group;

audio professionals, notably Walter Murch, Randy Thom, Ben Burtt, and Christopher Boyes, whose boundless creativity, ingenuity, brilliance, and expertise in audio have challenged, guided, and inspired me endlessly;

Bill, Gerry, Lynn, Kathy, Mark, Kate, Merrill, and Hannah for their unwavering support;

and most especially to Wendy Woodhall for all of the insights, questions, thoughts, comments, and commitment to me and to this text.

Truly, this book could not have been created without all of your steadfast help and guidance.

CHAPTER 1

PLAN FOR SOUND

OVERVIEW AND LEARNING OBJECTIVES

In this chapter, you will:
- Discover what is so important about sound
- Understand why so many low-budget movies can sound so bad
- Learn how to plan for location recording
- Acquire simple tips for great location recording
- Understand working with actors, directors, and crew

What Is So Important about Sound Anyway?

Motion pictures are a powerful artistic medium for storytelling. The combination of a giant screen reflecting larger-than-life images with pulsating sound from all sides can be a transcendent experience. With the advent of digital filmmaking the ability to make movies is finally in the hands of the masses. But even with all of the affordable technology and computer advances that are available today for digital filmmaking, the essential techniques required to create movies remain the same. Movies still require a camera and a microphone. They still require a production to create and record the images and sounds. They still require postproduction to manipulate those recordings into a finished product.

From the start they were called moving pictures, or movies. Film art began without sound and was often accompanied by live music.

1

No doubt you have seen clips of silent movies with title cards spelling out the key lines of dialogue. The acting had to be large enough to convey the emotions without the use of spoken dialogue. Silent movies were an extremely popular form of entertainment by the turn of the twentieth century. By the end of the 1920s, after a number of failed attempts, the technology had evolved to add reliable, repeatable audio to the playback of movies. Then movies became known as the talkies.

As you learn about sound throughout this text you will need to develop and exercise the skill of critical listening. Sound exists in layers, surrounding you every day. You must unlearn the subconscious masking of sound that you've developed over the years. Now you

CASE STUDY: WHAT ARE THE MAIN ELEMENTS OF A MOTION PICTURE SOUNDTRACK?

Motion picture soundtracks consist of several elements that are edited and mixed together to create the final sound. Soundtracks can be broken down into these elements:

Dialogue:

> Production dialogue tracks—the recorded location audio
>
> Dialogue replacement tracks—rerecorded and added dialogue or voice-overs
>
> Crowd dialogue replacement tracks—additional group dialogue recordings

Sound Effects:

> Hard effects—car crashes, door slams, planes, trains, and ambiences
>
> Designed effects—otherworldly elements created specifically for a given project; drones, eerie pads, unnatural sounds
>
> Foley—recreated human sounds recorded in sync with the picture, such as walking, fighting, body movements

Music:

> Score—the musical soundtrack usually written by a composer for a given project
>
> Source music—popular songs that may be used as score elements or as music played as through a radio or as background music in clubs or restaurants among many other uses

need to *listen for* and *hear* the sounds of passing traffic, household appliances, birds calling, and other noises that you normally excise from your conscious thought.

Developing a more acute sense of hearing helps you monitor and record the location audio. Exercises in critical listening to the soundtracks of movies will help you discover all of the elements that exist in a motion picture soundtrack. Have a look at the box "Case Study: What Are the Main Elements of a Motion Picture Soundtrack?" to see all of the essential components of a soundtrack.

The purpose of this book is to illustrate, in practical terms, the craft of successful sound recording and sound editing and to illuminate the practice and art of sound design and sound mixing. Sound is a crucial element to the total experience of cinema. It is our aim to teach the vocabulary and the practice of audio for film. George Lucas, indisputably one of the most influential and successful filmmakers of all time, once noted that sound is 50 percent of the motion picture experience. Its impact cannot be overstated. In this section we will explore the ideas that

- Sound Creates Place
- Sound Creates Mood
- Dialogue Moves Stories
- Sound Enhances Picture

Sound Creates Place

Imagine this hypothetical scene from a movie:

It is late into the night and we can hear the faint rhythm of chirping crickets. On a slow dissolve to the horizon the sun is rising and we begin hearing the faint chirp of morning birds.

We don't see a close-up of a cricket or a bird and yet we know where we are and what time it is. There are countless examples of these sorts of auditory cues that are used in films to create time and space with sound. We, as audiences, take for granted that crickets are what we hear when it gets dark outside and birds chirp during the day. These sorts of auditory cues are ingrained in the lexicon of film sound. They are so subtle that we are often unconscious of them. Start listening for these cues whenever you watch movies and sharpen your critical listening skills.

Prelapping is an editing technique where you hear the incoming sound of the next scene before the picture appears. This is an excellent example of sound creating place. For example, if we hear cows and other farm animals while the picture is showing the end of a scene of a car racing down the highway, the next picture cut will most likely be that of an establishing shot of a farm. Prelapping can be used to create place, mood, or both. Sound is a major player in storytelling, and goes well beyond just actors speaking lines of dialogue on-screen.

Often, much of a scene's sound may get replaced with new recordings later. Watch a motion picture scene that has a lot of wind and rain effects onscreen. Listen carefully to the overall sound mix of the scene and particularly to the dialogue within the scene. Chances are that every moment of that sound was recreated. It is more than likely that the actors had to perform the dialogue over again because the audio that was recorded on-set at the time of shooting was unusable.

Think about the actual recording situation on the set: the roar of the wind and water machines, the loud rocking of the set on a soundstage, the water pouring down over all the set pieces, the director and stunt director shouting commands to the performers. These elements required to capture the proper images have probably rendered the on-set production sounds useless. The wind, the rain, and the dialogue will all be replaced in the editing stage of the project. This is something that the casual moviegoer rarely realizes. Listen critically to the layers of sound within a motion picture soundtrack.

In science fiction genre movies often whole sections of the audio have to be created from scratch because the places that are created are imaginary. Ben Burtt, an Academy Award–winning, motion picture *sound designer*, is a master of such sound creation. He has helped create the sonic worlds of *Star Wars* and *Wall-E*, and the new *Star Trek* movie among many other top Hollywood blockbusters. A sound designer is in charge of the sonic universe of the project. Often in science fiction films sound designers must create special sound elements such as otherworldly noises, nonhuman vocalizations, and other noncompositional sounds and sound effects, literally entire universes.

Walter Murch, an award-winning filmmaker and a true pioneer in the world of modern cinema sound and picture editing, created the wonderful term and technique known as *worldizing*. Worldizing is the technique of amplifying sound elements through speakers in a real-world environment and then recording the resulting playback. The idea is to use the effect that the world has on the playback of the audio rather than trying to re-create the effect with digital technology. Worldizing puts the audience in the space of the characters on-screen.

This technique is ubiquitous now, but it was developed in part for Murch's work with George Lucas on the film *American Graffiti*. Music, specifically playing from radios in cars, plays a key part in the sound in this film. George Lucas thought it was imperative to hear radio disk jockey Wolfman Jack echoing off the buildings from the cars during the night. The sound of the radios in cars, on streets, and in neighborhoods created the space of that movie.

Murch defines the effects and options in sound worldizing as analogous to the effects and options in visual depth of field. Have a listen to *American Graffiti* and see how the use of worldizing created the sonic qualities within the soundtrack. Murch, whose work spans decades and many highly regarded films, is a sound designer of the highest order.

Sound Creates Mood

Imagine this scene:

We see a dark room and a woman slowly walks in with a frightened look on her face. She steps in cautiously, and we hear a loud crash; she and the audience nearly jump out of their skin. She trains her flashlight behind her and sees a cat jump out of the room, and she then hears a bowl drop to the floor. She heaves a sigh of relief, takes one last look around, and steps back out of the room and out of view. Just as she exits we hear a door squeak, and an ominous score begins to play. Then a shadow slowly moves toward her.

The combination of the visuals, the action, and the sound create the mood and tension of the scene.

Music is also, of course, a major component of the soundtrack of films. The music is a key contributor to the mood and feeling of a movie. In a later chapter we will be dealing exclusively with music and the score elements within a soundtrack. For the moment, however, think of the nonmusical sounds, sounds designed for specific moments in a movie, which are also very powerful and widely used for emotional effect. Often the nonmusical sound is a major and *subconscious* element within a motion picture soundtrack.

Imagine a thriller:

We hear the ominous flapping of a curtain near a previously unopened window; we hear footsteps approaching softly in a dark room, and suddenly the muffled screams of someone in danger are heard.

The sound elements all contribute to the feeling, mood, and experience of foreboding. Listen critically to the layers of the sound in scenes of your favorite films. Can you determine if the soundtrack, *outside of the musical score*, is affecting the mood of the scenes? This should be a fairly simple exercise if you focus on genre pictures such as science fiction or horror movies. Don't limit yourself to these films, however; also seek out comedy and drama films. With an observant ear it will be plain to see that sound cues are used in many different types of films to create and to maintain mood.

> **TIP**
>
> With the advent of the DVD format there are many offerings that include the "making of" or the "behind the scenes" features that profile the audio portion of the film. Some of the larger budget features show in depth how the audio was created for particular moments or scenes. I strongly encourage seeking out these video documents to better understand the techniques, technology, technicians, and artists who create these awesome soundtracks.

Dialogue Moves Stories

This book will devote a good deal of time and energy to the recording, rerecording, editing, and mixing of dialogue. Dialogue is a major part of the final soundtrack. It is the one absolutely essential element in a movie soundtrack. The dialogue moves the story and the plot points forward. Dialogue is usually the most clearly mixed element of a soundtrack.

In the *sound field*, or *panning*, of the mix, generally the dialogue will be mixed front and center. Panning is a term used to describe the mixing process of moving sound from speaker to speaker, for various effects. In the mixing of soundtracks, an imaginary *sound field* between the speakers is created for the listener. Panning is the action of sounds moving across the sound field.

Often panning is used to follow the action on the screen. For instance, if a car is driving across the screen from left to right, the sound of the car can be panned left to right matching its place in the sound field between the speakers, creating the illusion of movement. This example describes stereo sound that uses two speakers, mimicking the way humans hear. Today there are a number of other systems, where many speakers are used to surround the audience. With more speakers, the mixer can more precisely place and pan sound elements in the perceived sound space of the motion picture.

Since the dialogue track is so important, noisy production dialogue recordings will be rerecorded by the actors to be sure that the entire dialogue track is clearly audible. There are times of course, when the choice is made to obscure the dialogue in some way. But the hard and fast rule is that the dialogue track is the king track in a motion picture soundtrack. That is simply because the written word, translated on-set into spoken dialogue is what generally moves the characters through the plot and story.

Sound Enhances Picture

The famous Japanese film director Akira Kurasawa noted that cinema sound does not merely add to the viewing of images but rather multiplies the effect of the visual experience many times over. Think of a classic feature film such as Martin Scorsese's *Raging Bull*. Watch the fight scenes and hear how the use of the punching sounds, the flashbulbs, and the crowd are used to heighten the fight experience for the movie audience. Think of classic musical cues such as the shark motif in *Jaws* or the bell in *It's a Wonderful Life*. These sonic elements enhance the story and bring the audience into deeper levels of understanding.

As an experiment, find a favorite scene from a motion picture. Watch the scene but *without* the audio. Now, watch again, but this time listen to the scene *without* watching the picture. Now, watch the scene once more with both the picture and the audio. Were you able to determine the action of the plot without the sound? Were you able to determine the action of the plot without the picture? Try this with several different types or genres of films. During this exercise try to decipher the various layers of the soundtrack.

Imagine the same scenes without the score elements, or without the dialogue elements. Does the sound itself contribute feeling, mood, time or space more than just the dialogue does to the scenes you've watched? Did you feel that the visuals were adversely affected with the deletion of the sound? The art of filmmaking is the seamless blending of sound and image.

Why Do So Many Low-Budget Movies Sound So Bad?

The sad fact for lower-budget or do-it-yourself (DIY) filmmaking is that audio does not get the respect it deserves. There is an intense focus on the picture and the visual elements, usually to the detriment of the audio. First-time directors and producers are sometimes working under the misconception during shooting that the sound is not a priority or that the sound will be dealt with—later. The old cliché is "we'll fix it in the mix." This is a poor plan for filmmaking. As these blossoming directors and producers learn postproduction, they will appreciate the importance of capturing sound properly from the start. Sound issues on sets can often be quickly fixed, but there is a misguided notion that there is no time to "waste" doing it.

The frustration encountered in postproduction of replacing dialogue when there was a simple on-set fix can often be enough for a filmmaker to make on-set recording a priority on future projects. Compromising the audio at the start means that the audio will also be compromised at the end. You can kick the can of audio down the road, but sooner or later it must be dealt with. Sound is an integral aspect of the final product. The ideas discussed in this section include:

- Planning for Sound
- Tips for Great Audio
- Working with Directors, Actors, and Crew

Planning for Sound

Preproduction meetings and planning must include sound. Locations must be chosen or at least considered for their sound properties as well as their visual properties. Sometimes this is impractical because of the requirements of the visuals for a scene. If a scene calls for a location at a busy intersection or any place filled with sounds that cannot be changed or minimized, then that is the situation and it will just have to be dealt with later.

Often, however, locations are nondescript and generic. Optimal recordings should always be the goal. Sound must be planned for if it is to be useable in the final product, and time and care must be taken with the location recordings. Audio recording doesn't happen in a vacuum and isn't instantaneous. Audio setup should be given at least as much time as is given to the lighting and camera setups. The director of photography is generally given the time and tools required to get the shot, but there is often a mistaken assumption that audio is simply plug and play.

When scouting locations—listen. Listen to the traffic, listen to the birds, and listen to the surrounding environment. Are planes, trucks, or industrial noises heard? These extraneous sounds in the recordings will all come into play as the separate recordings are cut together by the editor during postproduction. If a plane is roaring in the wide shot that is then cut to the matching close-up shot which has no plane in the recording the edit will be jarring.

Try to minimize the auditory intrusions. Determine if it may be better to shoot at the same location at another time of day. Can the setup move a few yards one way or the other to minimize sound intrusions and still have the same visual integrity? Listen, listen, listen. It can save time and money exponentially in post.

Attention must be given to the quality of the sound in the spaces to be recorded in. You will live with these recordings forever. If shooting is taking place inside of a restaurant, for example, refrigerators and fans should be turned off for the shots. If it's a busy office, the air conditioning and the computers should be turned off. Part of the location recordist's equipment should be blankets that will help deaden reverberant spaces. Any nonessential sources of noise should be stopped!

Time spent locating and eliminating troublesome noise sources is worth the effort. Often the notion—we'll fix it in the mix—will come up again and again. There is sometimes a feeling that money is being wasted with so many people on-set "just waiting around" while the recordist determines the problem. Sometimes one needs to wait for a superintendent, office manager, or whoever controls the offending source to arrive and deal with the problem. A clean recording from the set saves money on dialogue replacement, Foley, and other expensive postproduction audio line items. That few minutes of "waiting" for clean audio recordings is time and money well spent!

Tips for Great Audio

Great sounding movies are no accident. They take enormous amounts of time, money, craft, and skill. Somewhere in the DIY filmmaking process audio got subordinated to image. First-time filmmakers may not yet understand the importance of getting things right the first time. But when the final picture edit hits the post-audio stage, all of the choices made along the way to compromise the audio will become apparent.

- Listen, Listen, Listen—Critical Listening
- Take the Time Needed for Sound
- Headphones
- Don't Settle for Mediocrity

Listen, Listen, Listen—Critical Listening

Listen to the sounds surrounding you. Wherever you are, take note of the layers of sound just within your normal everyday routine. Listen to the voices in restaurants. Listen to the music playing wherever you go. Listen to the traffic outside. Listen to the beeps of phones and machines.

Try to uncover all of the layers of sound as you move through the course of any regular day. No matter where you are, you are surrounded sonically in ways that you usually do not recognize without critical listening. Sharpen your skills every day by dissecting the sound environment around you. These skills will become crucial to your experience as you record audio on sets.

In the same way that a cameraperson must always be looking at the framing, the composition of the shots, the lighting, and the focus, so the location recordist must be equally alert to the sound and the recordings. Audio recordists are proud of their acute hearing sense. A sound recordist may hear a 2,000-hertz buzz tone on-set for example, and may voice this to another crew member in passing. Later, the same crew member might remark "I wish you hadn't mentioned that buzz, now it's all I hear!"

This critical listening skill is available to all of us, but needs to be developed. You need to tune your ears into being a delicate receiver capable of uncovering the intrusive sounds that we have learned to block out. Critical listening is a key skill for a sound recordist. The planes and trucks, hisses and rumbles, beeps and buzzes that you have learned to filter out of your auditory experience will show up in your recordings. Just know this: if it is heard in the headphones, it will be heard on the recordings later. Sooner or later these recordings will be the intense focus of the director and a small army of editors. Make sure that you have done everything to make the sound great.

Take the Time Needed for Sound

This can be tough, particularly if you are a novice recordist and you are working with more experienced crew members. It's difficult because you may not yet know exactly where the boundaries are drawn in terms of the limits of recording and in terms of where you and your crew fit with the other crew members. You may feel awkward or intimidated by other more experienced people on the set. But at the end of the day, you have one responsibility: to make the recordings as good as they can be. You are as key a member of the crew as is the director of photography.

Understand the scene and the action to be recorded; devise a plan for capturing the sound within the boundaries of your situation; and make others aware of problems, limitations, and issues. If you hear an airplane, always tell the director. This way it becomes the director's decision to wait, to obscure it in some way, or to just live with it. If during editing the concern is raised about the sounds of airplanes in the recordings, you will know that others were made aware at the time of the issue.

Within reason, encourage directors and producers to get it right the first time. They may not thank you on that day or even during the shoot, but in time they will recognize the contribution. If you are also the director, or if you are involved in the project with responsibilities beyond your recording duties, then soon enough you will see the wisdom of this approach.

Headphones

The importance of good-quality headphones cannot be minimized. You'll need headphones for yourself, headphones for the director, and headphones for the boom operator, as well as spares. Your trusty headphones will allow you to evaluate what is going to be recorded. They are to you what the viewfinder or location monitor is to the director of photography. You need to know them and be able to depend on them.

Proper headphones for production recording are closed-ear-type headphones, not earbuds and not open-eared headphones. They need to close out the extraneous noises nearby and to allow for proper monitoring of the recordings. Don't skimp on the purchase of headphones, these will truly be your ears for the recording process. And make sure that they are comfortable to wear; you may be wearing them for long stretches at a time.

If you look at photos taken on motion picture sets, you will often see the director with a pair of headphones wrapped around his or her neck. The best filmmakers are always monitoring and checking the audio. In fact, anyone who has a vested interest in the audio of a project should own a good pair of headphones, whether it is the producer, the director, or the picture editor. Don't leave home without them!

Don't Settle for Mediocrity

Time and money considerations can make every setup a challenge.

Situations constantly arise during production when the decision is made to move on from the location or setup even though the audio recordings were not ideal. Shooting can be a very difficult situation for all parties involved, and all you can do as the location recordist is make the issues known and move on with everyone else. Sometimes whole performances have to be scrapped and replaced later.

ADR, or automated dialogue replacement, also known as looping, is a process of rerecording actors' lines in sync with the picture. These new recordings will replace production tracks that are noisy, inaudible, or otherwise deemed unusable. Filmmakers might also choose ADR if they decide that a performance is not to their liking and will have the actor rerecord the line with a different emotional quality.

In ADR, actors record their lines of dialogue while watching playback of their performances. Contrary to its name, the dialogue replacement is not automatic. It is a demanding and painstaking task to re-create performances, as well as re-create the sound quality of the original location recordings. Some actors are just not good at it and many filmmakers just do not like it.

Therefore, location sound must always be taken into consideration when decisions are being made during production. Bad location audio will haunt the postproduction process. If a filmmaker is inexperienced in ADR, he or she may not fully understand the ramifications of the decision to move on from a location. Once a filmmaker understands the depth of the work involved in ADR, recording take after take with actors, watching takes for sync, matching the performance level of the scene as well as the sound quality of the location recordings, suddenly the extra five minutes required on-set to get things right doesn't seem so long to wait.

A very successful recordist I know, Fred Ginsburg, CAS, has a great trick for creating rapport with the director. He finds out what the director likes to eat. A specific candy, some sort of indulgent snack, whatever it might be, he always determines on the first day of the shoot what the director's particular weakness is. He then buys a supply of that indulgence and makes sure that the director is fully aware that these goodies reside on his location audio cart. It is a simple and highly effective way to get the director to spend some time with the mixer and with the audio crew. Between shots the director will get to know the audio crew better and, hopefully, in the process the acquaintance will help smooth the more difficult parts of the shoot.

As filmmakers, we are creating art. It is as simple as that. Whether it is a thirty-second commercial, a half-hour infomercial, a one-hour documentary, or a full-length feature film, we are striving to do our best to communicate ideas, feelings, and emotions. Give each shot and each shoot your all. Mediocre work on-set means that the work will just have to be done later. Don't settle for mediocre work. Not from yourself, not from your assistants or from other crew members. Do your best work always and those efforts will always shine through.

Working with Directors, Actors, and Other Crew

Motion pictures are a collaborative process. It would be nice to think that making films is a solitary process like writing a novel, but that is simply not the case. There is usually a cast of actors and a sizable crew for production and postproduction on even the smallest of film projects.

Great filmmaking is truly a team effort. In the spirit of this, we must think of cooperation and sharing as a key element in the process. Good humor and patience are valuable qualities to have as you navigate the production process. Everyone is there for the same reason, even if his or her individual goals may differ.

While creating a great working relationship with the director, a similar relationship must be created and maintained with the director of photography and the camera crew. They are in charge of the "frame," which the boom, mic cables, and other audio gear must stay clear of. This crew can be the recordist's best friends or deadliest foes. Guess which situation serves you and the project better?

Become friendly with the actors you will be recording. You will be "up close and personal" to many of these folks, so making friends is the best course of action. If you are *body miking* the performers, hiding and taping mic cables and transmitters to their bodies and arranging and rearranging troublesome microphones on their costumes, it is best to be in their kind regards.

Body mics are small packs that are a part of wireless microphone systems for recording performers. They can be hidden under clothes, in hats or glasses, or anywhere that can properly pick up the voice. The transmitters that are attached to the microphones must also be discreetly hidden from view. Sometimes they will hitch to a belt loop, reside inside a pocket, or affix to a bra strap or a belt that is wrapped around a thigh. Don't worry about any of this yet, we will be discussing many of the various aspects of body miking, such as the equipment, the protocol, and the occasional diplomacy involved, throughout the book.

Shooting on sets is a time-consuming, stressful, and often difficult experience. The best advice is to be patient and calm. Be a positive force during these stressful times. Have a smile and a laugh and, perhaps, a piece of chocolate to keep things moving. Over time, this approach and attitude will gain you friends and influence. An added benefit is that in the long run a happier set translates into a better project.

The rest of the film crew is equally essential and will be there to help or hinder you. The makeup crew and wardrobe department can be a big help if you are trying to hide microphones in costumes or in wigs or hairpieces. Every crew member is essential, and they are all there for a reason. Sooner or later your path will cross with everyone and you may need their assistance. So smile, laugh, and create good cheer, and you'll be the bright spot of the shoot.

Summary

Sound is a major, though often subconscious, part of the filmmaking experience. It has many layers and levels, and its impact cannot be overstated. Motion picture sound is made of many different elements. Dialogue elements, sound effects elements, and musical elements combine in the final soundtrack to create place, time, and emotions just as powerfully as the images and acting do.

Great sound does not happen by accident. It must be planned for, properly recorded, and finally artfully designed and skillfully mixed. It is the coordinated effort of a team of people working toward a common goal. Make friends with your collaborators. Although many will not be a part of your audio crew their aims are the same as yours—to create a great movie. You are all on the same team, and in difficult moments you may come to rely on them for their expertise and guidance.

Learn to listen to the world around you. Learn to hear all of the layers of sound that surround you daily. Listen in particular for the sounds that don't seem to be there, the birds, the cars, the fans—all the noise that you have learned to turn off. Develop these critical listening skills for your training in audio.

Use these same critical listening skills when watching motion pictures that you enjoy. Watch the scenes over and over and try to determine if there was ADR in a scene, how the sound design affects the overall experience, and how the music is carefully blended with all of the other elements. Listen, listen, listen. This self-training will expand your skills and your appreciation of the audio portion of the filmmaking process.

Review Questions

Questions like these are likely to appear on exams to test how well you understood and retained the information in this chapter.

1. What are the main components in a motion picture soundtrack?
2. What is critical listening? Use your critical listening skills now and describe what you hear.
3. Identify possible sound problems and recommend solutions for noise-generating sources on-set.
4. What sort of sound issues should be addressed to the director?
5. What is the importance of creating and maintaining camaraderie on-set?

Discussion/Essay Questions

Your instructor may assign you one or more of the following questions for discussion in class or as the subject of a paper.

1. Watch scenes from major motion pictures. Describe several examples of film sound, indicating time and location.
2. What is worldizing and why would you use it? Offer specific examples.

Applying What You've Learned

Research/Lab/Fieldwork Projects

The following lab exercises will give you practice and help you understand how important it is to keep the microphone in the proper place and to minimize external noises.

SLATE

For location audio recording, slating is the process of verbally stating and recording the scene and take name, and possibly other important notes such as the date, the time of day, what is being recorded, or any other valuable information. Typically slates are recorded just prior to each take's performance.

1. Take a video camera with an external microphone to a busy street corner. Point the microphone toward the street, stand in front of the microphone, slate your location, and record thirty seconds while speaking.

2. Now point the microphone away from the street, stand in front of the microphone, slate your location, and record thirty seconds while speaking.

3. Now move your setup five feet away from the street, stand in front of the microphone, slate your location, and record thirty seconds while talking.

4. Now move ten feet from the street, stand in front of the microphone, slate your location, and record thirty seconds while talking.

5. Critically listen to all of the recordings in a quiet, controlled space and note the quality and differences of the effects of the placement of the microphone and the change of location on the voice recordings.

Resources

The following resources have more information on the topics covered in this chapter.

The Cinema Audio Society (http://www.cinemaaudiosociety.org/). This is a professional organization that celebrates cinema sound. Here you can find online articles on sound, their quarterly newsletter, as well as podcasts discussing audio-centric issues.

The Motion Picture Sound Editors Guild (http//www.mpse.org/). Under their education link you'll find articles with award-winning sound designers discussing their experiences and their craft.

CHAPTER 2

TOOLS FOR RECORDING

OVERVIEW AND LEARNING OBJECTIVES

In this chapter, you will:

- Learn to choose the proper microphone for various shooting situations
- Understand the importance of microphone placement
- Learn about signal routing, cables, and connections
- Learn about gain and recording levels
- Consider the technical details: sample rates, frame rates, and bit depths

Microphones for Location Audio

The *location audio* is key to every other part of the sound process. Location audio is the sound that is recorded on-set during production. It is also referred to as the production audio or the production tracks.

The microphone is where location audio begins. There are several aspects that must be considered when choosing the proper microphone for location audio. Some of these considerations include: the type of space the recordings are being made in, how close the actors are to the camera, and the nature of the action being performed within a scene. This section will discuss

- Microphone Types and Polar Patterns
- Lavaliere Microphones and Their Use

- Shotgun Microphones and Boom Poles
- Phantom Power
- Wireless Microphone Systems

Microphone Types and Polar Patterns

There are several different ways that microphones convert sound into electrical energy for recording. The microphone type that is most useful in location recording is the *condenser microphone*. Condenser microphone types are sensitive to sound and are low noise in operation. One defining characteristic of a condenser microphone is that it needs additional power to operate. Modern digital filmmaking equipment typically can send the microphone this power through the microphone cable.

Another type of microphone is the *dynamic microphone*. Dynamic microphones are typically not appropriate for location recording. They are excellent microphones for recording loud sources, but they are not powerful enough or accurate enough to record properly on-set. Dynamic microphones are typically used on-stage for musical performances and do not require additional power.

Polar patterns, also referred to as pickup patterns, are diagrams that indicate how a particular microphone picks up sound. Some microphones will pick up sound from the front and reject sound coming from the sides, other microphones can pick up sound from all sides. It is important to choose the correct polar pattern to record the sound properly. Figure 2.1 gives examples of three common types of microphone polar patterns.

Here is how to read the polar patterns in Figure 2.1. The zero-degree position is indicated at the top of the pattern. This is where you point the microphone. The other angles are the sides and rear of the microphone. The diagrams indicate the width that the microphone will optimally record.

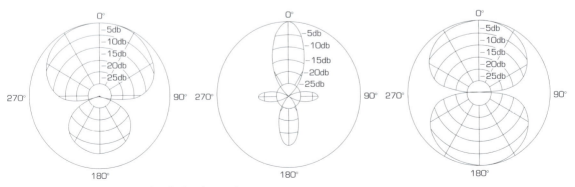

FIGURE 2.1 These are three examples of microphone polar patterns

The polar pattern on the left is called *hypercardioid*. Hypercardioid has a wide front pickup with good side rejection and a small rear pickup. The center polar pattern is a *directional* pattern. Directional patterns have a very tight pickup with good side rejection. Be aware that this pattern is extremely focused but that it also picks up sound from the rear. The pattern on the right is called a *figure 8*. The figure 8 pattern will pick up sound equally from the front or rear and has excellent side rejection. Always check the polar pattern of the microphone that you are using so that you understand how it picks up sound.

A popular polar pattern that is not depicted here is called *omnidirectional*. An omnidirectional pattern picks up sound equally from all sides. You can literally circle around the microphone from front to back to front again and it will pick up sound each step of the way. Omnidirectional microphones are quite useful in a variety of location recording situations.

Lavaliere Microphones and Their Use

A *lavaliere microphone* is a very small, condenser microphone that is well suited for video production recording because of its size, its great flexibility in mounting and hiding, and its excellent sound recording ability. Figure 2.2 shows an example of a lavaliere microphone. They are generally omnidirectional and can be hidden under clothing or hidden "in plain sight" on tables, desks, or any location that is close to the action and the actors.

When mounting or hiding a microphone on a performer it is imperative to listen closely for clothes movement, rustling, or scratching sounds. The microphone must be readjusted to minimize any such sounds being recorded. If a microphone is being planted or hidden on the set, it is important to see that the action does not bump or hit the mounting surface or the microphone itself, since these sounds will also be recorded.

In some situations it is appropriate to fit the lavaliere onto a small clip and then attach it to a lapel, shirt, or a tie. This is how many newscasts, talk shows, and interview shows use the microphone. Although the microphone is visible in these situations, care should still be taken with the cable, tucking and hiding it if possible.

Whenever mounting or placing a microphone it is always a good idea to determine the range of motion of the actor's mouth for optimal recording. When using lavaliere microphones, create a small loop in the microphone cable a couple of inches from the microphone head. This small loop will drastically cut vibration noise that will be picked up by the microphone and recorded. Also be sure to leave slack in the

FIGURE 2.2 A lavaliere microphone next to a coin to demonstrate scale

cable to allow for the performer's movements. Figure 2.3 is an example of a cable loop.

Many recordists prefer the sound of an overhead boom microphone because it picks up sound more closely to the way our ears hear. A properly positioned boom microphone will pick up more of the sound of the recording space and will generally sound more natural.

Shotgun Microphones and Boom Poles

Although the nicknames *shotgun* and *boom* seem interchangeable, in fact the "shotgun" is the microphone and the "boom" is the long pole that the microphone is attached to. Shotgun microphones are highly directional and have excellent rejection characteristics. The key to their proper use is in the distance of the microphone to the performers' mouths or to the action. In general, the microphone should be placed above and no more than three feet from the action or dialogue to be recorded. Figure 2.4 shows a shotgun microphone mounted on a boom pole.

Keep the boom as close to the scene to be recorded as possible. The farther away the microphone is from the action the more distant, "roomy," and "off-mic" the recording will sound. *Off-mic*, also known

▪▪▪ AUDIO PRODUCTION AND POSTPRODUCTION

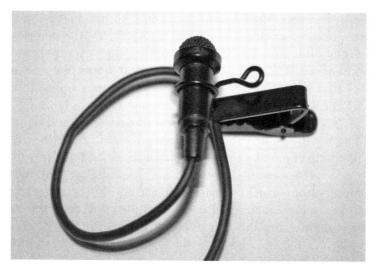

FIGURE 2.3 This is a standard loop when mounting a lavaliere microphone to a lapel with a clip

FIGURE 2.4 Here is an example of a shotgun microphone covered with a windscreen on a long boom pole

as *off-axis*, is a term that describes a sound source that is not hitting the microphone element properly. Put another way, the mic is pointed in the wrong direction. The sound is muffled, uneven, noisy, and low.

Booming is a skill and a craft. Although it seems like one of those positions that could be filled by anyone, the exact opposite is true. It is a physically demanding job. Balancing a microphone on a long pole over people's heads and following the action can take stamina. Depending on the shot, the crew, the equipment, and the size of the space, booming can make for some very interesting body positions!

Professional boom operators are highly skilled at keeping the tip of the microphone aimed squarely at the mouth of the performers throughout the movement of a scene. Unskilled operators tend to drift or sway, and since the shotgun microphone is so highly directional a swaying boom will be recording the scene off-mic. Great care must be given to the consistency of the recordings. In the quiet space of the editing room, away from the noise and hustle of the set, the quality of these recordings, crucial to the final film, will become apparent.

A great idea used by boom operators the world over is to place a white or brightly colored piece of tape on the end of the windscreen covering the microphone. That will make it clearly obvious that the boom has "dipped into the frame." Make friends with the camera operator and with the director of photography, you will all be working closely together.

Do not use a microphone attached to the camera as the recording microphone. Although these microphones are often called shotguns, the truth is they are simply too far from the action for professional recordings. Do not plan on relying on these recordings for anything other than guide tracks for editing. Unless the camera is in tight for a close-up, the microphone will be too far away for a proper recording. Also keep in mind that a microphone that is attached to a camera is prone to all of the noise from the handling of the camera. If the camera operator needs to zoom or shift focus or change settings, the microphone will also pick up these sounds. Get the microphone off of the camera and into the scene.

Phantom Power

Phantom power is a 48-volt current of power that is sent along the microphone cable to operate the electronics inside condenser microphones. The best policy is to turn phantom power off on any input channels that do not require it, since sometimes cables can be improperly wired and several microphone types will burn out if phantom power is activated. It is unlikely, but it could happen.

Typically, modern mixing boards and recorders today can send phantom power to a microphone. However, if for whatever reason that is not the case, there are also external phantom powering devices that can power the active circuits in a condenser microphone. Some condenser microphones will also accept a battery that will serve as the phantom power. If you are using batteries, be sure to have plenty on hand. They will get drained quickly.

If you are using a lavaliere microphone or a shotgun microphone and they are not working, check the phantom power. Neither of these microphones will work without it. Check to see if the mix board or recorder is sending phantom power. If it is incapable of sending phantom power you'll need to find an external device that can provide it, otherwise the microphone simply cannot operate.

Wired Microphones or Wireless?

Most modern microphones end in a connection that is referred to as *XLR*. XLR is a three-pronged connector type that is commonly used for audio purposes, most often for microphone connections. These connections come in male or female. Microphone cables typically have a male XLR plug on one end and a female XLR plug on the other. When referring to a *wired connection* we are simply stating that the microphone is attached to a cable that reaches all the way to the mixing board or the recording device. Figure 2.5 shows the XLR three-pronged connection.

FIGURE 2.5 This image shows the female and male ends of an XLR cable

A *wireless connection* refers to a wireless recording system. This system uses a microphone attached to a transmitter that then sends the signal out via radio waves to a matching receiver that is hardwired into the mixing board or recording device. Figure 2.6 gives an example of a wireless recording system.

Wireless microphone systems consist of several components. There is the transmitter, which is a small pack typically worn on a belt or inside a pocket. The lavaliere microphone attaches to this transmitter with a very slim cable. Then there is the receiver that picks up the transmitter's signal and is hardwired into the recording device or the mixing board.

In today's technological society many different types of devices send signals wirelessly, and in densely packed cities, these other signals can interfere with wireless microphone signals. Most modern wireless systems offer several different frequency channels over which to send signals back and forth between the receiver and the transmitter. If there is interference causing static or other noises, many times the solution is as simple as changing the channel frequency to eliminate it.

FIGURE 2.6 A complete wireless system consisting of a transmitter and microphone and a receiver

Most wireless systems use frequency modulation (FM) and are sent either VHF or UHF. These are defined bands in the wireless frequency spectrum. Be sure to look for models that offer "true diversity," which means that it includes an additional antenna to maximize the connection between the transmitter and the receiver.

Mixing Boards, Cables, Meters, and Levels

The mixing board, mixing console, or mixing desk is the hub of your location audio system. All of the signals come into and go out of it. It is the command center of your location-recording universe. It can power the microphones connected to it, add or reduce *gain* to the inputted signal, and take the signals that are input to it and send them out in a variety of ways.

Signal gain is the amount of level or volume that is supplied by a microphone amplifier in a mixing board. Mixing boards and recorders have a gain knob to control the amount of signal that is being recorded. The lavaliere and shotgun mics described here require lots of good, clean gain. Figure 2.7 shows the front of a mixing board.

Although they can look a bit intimidating, mixing boards are actually pretty simple to operate and understand. Think of them operating from the top down—the mic is attached at the top, under

FIGURE 2.7 This is a professional location mixing console

which is the gain control, under which are the frequency controls, under which is the *fader*. The fader controls the amount of signal being sent from one place to another. In a plumbing analogy, the fader is akin to the spigot: turn it up, you get more: turn it down, you get less. In this mixer the faders are the multicolored sliders. Large consoles simply multiply this one by eight, sixteen, twenty-four, or more faders.

The outputs of mixing boards are just as important as the inputs. You'll need to send the signal coming in back out—out to the recording device, out to the headphones of the boom operator, and out to the headphones where the picture monitor is being viewed by the director. Figure 2.8 shows the back panel of a mixing board.

You may also be called on to provide audio playback. Perhaps you will be asked to play back a musical track that performers need to lip-sync to or dancers need to dance to. These playback signals will be routed from the mixing board and sent back out to amplifiers, monitor speakers, and other appropriate places. This section will consider the following:

- Mix to a Recorder or Mix in the Camera?
- Signal Flow
- Channels: Splitting, Isolating, Combining, and Track Allocation
- Cables and Connections
- Understanding Meters and Levels

FIGURE 2.8 This is the rear of the console with many XLR ins and outs

■■■ AUDIO PRODUCTION AND POSTPRODUCTION

Mix to a Recorder or Mix in the Camera?

This question comes up often, so we will address it first. If the camera itself can accommodate microphone inputs and also send phantom power, why would you need a separate mixing device at all? Let's have a look at some possible scenarios for further information.

Today's digital cameras are small, and attaching cables and transmitters can be difficult enough, but how can you keep an eye on the recording levels if the cameraperson's eye is looking through the viewfinder? Generally the meters and gain controls are located on the side of the camera or on the viewfinder. That makes access to them while someone is shooting with the same camera quite difficult. One of your main jobs as a recordist is to keep an eye on the recording levels.

If you are working alone or in small spaces with few performers, an *ENG*-style mixing panel may be sufficient. ENG stands for *electronic newsgathering*, which means a single camera operator and a single audio person mobile team. The cameraperson is in charge of shooting and lighting, and the audio person is in charge of microphones, levels, mixing, and recording. This sort of shooting is also known as "run and gun," and the gear consists of only what two people can carry. ENG is widely used in news programming.

For the audio side, ENG is generally a boom pole and shotgun mic, a small, over-the-shoulder mixing panel, headphones, and whatever else may fit in a backpack. If you have more complicated setups and need to send the audio to numerous places, it is best to use a cart location recording station for your location audio. With a location audio cart the audio crew is free to power, route, cable, and set up their audio devices in ways that work best for them.

It doesn't take much imagination to see what a nightmare it can be to navigate the controls, the movement, meters, and levels while essentially attached to another person. That said, if you are the cameraperson and the audio person in one, then of course it would be much simpler to connect and control from your one central place—the camera.

Signal Flow

Signal is defined in audio terms as the actual material/electricity that is moving through microphones either wirelessly or in cables and ends up on a tape or some other storage media like drives or disks. *Flow* is where that signal is being directed. Understanding signal flow is key, since the recordist must determine what goes in where and what goes out where.

A simple illustration of signal flow would be actors lines spoken into a microphone (signal) down a lavaliere plugged into a channel on a mixing board (flow) out to headphones for the recordist (flow), out to headphones for the boom operator (flow), out to headphones for the director watching on a picture monitor (flow), into a recording device (recorded signal).

Understanding signal flow becomes particularly important when the situation arises where several microphones are needed for a particular scene and yet the recording device can only record two tracks at one time. What will have to happen is a combining of signals into one track.

For instance, you may have a microphone planted in a scene, two performers wearing a body microphone each, plus a boom microphone. In this example you have four signals needing to get to only two places. Your mixing board will have four inputs but you will need to mix those four signals down into two channels. Extra care will need to be paid to the recording levels, since you will be combining these all together. If there is something wrong on one of the combined signals, the entire recording will be bad.

Because filmmaking has become increasingly complex, and the technology can accommodate more channels today, it is not uncommon to find recorders that will record up to eight channels at a time, effectively eliminating the need to combine signals. The picture and sound editors would prefer to have all of the audio elements isolated on separate channels to allow for more precise editing. But as a resourceful recordist, you need to do what you need to do to get the scene recorded.

Channels: Splitting, Isolating, Combining, and Track Allocation

As a general rule for anything in filmmaking, the best tactic is to just use what is required. No more, no less. Things will expand exponentially as the shoot progresses. Bear in mind that if you just keep shooting and shooting, at some point, all of those takes will need to be sorted, transcribed, logged, inputted, and backed up. If you have four or eight tracks of audio accompanying these takes, things will increase substantially.

If you are shooting *double-system*, sooner or later all of these things will need to be synced up. Double-system sound is audio being recorded on a separate device from the images. A camera will shoot the images, and an audio recorder will record the audio. Double-system sound was the standard for many years in Hollywood, because motion picture film does not record audio.

Large sections of movies contain no dialogue, but be sure to record those scenes as well. The sound editor needs all the clean audio they can get. When covering action for location recording, use plant mics to get closer to the action. For instance, if the frame is a very wide shot and the action is a brawl, plant a few microphones around the area of action. It may not all be useable sound but a good sound editor can work wonders with short bits of audio.

Another great idea—if you are only using one microphone but have two channels of recording available: record the one microphone to both channels but lower the gain on one of the channels; it may save you in editing later. For instance, there may be a loud yell or crash that may distort on the louder channel but won't on the lower-gained channel.

A key consideration during location recording is how the sound will edit when the location recording is complete. For instance, if the filmmaker knows that he or she will need extreme isolation in the dialogue tracks for an effect they are trying to achieve in the storytelling, then be sure to use separate microphones and tracks for each performer if possible. Discuss strategies with the director if there is a particularly difficult scene with many actors speaking at once and you have only limited recording tracks. Determine a plan to combine them in a way that will be useful for the editors later.

One of the most common ways to record simple dialogue scenes is with both an overhead boom as well as a lavaliere. Often cameras and recorders offer only two channels of audio recording. By splitting the recordings to boom and lav, you get a good room recording of the scene as well as a close-up recording of the actors' performance.

Many times scenes don't require an army of microphones. Often scenes are between just a couple of people and are photographed in medium and close-up shots, so two channels are all that is required.

Cables and Connections

Cables are one of those pieces of gear where quality really does make a difference. They are one of the most common tools in the audio arsenal and are rarely considered until there is an issue. And be aware, there can be issues. In essence, a cable is simply a number of wires that are insulated, twisted, and terminated in various types of connectors. The issue with cables is that lesser-quality cables use cheaper wire with less stranding as well as cheaper connectors that may not be affixed as well as better-constructed cables.

Excellent cables can be bought or built inexpensively.

These cables are the workhorses of your location-recording outfit. They will get yanked, pulled, stepped on, rolled over, and connected and unconnected many, many times over. Cheaper cables just can't handle the wear and tear. Don't get into a situation where crackling,

FIGURE 2.9 Left to right are a male/male RCA cable, a male/female XLR cable, and a male/male quarter-inch cable

dropout, or other anomalies are occurring simply because the cable has been repeatedly mishandled. Use professional cables and connectors.

Wrap your cables properly before, during, and after each use. You want to prolong the life of the cables. They need to be reliable, and you certainly don't want to be replacing them again and again. Be sure to coil the cables in a loose manner that does not put any undue strain on the connectors. Figure 2.9 shows the common audio connectors: XLR plugs, quarter-inch plugs, and RCA plugs.

Understanding Meters and Levels

Meters are devices that display the visual rendering of the levels of signal that are being recorded. There are a number of types of meter schemes. *Decibel* (db) is the unit of volume measurement in digital audio. Meters in digital recording display levels measured in dbs. *Decibel full scale* (dbfs) means that 0 db is the absolute peak level of the digital audio signal. Since zero is the full scale, dbs are measured in the minus range, or below the full scale of zero. Simply put, a decibel is the measurement of how loud things are in the digital world. Figure 2.10 shows a decibel-type meter.

A meter that has long been in widespread use is called the *VU meter*. VU stands for "volume unit," and this type of metering is typically used with analog audio signals. VU meters spend some time "in the red." If you "hit the red" in digital, however, you've gone too far!

In general, zero VU in the United States is *calibrated* at −20 db. Calibration is a process of using a standard of reference—in the case

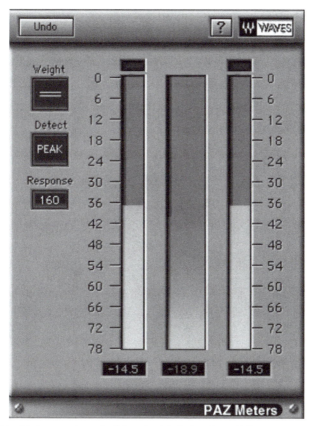

FIGURE 2.10 This digital meter shows the full scale of decibel ending at 0 db

of audio for filmmaking, a 1,000 Hz sine wave—to adjust audio levels uniformly from track to track, from deck to deck, or from media to media. Figure 2.11 shows an example of a VU meter.

In audio it is important to define the *standard operating level* (SOL). SOL is the operating level for a given purpose. A common SOL is −20 db. That means there is 20 db of *headroom* in the level. Headroom describes the range of audio level from the SOL to the maximum level before *clipping*. Clipping, also referred to as *distortion* and *overmodulation*, describes a signal that is recorded louder than the recording can support.

When signals clip, the resulting sound can be unpleasant, and it does not retain all of the characteristics of the original sound. It is impossible in most situations to repair seriously clipped recordings. A SOL of −20 db provides a good, solid recording level and lots of headroom for the occasional loud noise, yell, or otherwise loud dynamic in the performance and recording.

NOTE

Different countries and different systems calibrate things differently. For instance although the United States uses −20 db as the reference level, in the UK the reference level is set to −18 db. Always verify what levels you should be calibrating to.

FIGURE 2.11 It is common practice for VU levels to peak in the red zone

The location mixer should always be watching the levels, adjusting the gain, monitoring the recording, and understanding the dynamics of the scene. Learn the action of the scene so you can "ride the faders" during the recording. If the actors are quiet or whispering, be sure to add a bit of gain for a better recording. If there will be a loud action or yell, it must be anticipated so the gain can be lowered for that moment. Keep an eye on the levels and keep the audio from clipping.

Location mixing and recording is not a "set it and go" experience. It is hands-on all the way; you must be an active participant with the performance, making sure to keep the levels consistent and not allowing them to clip. Keep an eye on the levels at all times and make sure to be listening to the takes, to the quality of the recording, and for background hiss or noise.

Recorders, Tracks, Media, and Tone

With the advent of digital recording and fast computing power, a vast number of different recording devices have become available to filmmakers today. Currently, relatively inexpensive handheld digital recorders are very popular. These recorders have built-in microphones and record to magnetic media such as memory cards or memory sticks

■■■

instead of tape. Today, professional hard disk recording devices record two, four, eight, or more channels simultaneously. Ideas to be explored in the section are:

- How Many Tracks?
- Tone and Slating
- Media—Tape, Disks, Drives
- Backing Up

How Many Tracks?

Smaller productions tend to use the camera as the recording device for audio. If this is the case, you will most likely be locked into two channels for audio recording. The ideal would be to have one channel for each microphone or sound source. Some of the more professional cameras will allow up to four channels of audio recording. Always check the camera's audio specifications to verify that you are recording audio in the best quality available.

If you are recording double system, then record what you need for each scene. Several digital recorders offer up to eight or more tracks of simultaneous recording.

Tone and Slating

Tone is used extensively for audio in film and digital filmmaking. Specifically to filmmaking, tone is defined as a 1,000 Hz sine wave signal that is used to calibrate gear. It is an unwavering, occasionally annoying sound that is easily identifiable once heard. Its steady state and pitch make it an ideal sound for levels and calibration. It is also the sound used for the "beep" when audio is censored for public broadcast.

Things have changed drastically and rapidly in the new era of digital technology, but a serious recordist must still put tone to tape. As mentioned, tone in the United States is generally recorded at −20 db. This provides a reference level if there is a need for an analog duplicate of the media.

Always check to see that you have a tone generator on-set. Most recorders have a tone generator built-in. In today's increasingly professional camera gear, cameras also have tone generators. If one is not in the camera or in the mixing board, then an external tone generator will be required to create tone. Tone is quite a useful sound source. Besides calibrating decks, it is used to send signal down various paths to check cables, headphones, connectors, and routing.

To record tone, simply press the tone button, calibrate the gain to the correct calibration level and record it. If you are recording tone to tape, for example, you will put thirty seconds to one minute of tone at the top of each new tape. It's very important to notate on the tape the level that the tone was recorded at. Since not all tone is calibrated to the same level, it is important to write the recorded level on the labels and sound reports.

To have a proper frame of reference to what the original levels were, we use the standard of tone. In the analog world, the same material must be reamplified to be sent to another media source. In the digital world, media copied from one place to another is called a clone. It is an identical duplicate of the original. It does not go through any sort of processing to be re-created, copied, or moved.

Slating is the process of announcing the scene and take number for the upcoming shot. Various nomenclatures are used to describe scenes. You will be using either a built-in microphone in the mixing board or an external microphone for the slate recording. Slates are recorded prior to each recorded take of a scene. For instance, if a scene is at take one, you may slate the take as "Apple—take one." Then you would slate the next take as "Apple—take two," and so on, until the scene is moved to scene B. Then it may be slated as "Baker—take one," and so on. In a later chapter, we will discuss sound reports. These reports will notate the take name, notes, and other vital information relating to the audio recordings such as: "Airplane low during second half of scene." "Actor hit microphone during take." "Action of actors hugging distorted the recording." Keep the notes short, relevant, and clear. These will be used later and can be very helpful to those who never set foot on the set.

If there is a *script supervisor* on the set, then you will work out the slating nomenclature with that person. The script supervisor has a complicated position, being responsible to a number of departments within the production. The main task of the script supervisor is to watch for continuity errors. Continuity means consistency in each take, for instance, if an actor is holding a glass in his right hand, in all subsequent takes he is using the right hand for the glass. A continuity error would be if in several takes the actor mistakenly used his left hand.

For the sound department the script supervisor works with the production sound mixer to make sure that each sound report take has a proper slate and that it matches the picture slate. Another task is to note the duration of each take and log the action of the take and whether the director indicated a take as good or not good.

For the editing team, the script supervisor creates the *lined script.* A lined script is a version of the shooting script that has been drawn with vertical lines notated with the take names of scenes that have been shot in that part of the script. It is a map for the editing department to determine which takes correspond to the written text. By utilizing the lined script the editors can find where the media is located for any given take.

Media—Tape, Disks, Drives

For a very long time it used to be all about film. And tape. Period. A cameraperson was filming the scene with a film camera, and the medium was film. The location recordist was recording to magnetic tape, be it open reel, DAT (digital audio tape), or other types of tapes. In today's digital world, media means a lot more than only tape and film. There are optical disks, memory sticks and cards, hard drives, and more. All of these serve the same purpose as tape did, to capture moments on a set.

Recorders and cameras will record to any and sometimes to all of these types of media. A key consideration when using material that is not tape is *backing up*. We will explore this idea in depth later, but bear in mind that media such as memory cards or hard drives will be erased to be reused. All of that data, the location recordings, must be transferred to another media. If the recordings were done to tape, then those tapes become the master recording tapes that should be backed up.

Media other than tapes are nonlinear in nature and can be quite useful in retrieving recordings. Tapes are linear, they must be fast-forwarded or rewound to reach any particular point in the recordings. Nonlinear media such as audio CDs can skip from point to point across the data. Also tapes over time have a tendency to sag, shed, or otherwise degrade. Non-linear recording media have no moving parts, so they won't jam, break, or get stuck in a tape mechanism. The downside is that they are used and reused so care must be taken that each day's recordings have been properly captured, logged, and stored on other media.

Be sure to properly label all of your media. If you are using tapes, label each tape consistently for easy retrieval later. If the media is magnetic memory media, such as memory sticks or cards, then be sure to back up and label all of this material in a clear and consistent manner. There is nothing more frustrating than knowing that a piece of audio was recorded but not being able to find it! Many hours of valuable time can be saved when things have been properly labeled.

Backing Up

There is an old saying that nothing is backed up until it is in three places. And not just three copies of the material but also in three separate places. This is important because if there is a fire or a theft, the material will be secure in a separate place. In today's digital world hard drives often become the backups for our media. Since drive media are so inexpensive these days, hard drives are an excellent choice for backups.

Don't just back things up to tapes or drives. It is important to keep a "hard copy" of the original recordings. Today DVD media can hold almost 8 gigabytes of data. In the high-definition world of video that's not much storage, but for audio, 8 gigs will hold a lot of material. Be sure to create a data DVD backup of the material. Data that is stored this way is not prone to erasure, mechanical failure, corruption, and other problems that can plague other media. One copy of all of the recordings should be created on this sort of optical media and stored in a secure place.

When backing up to hard drives it is often a good idea to create folders in whatever way makes best sense for the production. If tapes were used to record the scenes, then create a folder named for each tape to hold the media from that tape. That way if you need to look back at the master tape for some reason you'll know exactly which master to look for.

If you are recording to memory cards or removable media, then sometimes it makes sense to organize by shoot date. The original reports will have dates that can refer back to the media. Sometimes it is best to organize by scene number. Every production and postproduction scheme is different, and the needs, desires, and expectations of each team can vary wildly. The key is to properly label all files and backups and keep documentation that matches as well.

Important Concepts for Great Audio

It would be nice if making movies was as simple as "point and shoot," but we know that is not the case. There are many considerations that go into creating movie magic, and technical considerations are at the top of the list. The levels must be recorded properly and the microphone must be in the right place. Technically, the audio must have the same settings as the camera recording settings. Additionally, there needs to be an understanding of how the project will be posted so there is consistency for the editors. In this section we will discuss

- Recording Levels—Know Your Performance
- Microphone Placement—Know Your Shot
- Sample Rates and Bit Depths: The Technicalities
- Frame Rates and Post Considerations

Recording Levels—Know Your Performance

So now you have the correct microphone and a useful mixing board, and you've calibrated your gear with tone. A major exercise in audio work is keeping the recording levels high enough so that the recordings are "hot" and clean but not so hot as to go into distortion or clipping. This is no easy feat. It requires constant attention to the meters and to your ears.

Sometimes meters don't show what your ears can hear. Since your ears are now tuned with critical listening, you must use your hearing, your meters, and your judgment. In general, try to keep the recording levels somewhere between −25 db and −10 db. This is in no way a hard and fast rule, since all situations are unique, but it is a great range to bear in mind when recording on sets.

This gives a good amount of headroom and allows for a good *dynamic range*. Dynamic range is the ratio of the lowest to the highest. In audio, dynamic range is most commonly referred to as the ratio of the softest to the loudest. In this context, dynamic range is measured in decibels. The larger the number, the better the dynamic range. Some idea of the dynamic range of various recording formats includes: vinyl LP dynamic range: 40 db; cassette tape dynamic range: 55 db; compact discs dynamic range: 96 db; DVD dynamic range: 144 db.

It's always a good idea to keep your fingers on the faders ready to change the levels. Always pay close attention to the scene and to the performances. There are times when the level recorded may be too high or too low. Be sure to tell the director if a scene was not recorded properly.

Often cameras, recorders, and mixing panels have built-in *limiters* that will limit the recording signal set to a particular threshold. For instance, a limiter set to −2 db means that no signal will go beyond −2 db. This is very useful for the occasional peak of audio. Beware, however, because too much limiting can sound bad.

In the case of limiters for location recording, if you do use them, less is more! Too much limiting can severely affect the quality of the recording. They can be quite effective, but they can also destroy otherwise wonderful recordings with improper use. The best use of a limiter is to maintain a signal threshold that it is activated only very rarely.

Microphone Placement—Know Your Shot

If booming overhead, get the microphone about three feet over the performer's head pointed at the bridge of the nose. This is a simple enough feat if the actor is merely standing in place. The real challenge comes when the performance requires the actor to move throughout the scene. The boom operator must keep pace with the actor, keeping the proximity of the microphone relatively in the same place and also keeping the perspective of the sound matching the shot. It would sound odd if an actor was walking toward the frame and yet their audio was fading down.

Not all overhead booms are held by hand. For many years, Hollywood productions have used what is called a *Fisher boom*. This is a device that is operated on a dolly platform with levers and pulleys that can maneuver the boom remotely. It takes some skill and practice, but it is a wonderful device for studios or large sets with the room for it. Fisher booms can also be affixed to the catwalks over a stage for an even more convenient way of working.

When planting microphones the key concerns are acoustic noises and contact noises. Plant mics are very useful and can be kept quite close to the action. The type of microphone depends on the hiding choices. Large boom mics can't be hidden as well as small lavaliere mics. Lavalieres are excellent for planting, since they tend to be omnidirectional and can pick up sound from all sides. Also, lavalieres are great for hiding since they are so small.

The choice will depend on whatever the scene is, the action of the scene, the proximity to the actors, and the frame of the picture. If a scene calls for a lot of table pounding, then placing the mic on the table might not be the wisest choice. However, hidden next to a lamp just overhead may do the trick. The biggest concerns here are keeping the microphone away from contact with the performers or the action in the scene.

There are also other obvious matters such as keeping the microphone element away from heat or water or hiding the mic so well that you have covered up the microphone in the process, giving a muffled or otherwise compromised signal. All of these tasks require some planning and thought. Plant mics can provide excellent recordings because the microphone is right where it needs to be.

If you have concerns about microphone placement follow your instincts. Sometimes due to the stress of the situation or the speed at which you are working you may make choices that you might later reconsider. Do not be shy about changing your mind about where things are located. If a plant microphone keeps getting bumped, move it. If the plant mic is too far from the action for an excellent recording, move it. Trust your gut.

If you are a novice it may seem awkward to change and move things. Just remember you are the sound expert at that moment and everyone is relying on you to make these sorts of choices. Move decisively and with passion, watch the other more experienced crew members around you and see how they approach a change. You'll see that if the cameraperson decides that a shot is not working he or she will get up and change things until they are right. Do what you need to do to get the best recordings possible.

When hiding lavaliere-type wireless microphones on a body, be sure to keep the element as close to the performer's mouth as possible. Location recordists hide these microphones in hair, in brassieres, under neckties and jackets, on eyeglasses, and so on; just be aware of the actor's mouth and head movement. If the best place is to conceal the microphone is on the actor's left side and she keeps turning her head to the right, you will not get an excellent recording.

Omnidirectional microphones are wonderful, but they will still lose their capabilities the farther they are from the action. Concealing microphones is an art and a skill. It also requires tact and diplomacy. There will be numerous times when male and female performers will need to be miked in a way that puts you up close and personal. We are often running cables up and down performers' costumes and inside their clothing and undergarments, so it is always best to be as professional and neutral as possible.

You must make sure the microphone is properly positioned and won't be affected by contact noise and that the cable has sufficient slack. And while you are doing all of that, remember that the performer is there preparing for a performance and you will need to give him or her proper space and respect.

Sample Rates and Bit Depths: The Technicalities

The *sample rate* of digital audio refers to how many times the device samples the values of a continuous signal. These samples are turned into binary code, or ones and zeros, to be later turned back into electrical signals and then amplified to produce sound. A waveform is the digital representation of a sampled signal. Figure 2.12 gives an example of an audio waveform.

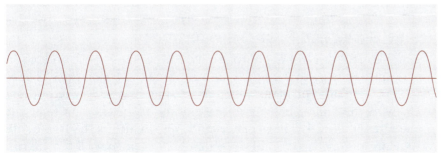

FIGURE 2.12 This is the image of a simple sine waveform of tone. Signal is depicted under and over a centerline that is called the *zero crossing*

There are a number of common sample rates used in digital audio. The two most common sample rates are 44.1K and 48K. Those terms mean that a signal gets sampled either 44,100 times per second or 48,000 times per second. If we think of it in terms of motion pictures, then film "samples" the action 24 times per second.

In digital video (DV), the most common form of video today, the audio sample rate is set to 48K. In audio CD (compact disc) recordings, the sample rate is set to 44.1K. Some cameras and recorders will record at 32K, which is not acceptable as a professional standard. It is used because it takes up less space and creates a smaller file. But it is not a clean and clear recording sample rate.

Some equipment specifications indicate a 32K sample rate. For instance if you record four channels on a DVCam tape, it defaults to changing the sample rate from 48K to 32K so it can fit on the tape. This is not desirable, since it is sampling 16,000 times less than 48K. There are also other sampling rates that double or even triple those rates. There are sample rates of 96K and even 192K, but these rates are left to the audiophiles and are not relevant to our discussion on location audio.

The *bit depth* of a sample refers to the resolution of that sample. Each bit refers to 6 db of dynamic range. In digital audio the bit depth refers to the resolution for the sampling rate. The higher the bit depth, the better the resolution. For audio, that means higher sample rates and higher bit depths create better sounding audio recordings. Available bit depths include: 8 bit, 12 bit, 16 bit, 20 bit, and 24 bit. The sample rate and bit depth of a CD is 44.1K sample rate and 16 bits of resolution. A 16-bit resolution has the theoretical dynamic range of 96 db. I say theoretical because in the real world playback systems and human ears are not made alike!

DVD audio uses a higher specification of a 48K sample rate and 24 bits of resolution. This gives DVD audio the theoretical dynamic range of 144 db! Now that is beyond the comprehension of human hearing!

Frame Rates and Post Considerations

The director, the director of photography, and perhaps a postproduction supervisor or the picture editor will determine the frame rates. Those decisions are made for many different reasons that will have nothing to do with the audio. If the project is going to be shot on film, the frame rate will be 24 frames per second (fps), which is the frame rate of film: 35-millimeter (mm) film, 16 mm film, even Super 8 film all run at the speed of 24 fps.

U.S. video runs at 29.97 fps, UK video runs at 25 fps, and modern video and high-definition cameras offer a dizzying array of frame rates. The digital filmmaking revolution has created many different frame rate choices. The producers and director will choose the frame rate on any number of factors from the camera system being used to the *deliverables*. Therefore the location audio recordist needs to verify and record the audio with the same settings as the camera.

Deliverables is the term used to describe what the producer will need to deliver to have the final project distributed. The items provide a range of options for the distributor to repurpose the program for different markets. Deliverable items include: several different master tapes of the final program, including subtitled, with graphics, with no graphics, in letterbox format, and in standard definition television format; the camera tapes; the sound tapes; a final script that matches the edited picture; and all of the signed releases, contracts, and agreements. Compiling the final deliverables can be a daunting task!

Fast computers and digital audio have revolutionized the way audio files can be altered to match frame rates, sample rates, and bit depths of any given project. Postproduction processes and equipment have changed drastically with computers. Although these technological changes make changing audio later to conform to the rates determined by the camera easier, the best practice is to use the same settings that the camera is recording with throughout the post process.

Summary

Good location recording requires an understanding of microphones, mixing levels, microphone placement, and technical requirements. Location recording is a hands-on, demanding task, requiring attention to detail and staying flexible to changes as the shoot progresses. Understanding signal flow is essential to properly monitor and record the audio. Tapes and media should have tone recorded as a reference, and the tone level needs to be logged. All of the media and the documentation should be well organized and properly labeled. Last but not least, backups need to be created and stored in discrete locations.

Review Questions

Questions like these are likely to appear on exams to test how well you understood and retained the information in this chapter.

1. List various microphone types and polar patterns and their application and use.
2. What purposes does the mixing board provide?
3. What is tone, and what is its purpose?
4. What are the elements comprising a wireless microphone system?

Discussion/Essay Questions

Your instructor may assign you one or more of the following questions for discussion in class or as the subject of a paper.

1. Describe the key elements for excellent location recordings, from required gear to proper recording practices.
2. Describe signal flow and the various inputs and outputs that might be necessary during location recording.

Applying What You've Learned

Research/Lab/Fieldwork Projects

The following lab exercises will give you practice in understanding the importance of microphone placement for location recording.

1. Take a portable recorder to a quiet environment. Set the recorder down, stand three feet from the front of the microphone, slate "on-axis," and record thirty seconds while speaking.
2. Now set the recorder down, stand three feet to the side of the microphone, slate "off-axis side," and record thirty seconds while speaking.
3. Now set the recorder down, stand three feet to the rear of the microphone, slate "off-axis rear," and record thirty seconds while speaking.
4. Critically listen to the recordings in a quiet controlled space, note the quality of the voice recordings.

Resources

The following resources have more information on the topics covered in this chapter.

Coffey Sound (http://www.coffeysound.com/) A leading Hollywood sound rental facility. Here you can find online articles about location recording equipment and various systems available as well as their excellent magazine, *The Coffey Files*, which has gear reviews, interviews, and opinion pieces dedicated to location recording. It's free!

Equipment Emporium (http://www.equipmentemporium.com/) Esteemed Hollywood location mixer Fred Ginsburg, CAS, hosts this website. There are numerous articles and video clips that detail many of the finer points of location audio, from equipment to excellent recording practices. This is a pay site; however, if you use the unique code 879E67 for readers of this text, you will receive a 50 percent discount off the annual price.

CHAPTER 3

RECORDING AUDIO AND WORKING ON-SET

OVERVIEW AND LEARNING OBJECTIVES

In this chapter, you will:
- Understand the members and duties of the location sound crew
- Learn tactics for the proper recording of location sound
- Utilize sound logs, slating, timecode, and metadata
- Understand the importance of staying organized

The Location Sound Crew

Three main location sound positions need to be considered. The mixer is the head of the location recording crew, the boom operator handles the microphones and the boom, and a utility audio assistant assists the team as the needs arise. Sometimes these jobs are held by three people or more people; often, a crew of one performs all of these duties. Each project, each shoot, and each day has different challenges. In this section we will discuss

- The Mixer, the Boom Operator, and the Utility Person
- Going It Alone
- Making Friends with the Other Crew Members

The Mixer, the Boom Operator, and the Utility Person

The *location recordist*, or *mixer*, is the main person for audio on sets. The mixer determines the equipment, the crew, and the other requirements needed for each shot. Mixers own, rent, or acquire the equipment needed to record the audio for the project. They will troubleshoot, interface with the director, and work with the actors and director of photography to find the best microphone placements to create quality recordings.

It is important that the location recordist reads the script, meets with the director and the director of photography, and sets a plan for each day's shooting. If the recordist is you, express yourself about the issues you hear and the possible difficulties you see ahead, and always offer a solution with each challenge. Filmmaking is a seat-of-your-pants situation, and not just for the sound crew. There are a lot of other collaborators working in their respective crafts contributing to the project. They are facing their own challenges, and there may be problems outside of your department that will take precedence over yours.

Redundancy is an important aspect in a location sound kit. There must always be extra batteries, extra microphones, extra headphones, and extra cables—things always go wrong! If you have been tasked to rent the equipment that will be needed for the shoot, be sure to have the rental facility pack in extras as you see fit. Extra cables and connectors are usually included in the rental package.

Always think of contingencies. A recordist's gear will consist of microphones, a mixing device, cables, and a recorder. But the list does not stop there. It's always a good idea to have extension power cables, adapter plugs for interfacing various pieces of audio and video gear, and a box full of good headphones. You'll also need safety pins, various types of tape, paper, pens, Velcro, Band-Aids, rubber bands, and paper clips. Be sure to have a box of batteries, a good flashlight or two, some simple tools like a screwdriver and wrench, and a Swiss army knife. Never assume that someone else on the set will have something that you need. Chances are they brought it for themselves. They may help you out in a pinch, but plan for your own contingencies. On a movie set you can never be too prepared. See the case study "A Professional Location Cart" in the sidebar for more information on a location workstation.

The *boom operator* position of balancing requires great skill. The microphone must be close enough to the action and the actors to capture an excellent recording, but the boom must be kept from dipping into the shot. Also the microphone must be balanced and pointed in varyingly difficult physical positions. It is a widely misunderstood and underappreciated skill.

If there is one boom for a scene with several actors, the boom microphone must be repositioned toward each actor as they speak. This is a very active, focused process and requires patience, strength, a steady hand, and physical agility. There is a mistaken assumption that the job is simply a matter of presenting a microphone near the activity and that this position can be filled by anyone. But the mistake of using an inexperienced boom operator will become apparent when the project reaches editing. The recordings will be filled with the sounds of "fingers on the boom pole" and odd thumps and bumps due to awkward boom movements.

With an unfocused boom operator, off-axis recordings are the result because of improper microphone positioning. Boom operators also assist the mixer throughout the shoot with the placing of body microphones, planting microphones on the set, running cables, and doing anything that needs to be done for any particular shot.

The *sound utility person* is the general assistant for the sound crew. This person helps the mixer and the boom operator in whatever way is needed. If the boom operator has a complicated following shot, the utility person may follow closely behind to untangle cables or keep areas free. They can help with miking, cables and plant mics, and just about anything that the sound crew will need assistance with during the shoot. This is a popular way to begin a career in location audio. Since sound utility persons will, over time, be present during many different types of situations with more experienced audio crewmembers, they are in an excellent position to learn location audio.

Going It Alone

The basic functions and duties of the mixer, the boom operator, and the assistant all still need to be fulfilled even when they are performed by only one person. ENG shooting utilizes a solo audio crew member. ENG is short for electronic newsgathering. As previously discussed, ENG crews usually have two members, the cameraperson and the sound mixer. Make no mistake about it; ENG location audio is a challenging situation. You'll be monitoring the recording levels, positioning and holding the boom, tracking the shot, and listening for any sonic intrusions that may render the recording unusable.

In DIY and low-budget filmmaking the audio crew often consists of only one person. Critical listening skills will be highly valuable in this situation. A pair of high-quality headphones will be a key piece of equipment. The location recordist will be in the center of the action as the boom operator and will have the responsibilities of the mixer and the utility person as well! This is generally a very mobile position. You will be an integral part of the shoot. Location audio is often an underappreciated skill—unless it is not done well!

Making Friends with the Other Crewmembers

We all have our own style, our own personality, and our own way of interacting with others. People respond to smiles and niceties. People respond to kind words and helping hands. People respond to constructive advice. It is more effective to be a problem solver than to be an obstacle. Shoots are complicated team efforts, and your helping hand one day just may encourage a helping hand from someone else when you most need it.

Try to think of everything that you might need during the shoot—and then bring more. Remember to share and share alike. If someone needs a piece of tape, a battery, or a stick of gum, have it handy. Little acts of kindness can go a long way during a shoot. It always helps to make friends with others on a movie set.

If you are the lone audio person on a shoot, then your preparation and planning is even more crucial. It just cannot be overstated. When the director calls "action," you must be as ready as the actor for that take. You cannot miss a take of an actor giving a perfect performance of a deeply difficult emotional scene. Miss a couple of takes in a day and things can get very difficult. Actors can occasionally blow takes, miss their cues, or move to the wrong position, and the shoot will proceed forward. The crew however does not have that luxury. Plan for every contingency! Plan for things that may probably happen. You may even want to plan for things that will never happen. Don't be caught unaware—eventually the unexpected will happen!

Other crew members are a great resource for what's happening in production and may know of other projects coming up. Sets are always looking for great sound people. Firsthand recommendations are the best recommendations. Make friends and influence people.

Strategies for Recording Location Sound

The actual recording process is simple; we've all done it—plug in a microphone, turn on a recorder, and hit record. The process of getting quality, usable, location audio, however, is quite a bit more involved. The shooting situation and the locations and the type of equipment and the costumes will dictate how any one particular situation will be. However, in the most general sense, at a minimum, a microphone will need to be plugged into a device that records audio. The microphone can be wired or wireless. The microphone will be boomed from overhead or it will be hidden on-set or on a performer. The location recordist and boom operator will rehearse the scene with the performers. Proper gain and levels need to be maintained to create excellent recordings. In this section we will discuss

- Hiding Wireless Microphones
- Working with a Boom Microphone
- Planting Microphones
- Deadening Reverberant Spaces
- Listening—Hums, Fans, Airplanes, and More

Hiding Wireless Microphones

The hiding of body microphones on performers can be a tricky task. If it is improperly mounted, it can pick up clothing rustle, microphone contact noise, or other unacceptable sounds. If the microphone is in the wrong position, it will create a bad recording—muffled, low, or off-axis. Care must be taken with the cable as well, since it can show either by falling out of its hidden place in the costume or making a bulge under tightly fitting clothing. If a wireless system is being used, the transmitter pack must be securely fastened to the actor. If the costume is tight, small, or has no easy way to hide the pack, it can be a challenge.

There are several approaches to mounting and hiding microphones on actors. One excellent approach uses tape and safety pins. Create two triangles from sturdy tape with the sticky side out. Place the microphone head inside. Figure 3.1 shows this type of technique.

These triangles will firmly hold the microphone steady so that clothing rustle will be kept to a minimum. Once the microphone is secure in the triangles, safety pins can be used to assure a solid mounting. Have a good look at the hidden microphone to be sure there are no bulky bulges and that the cable is hidden.

The hidden microphone cable itself can create recordable noise. Appropriate slack in the cable should be accounted for, and a small loop of cable should be made near the head of the microphone capsule. This loop will cut vibration noise from the cable to the microphone. Be sure not to tape over the grill of the microphone!

Since lavalieres are generally omnidirectional in nature it does not matter if the microphone is pointed in any one direction. What does matter is that it is placed as close as possible to the performer's mouth. The center of the chest is ideal. Take note of the head movements for

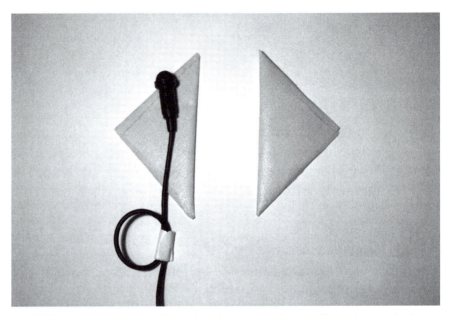

FIGURE 3.1 Once the microphone is placed, place the other triangle over it. Notice that there is also a cable loop to minimize cable noise

the scene because the microphone may need to be repositioned for a better recording if the action calls for it. Some situations may require the assistance of the costumer, depending on the particular garments. Supervise this, because clothing noise, static, or other sounds can get picked up from a poorly positioned hidden mic.

Practice creating the triangles and mounting the microphone. This is one of those things that will need a bit of practice. Don't show up on a set with this in your head as theory. Get some tape, create some triangles, and experiment on yourself and on friends. Practice this until it is second nature. After affixing the microphone, be sure to have the performers move around while you monitor the microphone, listening for clothing rustles, static, or other unwanted noises.

Working with a Boom Microphone

Shotgun microphones mounted on boom poles provide very natural-sounding recordings. The overhead boom allows the microphone to pick up the sounds of the action as well as the dialogue. An experienced boom operator can cover a two or three shot relatively easily with just one boom. It is more challenging for the operator to continue to adjust the boom from actor to actor, but in skilled hands it can sometimes be easier than hiding three separate microphones on three separate performers.

CASE STUDY: A PROFESSIONAL LOCATION CART

Eric Pierce is a professional location recordist working in Hollywood. Eric's extensive recording experience includes recording live television, feature films, game shows, live audience sitcoms, and episodic television. I asked Eric to talk about his location cart and equipment. See figure 3.2 for a photo.

ERIC: "The 01V mixer (Yamaha Digital Mixing Desk) is the heart of it. I can route anything anywhere that I want to. It has a sixteen-channel in-out digital card that is connected to my recorders, which are a Zaxcom DEVA V with eight digital and eight analog inputs with ten tracks, and a Sound Devices 744t four-track. I can also digitally feed external video decks whenever I need to. I have a computer on board for monitoring and storing backup snapshots of the Yamaha 01V, dialogue, or music playback, and using a capture card I can monitor video feeds from the cameras. Oh yeah, I can e-mail and Web surf during setups as well!"

"For microphones I use Schoeps CMIT-5U shotguns primarily. I also have Schoeps CMC6's with a variety of capsules, such as MK4, MK41, and BLM boundary mic, and a Neumann KMR 82i long shotgun. For wireless, I have six Lectrosonics 400 series, and I'm a strong believer in wireless booms, especially for television. It just moves too fast, and sometimes a light will be placed between takes without the camera cutting, and the boom operator needs to reposition in a few seconds. In a wired situation, this could easily turn into a 'Keystone Kops' moment. . . . Wireless boom is also very handy for steady cam 'walk and talks,' where the whole crew is walking backwards in front of the actors. We use "butt plug" transmitters that plug right into the booms so we don't even have to worry about cables from the boom to a belt-mounted transmitter."

"I had my Yamaha 01V's power modified so it will run from a battery. I have a 105 amp battery that sits in the bottom of my cart and it can keep everything except the computer and speakers going for about eight hours. Normally there is always AC power available on any set, but there have been more than a few times that being able to record without mains power has saved the day."

Keep the boom as close to the performers' mouths or action as possible. Try to be consistent with the distance from shot to shot within a scene. Try to keep the appropriate perspective with the microphone. Different axis recordings sound different, and although in the hustle of a busy set it may not be so apparent, in the quiet of the editing

FIGURE 3.2 Eric Pierce at his location cart mixing a feature film

room these shifts will be as clear as a bell. Monitor yourself with good headphones. Listen to any noises that your actions are causing and anticipate and minimize those.

If booming from overhead is unfeasible, then try booming from underneath. This can lead to some odd recording perspectives and sound reflections, so care must be taken with this approach. Listen closely to the microphone placement to be sure that the quality of the recording will be usable. Be aware of the polar pattern of the microphone and use it to your advantage. Keep the pattern focused where it is optimal and understand the limitations, such as the small pickup area behind a directional microphone. Always be listening to your recording!

Always try to keep the boom pointed away from noisy sources. Wind can be a challenging noise to maneuver around on location at times. Bear in mind that recorded wind sounds are difficult, if not impossible, to remove from the recordings later. Always try to use a windscreen or windsock in these situations. If booming on busy streets, point the boom from the street to the action not into the noisy car lane. Always try to position the boom to minimize noise while getting the optimal recording of the performance. Figure 3.3 shows a shotgun microphone with a mount and a windscreen.

Planting Microphones

This is a practice that every digital filmmaker should know. Plant microphones are hidden in a central location that should be in good

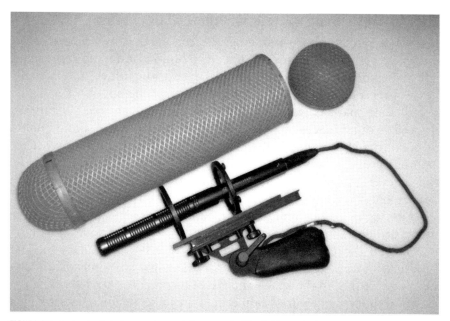

FIGURE 3.3 A standard shotgun and mount that goes inside of this particular windscreen, known as a blimp, which is then capped with only the cable dangling out

proximity to the action and the spoken dialogue. Plant mics can be wired or wireless. Omnidirectional lavaliere microphones are excellent for this, since they can pick up a number of performers and the action over a wide space. Of course more than one microphone can be planted, extending the coverage range considerably. Since lavaliere microphones are so small, they are easy to hide.

Shotgun microphones are also used as plant microphones, and since they are highly directional, they can help cover a noisy or difficult scene. These plant microphones can be hidden in plain sight, disguised, or obscured among the props. They can be on tabletops, sides of desks, lamps, shelves, and walls. Many awkward body situations required of boom operators are simply impossible. Plant mics can be an excellent remedy for these tight situations. And it's easier on the arms!

Listen closely to the incoming signal from the microphone. Be sure that it is close enough to provide an excellent recording. Watch the action of the scene and be sure to listen to and watch for any potential contact from the performers or from the action. It is imperative that there be no bumping, rustling, or other movements of the microphone or the cable. Seek an alternate microphone location if there is a chance of that. Directors will not change the action of scenes to suit microphone placement. Nor should they be expected to.

Deadening Reverberant Spaces

It is often preferable to minimize the echoes that are cast in large, empty spaces. Reverberation can lead to hollow sounding recordings, and the recordings can sound off-axis even though they may actually be well recorded. In some stories and scenes the sound of a highly reverberant space is wanted. Often however, the shooting locations, dressed as other places, may lose their illusion when the sound quality does not match the image. If the image shows a small confined space but the actors' voices sound as if they are speaking in a warehouse, this will jar the audience, and the sound must be adjusted. How much adjustment is needed must be determined on a case-by-case basis.

Although it can be a bit time-consuming on set, properly deadening the recording location can be a lifesaver in postproduction. Deadening is achieved by hanging sound blankets. The types of blankets that furniture movers use are excellent choices for this purpose. Do a simple recording in the space and listen to playback to determine the extent of the work required. Sometimes it can be as simple as affixing a blanket over the acting area with stands and clamps. This can deaden the voices before they reach the ceiling and walls of the space.

Sometimes it is not the voices that reverberate but rather the action. If it is a quiet scene close-miked, it is possible that the large empty space will not be a problem in the dialogue recording. However, high heels on a wooden floor in the same space may reveal the issue. In this case it may be appropriate, if the shot allows, to instead put a blanket or carpeting on the floor to deaden the footfalls. Even though these scenes can be filmed over many hours or even over many days, sooner or later they will be edited together and any inconsistencies in the levels of reverberation will become apparent.

The proximity of the boom can help reduce the reverberant space as well. The closer the mic is to the source, the less room will be present in the recording. Capturing some room sound is desirable; hence a preference for the overhead boom, but too much room sound or the wrong kind of room sound can render a recording unusable. There is simply no way to reduce that reverberant quality in a recording after the fact. If all of the recordings for that scene sound that way, then the editing match becomes easier. During final mixing, reverb can easily be added to a recording; however, it is nearly impossible to remove it from the location recording. Keep the mics close!

Since reverberant recordings can be problematic it is important to make the filmmaker aware of the issue. Although it can take a few extra minutes to set stands, clamp blankets, or cover flooring with carpet, the savings in postproduction can be substantial. At the editing stage, if the director deems that the location recordings are not usable, the only other option is dialogue replacement. We will be dealing with this in a later chapter, and you will find that it is a sophisticated, complicated, and costly art that requires participation from a number of people. I have witnessed actors' distress over having to perform dialogue replacement. One well-known actor explained to me that his performance on-set was perfect and that there would be no way recreate his performance in ADR, or as he put it, "you can't catch lightning in a bottle twice." Take the time needed for excellent recordings on-set.

Listening—Hums, Fans, Airplanes, and More

Listening is an aspect of sound work that will be covered many times in this text. Learning critical listening skills is fundamental to working effectively in audio. The tendency to tune out the sounds of everyday life needs to be overcome. Actively listen to the sounds that surround you daily. Unless you sharpen your hearing and attention to sound you will be like a cameraman with faulty vision or who has difficulty seeing things in the shot.

Many recordings reach the postproduction stage having sound issues that could have been easily avoided on the set. If a scene is being shot inside of a restaurant after hours, and the microphone is in close proximity to the refrigerators, they should be turned off or unplugged from shot to shot. If the air-conditioning is clearly heard over your headphones it must be turned off for each shot. These situations can be easy or difficult depending on the location, the time of day, and the access to the controls governing these things. In any case, many of these noises in the recordings will be near impossible to correct in postproduction. Do what you can to eliminate or at least minimize these issues.

Always make the director aware of the noises that you hear. The director is in charge of the shoot and in fact is generally in charge of the show, so if he or she says to "live with it," then do just that. It is important to let the issues be known so that the person in charge is making decisions about things that may cost time and money later in the process.

Every set and every director is different. Some directors want to know about every creak, every fan, and every airplane that you hear. Others do not "want to be bothered" by your reports of less-than-ideal recording situations. You'll have to assess each situation and act accordingly. In time you will learn to identify which noises can be easily filtered out and which will require the recordings to be replaced.

> **TIP**
>
> Stand in a quiet room. Listen to your surroundings—critically. Can you hear birds outside, cars rumbling past, neighbors speaking, or distant radios? Listen closer—can you hear fans, the refrigerator humming from the kitchen, the computer in an adjacent room? Listen closer still; can you hear the shrill whine of a light fixture or the soft push of the air through the central air and heating? Do this exercise often—inside and outside. Learn to listen for the layers of sound that surround you at all times. Learn how to call this new hearing power to your senses at will. You will need these new perceptions when critically listening to a set.

It is important to hold your ground if you believe that problems exist that can be readily solved. If it is a first-time directing and producing team, they may not yet understand the ramifications of what you are telling them.

If you have been critically listening, getting the mics where they need to be, and minimizing sound issues as they arise, that effort will be recognized. You may be on another set, with another inexperienced team, but you'll be building a reputation as someone who cares about doing quality work.

Besides the types of noise created outside of the production, there are also many unwanted sounds created from the production. Some examples are loud shoes on wood floors, actors crinkling a newspaper near their microphone, someone working at a stove with sizzling sounds and metal bowls and utensils, and actors hugging and hitting the microphone in the course of their action.

A location recordist must also pay strict attention to these sounds. Loud clangs from silverware or rustling paper will destroy a quiet performance and will be difficult to edit later. There are many instances where actors will need to be aware of their movements and their handling of props. Listen closely and make your concerns heard to the director. Although it is a team effort on-set, you are likely the only one hearing exactly what is going on.

Keeping Logs

Sound logs, sound reports, or location sound notes are the documentation that the location recordist creates to keep track of what scenes have been recorded, the tape or media name, which takes are good or bad, the date and time, the file type, and any additional information. In this section we will discuss:

- Writing the Sound Logs
- Slating, Timecode, Metadata
- Penmanship and Labels
- Staying Organized

Writing the Sound Logs

The key to good location sound logs is in their completeness. This log will be the first place editors will go to find out where the recordings are located. It is important to include all pertinent data so that things are easy to find. Most log sheets have perfunctory information filled in. Although on-set it may seem redundant to write the information over again, in editing, log sheets may be

SOUND REPORT

MEDIA GROUP
SANTA MONICA, CA 90404

MIXER: Donelly   PHONE: -See Contact
TITLE: Morgan   DIRECTOR: Woo   PRODUCTION COMPANY: AMG
RECORDER: DEVA   SAMPLE RATE: 48   BIT RATE: 24   FILE TYPE: BWAV   TIMECODE: TONE: -20   METADATA:

SCENE	TAKE	PNO	NOTES	TIMECODE	TRACKS 1	2	3	4	5	6	7	8
21A	6	26	Good	04:20:10	M lav	F lav	Boom	Boom				
21A	7	27	Airplane	04:24:35	M lav	F lav	Boom	Boom				
21A	8	28	Good ✱✱	04:27:44	M lav	F lav	Boom	Boom				
21B	1	29	Flub line	04:29:10	M lav		Boom					
21B	2	30	Noisy Grip Move	04:30:29	M lav		Boom					
21B	3	31	Good ✱ ✱	04:32:15	M lav		Boom					
21B	4	32	Good	04:35:16	M lav		Boom					
22A	1	33	Airplane	04:38:50		F lav	Boom	Boom	Plant 1	Plant 2		
22A	2	34	Good Perf	04:39:59		F lav	Boom	Boom	Plant 1	Plant 2		
22A	3	35	Good Perf	04:43:28		F lav	Boom	Boom	Plant 1	Plant 2		
22A	4	36	Truck Noise	04:46:11								
22A	5	37	Good ✱✱	04:48:37								

FIGURE 3.4 This sound report is from a multichannel on-set recording, notice the notes and track assignments

distributed to a number of different people, and a sheet without all the information may be missing something that is needed. Figure 3.4 gives an example of a sound report.

The standard items should always be included: sound roll name, date, time, file type, media, take number, scene name, frame rate, sample rate, and bit depth. In today's digital world, instead of a sound roll, it could be a media stick or a drive. No matter what the medium, create a nomenclature that is consistent throughout the shoot.

Since the items on the report will be generally the same, it's easy to neglect filling them out over and over again on each sheet. However, if you imagine that any one sound log is the only one available, you will see the wisdom of including this information on every sheet.

There are plenty of different types of sound logs available commercially online. They are usually in PDF or doc formats, so they are universally readable. However, if you know that the entire shoot will be using the same specifications, such as the sample rate or the bit depth, you can easily create a custom log that has those pertinent details already filled in.

Slating, Timecode, Metadata

Slating should now be a familiar process from your prior exercises. Typically, audio slates are recorded for each take, prior to the performance.

Why record an audio slate when there is a slate on a sound log and also on the lined script? Audio slates make things easier when editing. There are times when it is simpler to use the recorded audio slate than going through logs and scripts.

If you are shooting double-system sound, then the slate will include some sort of *clapper* to create a sync mark. A clapper is a slate that has a wooden bar across the top. The slate has important information on it, such as the take name and some crew member names. It is held in the shot and the wooden bar is clapped creating a loud clack. In postproduction the audio spike of the clack will be synced up with the visual image of the exact frame of the hit. Once the two are placed together, the separate sound and film or video files will then be in sync for that take.

Timecode can be a scary subject for those not familiar with it. Timecode is simply the counting of frames, be it film or video. Film is counted as twenty-four frames per second (fps). Video can be counted any number of ways. Separate audio recording devices should always follow the camera settings. Timecode is very important because it is used as a reference in many aspects of the post process. Timecode will also assist in the syncing of audio and video.

There are various ways of counting the video or film frames for post purposes, and there are also a number of ways to create timecode. For location audio, the most widely used scheme to generate timecode is called *jam-sync*. Jam-sync timecode means that one device is originating the timecode and all of the other devices—other cameras or the location audio recorder "jam-sync" to that device and then generate the same timecode.

Since jam-sync forces all of the devices to generate the exact same timecode, no external timecode generators or cables between devices are needed. This way, the devices can all run independently of one another and yet still have matching timecode. The subject of frame rates, timecode generation, and sync can fill a full volume of its own. For location audio, the easy answer is to follow exactly what the camera is using and it will all match.

Timecode can be a dizzying topic. There are various frames rates, for example, 30 fps, 29.97 fps, 24 fps, 23.976 fps, 60 fps, 59.97 fps, and others. There are also different generating schemes for timecode. There is jam-sync, which has already been discussed, and there is also "time of day," which uses a real-time clock as a basis for generating timecode. There are also "free-run—user generated" timecode schemes, which means that the operator chooses a timecode number to start with. For instance, each tape can start with a new hour. Thus, tape 1 can start at timecode of hour one, or 01:00:00:00, and tape 2 can start at hour two, or 02:00:00:00, and so on.

Since the frame rate and the timecode schemes are mainly the domain of the edit process and the camera choices, for our purposes in audio, the best advice is to follow the camera. Some people refer to 30 fps but actually mean 29.97 fps and sometimes people refer to 60 fps but actually mean 59.97. The best advice is to ask the camera department to provide all of the appropriate settings in writing. Then verify with the operator on-set.

Metadata is data about data. For instance, on the very popular audio format known as *MP3* the typical metadata included will be the artist name, the song title, and perhaps the album title. In broadcast audio, metadata has other important functions. The metadata can include information regarding the way dialogue levels are reproduced as well as the way the files are handled from the broadcast station to your television.

Metadata is a new phenomenon since the advances in digital audio technology. What use is there for metadata for the location recordist? Depending on the devices used to record the location audio, the recordist can add metadata to the recorded files, such as the character name, the scene name, and the take name, all embedded right onto the recordings!

Penmanship and Labels

It is often noted that physicians have terrible handwriting. In the case of a physician the impact can be dramatic. An improperly interpreted prescription can be a real problem. In audio, the results will usually not involve life and death, although in the heat of the moment it may feel that way! Try to write all of the labels, sound logs, and notes as legibly as you can.

It seems like a small point to be making, but the truth is an illegible note or sound log is just as bad as not having one at all. Try to make things readable for your colleagues. By the time the recordings you've provided are in the hands of editors, you most likely will be off on another shoot. Make the searching of recordings easier for editors; they must sometimes go through hours of material.

In the same vein of thinking, keep things organized and labeled properly. Filmmaking is a highly collaborative process, and many individuals will be going through the sound reports, tapes, and drives that you provide. Time is money, so label everything clearly and simply so that the meaning of the notes and labels is crystal clear.

Staying Organized

Finally, one last word to address the issue of organization. This is not only regarding the tapes and recordings but the location kit and personnel as well. Plan for the shoot, plan for the day, and plan for the shot. Be organized and understand the rigors of what needs to be accomplished.

Organize the microphones, the headphones, and the cables. Organize the sound reports, the tape stock, and the media. Organize the team, the responsibilities, and the tasks. Making movies is "all hands on deck." Life will be very difficult if you are sifting through boxes of cables searching for a plug and your assistant can't find batteries for the lavaliere body pack and the script supervisor wants to review the sound report while the director and director of photography are expecting you to be present on-set to discuss an upcoming shot.

Have boxes sorted and labeled correctly for the gear; keep batteries, clips, and mounting tape easily accessible; have notebooks and clipboards for logs; and create the space needed for easy retrieval of whatever is needed. The demands during a shoot can pull you in any number of ways—all at the same time! Don't let the easy things get away from you.

Keep the simple things simple to allow you time to concentrate on the important things—like setting the microphones and recording levels, conferring with the other crew members, and properly recording the shot! You will do a better job if you and your gear and crew are organized and ready to go.

Summary

The duties of the location sound crew include mixing the levels properly for the recording, getting the microphones in the proper places, and handling cables and equipment. The main individuals are the location mixer, the boom operator, and the utility person. Sometimes it is a crew of three or more, but often one person performs these duties.

When hiding wireless microphones on performers it is important to listen for acoustic noises from the costumes as well as contact noise from the placement or the action. Also be sensitive to the performer when hiding and placing microphones, and remember that they are there ready to give a performance. Be courteous and professional.

Plant microphones are a good solution for difficult miking situations; however, great care must be given to acoustic or contact noise as well. Listen closely to the recording whether you are the boom operator or the mixer. And be particularly attuned to the sounds created from the performances themselves. Let the director know about the need to reduce and minimize loud properties like utensils and paper shuffling.

Recording spaces should be deadened if the reverberation is marring the effect of the setting. Reverberation can be added later in the mixing process if needed, but it is close to impossible to remove unwanted reverberation from recordings. It is important to stay focused and organized during the shoot.

Listen closely each step of the way. Take excellent notes and create intelligent documentation as the shoot progresses. And make use of today's digital technology that allows for the inclusion of metadata to assist in the postproduction stage.

Review Questions

Questions like these are likely to appear on exams to test how well you understood and retained the information in this chapter.

1. Who are the main crew members in a location audio crew?
2. What are the main responsibilities of the location audio crew?
3. Why are reverberant spaces a concern of location audio recording?
4. Who determines the sample rate and bit depth settings for a shoot?
5. What is metadata?

Discussion/Essay Questions

Your instructor may assign you one or more of the following questions for discussion in class or as the subject of a paper.

1. Explain the various reasons why developing critical listening skills can assist a location recordist.
2. Put together a list of items needed for a three-person scene, set in a backyard, shot in wide shots and in close-up. Discuss possible miking and recording scenarios.

Applying What You've Learned

Research/Lab/Fieldwork Projects

The following lab exercises will give you understanding of the space reflection while recording location audio.

1. Take a portable recorder to a reverberant room. Set the recorder down, stand four feet from the front of the microphone, slate location, and record thirty seconds while speaking.

NOTE

Students who have ongoing projects may elect to use their own source material, such as video clips, with the instructor's permission.

2. Set the recorder down, stand six feet from the front of the microphone, slate the location, and record thirty seconds while speaking.

3. Set the recorder down, stand twelve feet from the front of the microphone, slate location, and record thirty seconds while speaking.

4. Critically listen to the recordings in a quiet controlled space; note the quality of the voice recording and the effect of the proximity to the microphone in such a space.

Resources

The following resources have more information on the topics covered in this chapter.

Audio Engineering Society, "An Audio Timeline" (http://www.aes.org/aeshc/docs/audio.history.timeline.html). This is a timeline of audio from its humble beginnings as sound on wax cylinders to the digital audio of today. Check out the entire AES website, it is filled with wonderful information.

Ron Dexter, ASC, "Set Etiquette" (http://www.rondexter.com/intermediate/production/set_ettiquette.htm). This is an excellent article on proper set etiquette. The website, from a veteran cinematographer, is filled with great articles about frequently asked questions.

CHAPTER 4

DON'T JUST GET THE SHOT

In this chapter, you will:

- Discover the prime importance of room tone
- Learn about "B-Roll" audio
- Understand capturing the "universe" of the set
- Understand on-set dialogue replacement and on-set foley

Room Tone

New or beginning location recordists sometimes think that their only requirement is to capture the dialogue for each scene in a project. While it is true that this is the main concern, there are many other recordings that will be required as well. In filming there is a term called *coverage*. Coverage, for location shooting, is all the various angles and shots to offer a good range of possible edits. Think about coverage for audio as well. You will need to cover the entire sonic universe created on-set and not merely the lines of dialogue.

Room tone, sometimes referred to as room noise, is a recording of the natural sound of any particular space that is being recorded in. Room tone is a recording of the sound of the space but with no talking, no movements, and no sound other than the space itself.

Room tone is a requirement for the proper editing of production tracks. In soundtracks, generally, there are no moments of "true"

FIGURE 4.1 This room tone was recorded in a controlled space

FIGURE 4.2 This room tone was recorded at a booth table at a restaurant

silence. Between recorded bits of action and dialogue is room tone. Room tone can be thought of as the glue that holds many tracks together for the illusion of a seamlessly mixed soundtrack. No two rooms sound alike, so you can't simply use a room tone effect from a library. With critical listening skills the different room tones of spaces will become apparent.

Figures 4.1 and 4.2 are images of waveforms of two different room tones. The waveforms look different, and they sound different. This is because the sound of every room is different. When editing location audio and making changes or deletions, room tone is needed.

Unfortunately, capturing room tone is often thought of as a time waster on a busy set. Without the proper understanding of the role that room tone plays during the sound edit, filmmakers will often wave off a location recordist's desire to record room tone. Room tone is one of the easiest ways to contain costs in audio postproduction. The reason for this is simple—if room tone has not been recorded it must be created.

Make no mistake about it, no matter how big or small the project, room tone will be required. The choice then becomes: Do we record the room tone here for one minute and be done with it, or do we pay a sound editor to spend hours and hours to create room tone from the production tracks for each and every scene?

- Why Is Room Tone Important?
- Proper Recording of Room Tone
- Logging the Room Tone

Why Is Room Tone Important?

For many filmmakers room tone is a misunderstood element in location recording. Room tone is *not* an optional requirement to the filmmaking process. Room tone is essential to properly edit the location production tracks. For example, in the best take of a scene there is a loud crash that happens between the lines of spoken dialogue. An editor will take a small bit of room tone and paste it over the crash. This will seamlessly cover the problem and continue the illusion of a continuous take. Room tone, often referred to as *fill*, is used to cover the spaces in the production tracks to fill moments of unintended true silence, and is also used to cover unwanted sounds in the production tracks.

Why not just cut out the offending noise and be done with it? If a noise or crash as described above is simply lifted from the track, a gap, a bit of true silence, will make the track feel as if something has "dropped out." Room tone gives the editor the ability to smooth things and change things so there is never a dropout of the production audio. Room tone shifts and room tone dropouts will take the audience out of the viewing experience.

There are other uses for room tone as well. Room tone is an important element when adding rerecorded lines of dialogue into the sound edit of the location recordings. The room tone allows a final sound mixer to blend the room tone and the new recordings. This creates the illusion of a seamless edit and replacement.

No two rooms sound alike. It is as simple as that. Microphone placement, the specific equipment used to record the scene, the furniture in the room, the time of day, the proximity to exterior sound—all of these elements contribute to the room tone. To an ear untrained in critical listening it may seem that all of these rooms sound similar. Unfortunately, in the exacting art of sound editing and sound mixing, similar is not good enough. These differing room tones will audibly shift and will affect the experience of the audience.

Room tone is also used extensively for the *production effects track*, or the *PFX track*. The PFX track is an edited audio track that contains production effects that were recorded on-set in sync with the picture. For an example of a production effect, think of a dialogue scene that takes place in a kitchen. During the dialogue interchange the characters are running the sink, placing dishes and silverware and moving around the room. A sound editor will snip out the bits of action between the lines of dialogue in the location recordings. All of those elements will be placed onto the PFX.

These PFX tracks will be combined with other elements of the soundtrack to help create a deliverable item called a *music and effects track*, or an *M&E track*. An M&E track is a track devoid of all dialogue elements. It is a final mixed track that only contains the mixed effects tracks and the mixed music tracks. A distributor can then hire actors who will rerecord the dialogue in other languages and then mix the M&E track with the new dialogue recordings to re-create the soundtrack in another language.

Room tone is used to properly fill in the PFX track as well as give the *post sound mixer* the ability to transition from the various sound elements in a smooth manner. The post sound mixer, also called the *rerecording mixer*, is the sound crewmember responsible for the final mixing of the soundtrack in collaboration with the filmmakers. The post sound mixer creates the final mix of the project and creates the audio deliverables.

Proper Recording of Room Tone

Room tone should be captured in each location. As a bare minimum thirty seconds of room tone should be captured for each setup. A key element in the recording of room tone is that the "room" must be exactly as it is in the shots. Same crew, same props, same furnishings. It would be ideal to get one minute's worth, but getting any at all can often be an accomplishment.

Imagine a simple dialogue scene around a table. To properly record the room tone, position the boom where it will be during a take, set your levels similarly to the scene to be recorded, and hit record. That's it. The concept is simple enough; the reality is the difficult part. Try to get all the people working on-set to pause their activity, turn off their cell phones, stop talking, stop walking, and stop making any noise for the duration of that thirty seconds.

The key to useable room tone is that it has nothing in it except the ambient sound of the location. It will be rendered useless if there are bumps, beeps, clangs, foot falls, and so on through the recording. The room tone recording, by definition, has to be free of any of these sorts of sounds.

Room tone is a recording that will be looped and replayed over and over again, and even something as faint as a cloth rustle, a footstep, or a cough will mar the recording. Instead, it will have what I refer to as the "washing machine effect." When looped and replayed it will instead—whoosh, whoosh, whoosh, or click, click, click, or whatever the sound was. This repetition will be useless to create the illusion of a seamless, uninterrupted sound. This is one of the main reasons why creating room tone can be such a difficult task.

Room tone that is created, from scratch from the location recordings, is a labor-intensive process. The location recordings must be searched for moments where there is no talking, no moving, and even no audible breathing. All of these elements will distract from the illusion of room tone. Finding useable bits of room tone in the production recordings can be tough indeed.

Briefly, here is how room tone is created from the edit: A few frames of useable room tone in a location recording are found, and then three more clean frames are found, then five more, and so on. The sound editor is looking for bits of room tone between lines of dialogue or before or after the actual edit begins. These are then all pieced together to create a second or two of "clean" room tone.

This process can be extremely time-consuming. Multiply that process of searching for frames of audio to create room tone for each and every scene in the movie and you can see how arduous a task this becomes. It can take many hours or even days to create all of the room tones necessary for any given project. This is a true waste of time and money. Particularly if you understand that it can be completed in thirty to sixty seconds on-set. Remember, room tone must be free of any noticeable noises; oddly, the recording of the room must be "silent"!

Logging the Room Tone

Logging clips in professional environments is a duty generally tasked to the assistant editor. Here I am referring to assistant picture editors. Accordingly, they excel at logging all the extraneous bits of picture that were captured on-set. Often some of the necessary elements required for audio are left on the drives, on the tapes, or somehow misplaced with other "nonessential" things. Unless told otherwise, the picture editors and their assistants are naturally focused on the images. They may not understand the importance of things that were recorded by the location recordist and thus may not log, capture, and label them.

During the logging process I encourage the creation of what I call the "additional audio elements" folder. This should be the "go-to" folder when cutting the sound. I suggest placing all of the room tones for each location in this folder. We'll discuss this folder in detail in a later chapter, but basically this folder will contain all sorts of terrific material recorded by the location recordist for the sound edit. It is a great idea to keep all of the room tones and additional audio elements in one place.

When the assistant editor is logging and capturing takes, be sure to make him or her aware of the room tones so that they actually do get logged and put aside for later use. Often after the material has been sorted, logged, and captured it is not looked at again. This is the prime and sometimes the only time to log and capture all of those sound elements. They may not seem important to a picture editor, but they

TIP (continued)

a decent room tone. Everyone is waiting on-set for him to call speed before the action begins, and he uses that momentary pause to force room tone to be recorded! He also told me he was admonished on-set several times for "the wait" but later was told that his simple technique saved many hours and dollars in the editing room by eliminating the usual process of creating room tone tracks in postproduction. Because of modern technology there is less of a need to "wait for speed" in digital filmmaking. Soon you will need to find another stalling tactic to record the room tone!

are essential to the sound editor. Log those room tones and make a file for them in a place for easy retrieval.

In my professional experience, I have found that the very finest picture editors are also excellent sound editors. They share similar concerns with the sound-editing team regarding the quality of the audio, the need for dialogue replacement, and the importance of room tone from the production tracks.

On the other hand, some picture editors have said to me, "I don't do sound," and their edits confirm this statement. If you are cutting the picture as well as the audio, you will find that having those room tones handy and easy to find will speed the more tedious work of cutting the production tracks.

B-Roll Audio—Every Set Is Unique

There is a term that directors of photography or camerapersons use called *B-roll* footage. B-roll is footage that is used to establish location or is additional footage that is edited within scenes and interviews. For instance, if there is an interview of a pilot, seated and speaking about flying airplanes, B-roll of them boarding the plane, entering the cockpit, and preparing the plane for take-off can be intercut with the interview.

B-roll is an important element in the final picture edit. Sometimes sound is recorded with B-roll, but often only with the camera-mounted microphone or without silencing extraneous sounds while the camera rolls. Since B-roll is typically not scenes with actors or spoken dialogue, there is a misunderstanding that the audio is unimportant. The thinking is that what is important is the shot.

However, if the footage is captured silent, then often the accompanying sound may have to be created. If there is talking or other sounds in the B-roll, then the sound will also have to be created, since the audio will be unusable. This can be a great loss, since often these are very unique locations with very unique sounds around them. In this section we will learn the proper techniques for

- Capturing Sounds Unique to Your Production
- Field Sound Effects Recording
- Recording Hard Effects

Capturing Sounds Unique to Your Production

Think of this example: The location is a remote house, built back in the woods, surrounded by forest and wild animals. It is a wet and windy place, and the photographed scenes contain the effects of the wind and the rain. During the time spent filming at the location, the crew complains that the place is eerie and the sounds in the house are quite spooky. Stories abound that late at night the wind howls through the house and creates a sound that sends shivers down everyone's spine. However, these sounds are not specifically recorded, since they were not included in the script's lines of dialogue. The only recordings of this eerie sound are between the takes—at the start or stop of each take of recorded dialogue.

When the project reaches the sound-editing stage, the sound editor hears wonderful stories from the filmmakers about the location and how eerie the location sounded. The creaking floors, window shutters slamming in the wind, the way the rain pounded on the roof, and so on. The sound editor responds, "Fantastic! Where can I find all these great sounds?" Often the answer is—"Well we didn't record any of it, but they are ideal for the soundtrack. You'll just have to re-create them." Does this seem like a wasted opportunity? It certainly does to any good sound editor.

In this example, an opportunity is lost to capture a sonic quality unique to the location. Multiply that many times over at each location on each motion picture made. On a remote island, inside an ocean liner, downtown in New York City, or even on the roof of a skyscraper, these sounds are unique to their place and are often vital elements in the final sound edit and mix of a movie. In pursuit of "the shot" there is often a disregard for the wonderful *sounds* that are just as special and particular as the look of any specific location.

Find the time to record the sounds specific to the location that is being filmed. Or if there is simply no time for you to do it, encourage the production to hire a separate crew to capture this audio. It may seem to a producer that the money could be better spent elsewhere, but a different case can be made. Since this audio will be required at one point or another, if it is not in the picture edit, then it will need to be captured, created, or found during post. And that will begin to get expensive.

Similar to room tone creation after the fact, coming up with proper sounds for a particular location will be time-consuming, difficult, and expensive to do later. A sound crew hired for a day during a long shoot will cost many times less and produce a better representation of the location than paying crews to re-create it later. Capture the sounds that only exist in that particular location. It is time and money well spent.

Directors are often extremely literal in their expectations and desires for audio as they complete their projects. They might remember a howl of wind flapping sails on a boat, or the way the boards creaked every time a sailor walked on deck. The sound editor and mixer are then tasked to re-create the exact sound that was present during the location shooting! It can be quite a challenge to achieve these particular sonic elements.

If you find yourself in a situation where location sounds are unique, they must be captured clean. These recordings will have to be captured in a way similar to room tone recording. No cell phones, no talking, no moving about—unless of course that is a part of the location sound that you want to capture. These recordings will be used as an element of the final sound edit and mix. Just like room tone, they will not edit properly if they are filled with extraneous sounds.

Field Sound Effects Recording

Field sound effects recording is taking the idea of B-roll audio just a bit further. Thinking again about the unique locations productions find themselves in offers many more possibilities for capturing distinctive sounds. Once again, the task is to listen. Listen to the spaces that you find yourself in—busy streets and busy markets, schools, hospitals, wherever the script has taken the story. Often, when projects reach sound editing, all that the sound editors have is the audio that was captured on location for the dialogue scenes. When the picture edit is complete, then sound effects, ambient sounds, and other audio get pulled from sound effects libraries. For good directors who remember the sounds that they heard during production, many of the library sounds won't be satisfactory.

Take, for instance, an exotic locale that has many migratory birds. Perhaps the birdcalls are very unique and not easily found in sound libraries. If the location recordist captured several minutes of these sounds, they could then be used as background and ambient sounds under specific scenes. Sound effects libraries are wonderful resources for filling backgrounds, but they are no substitute for the real thing. As good as commercial sound effects libraries can be, they are quite generic in the sounds that are available. Often many unique sounds will have to be re-created because there will not be an exact fit for the particular scene that you may be editing.

When listening to the unique character of the spaces used during the location shooting, think about the totality of the script and the story. If outdoor scenes are a large component, be sure to get various background recordings from the locations. If there are many extras and crowd scenes, be sure to capture those sounds outside of and above and beyond what is called for in the dialogue scenes. It is imperative to have these additional recordings available for the picture editor and the sound editor to fill this newly edited world with just the right sounds.

Recording Hard Effects

Hard effects, in the sound-editing world, refers to nonhuman sounds that are in sync with the picture, such as car door slams, plane crashes, or other types of similar sound elements. For films that are special-effect oriented or are dominated by sounds such as car driving, mechanical devices, machines, and so on, it is imperative to capture these sounds as much as possible.

Often it is impossible to get close enough to large explosions or to find a way to record them effectively. The sound recordist must find solutions to capture these recordings. Perhaps you can be at the ready and record all of the rehearsals of a specific stunt or explosion. If there are several location recordings of an event, a sound editor may be able to piece them together to create the illusion of it being a single event. As we will discover in a later chapter, sound effects are often stacked upon one another and mixed together to create the final sound effect. Having location production elements mixed into that effect can heighten the illusion.

During a fistfight scene between actors, the performers actually make no or very light contact. And yet an illusion is maintained that real punches are landing. Surrounding that fight there may be breaking glass, crunching metal, or other sounds that can be captured. In these situations it is important to focus squarely on the sounds that can be recorded well and realistically.

Continue to think along the lines of capturing more than what is needed. If the scene calls for someone destroying a car with a baseball bat, for instance, perhaps you can capture additional sounds when the camera is not rolling. You may not be able to get close enough to the action for a great recording during the actual camera takes. If that is the case, see if you can record more of the action with audio only. This may allow you to get the microphone in close for really clean, hot recordings. With the intense emphasis on the picture and "did we get the shot," the idea of "did we get the sound" is generally not even a consideration. Don't let these choice opportunities pass.

Always maintain the highest quality of the audio being recorded. Since the camera may need very specific locations and angles for the picture composition, it may be tough to impossible to get the microphone where it is needed for the best recording. Keep tabs on any audio that might need to be rerecorded if time and the situation permit.

If there is a lot of car activity in the show, it's important to get the hard effects. Slam the doors, rev the engine, do drive-bys, record the wheels squealing on the pavement, try to cover the various situations that may be required for the edit.

In the course of production often these sorts of recordings are compromised in one way or another. The production is focused on getting the best possible recording of the dialogue. Stay on top of the larger picture, the sonic environment of the universe being created on-screen. Be sure to log all of these recordings and file them in the additional audio folder.

On-Set Dialogue Replacement

On-set dialogue replacement is a wonderful technique for being sure that clean recordings exist of all of the required dialogue. There are many instances where the dialogue recording gets compromised, be it from on-set noises, one-time sound discrepancies, or sometimes something as simple as slurred diction or unintended moves by an actor that put the boom or a plant mic in a wrong place. In this section we will discuss

- Keeping Track of Bad Takes
- Replacing Dialogue Scenes with Audio Only
- Capturing Wild Audio

Keep Track of Bad Takes

Everyone on-set has a job to do and must stay focused on his or her area of expertise. The makeup person is always looking for sweat or smudges; the property person is always checking to see that the correct items are on-set. The location recordist is the person who is the authority on the quality of what is being recorded. That person will know all of the dialogue that has been recorded and whether there was a mic bump, an airplane passing, or a flubbed line.

Keep a pad handy and keep notes regarding each scene as it is recorded. Your goal is to present the best-quality tracks and recordings possible in whatever the circumstances are at any given moment. Always be sure that there are clean recordings for each element of each scene. Jot down any lines that were not optimally recorded so that you can make the director aware of any possible issues for later. Also keep an ear out for unique sounds, hard effects, and ambience that can be captured and notate these as the shoot progresses.

During production meetings it is imperative that you take an active role along with other crew members, the script person, and particularly the director and voice your concerns or thoughts regarding the audio. You are the point person, and you are the ultimate authority regarding the recordings. You may be vetoed or otherwise overruled, but it is important to make the issues known for the good of the project.

And being proactive shows how much you care about your work and the project.

Replacing Dialogue Scenes with Audio Only

Dialogue replacement is a true craft and art. How is it done and what is the process? Dialogue replacement, also referred to as *ADR* (automated dialogue replacement) happens after the picture edit is complete. An assessment is made as to what lines of dialogue may need to be rerecorded in ADR.

Once the lines have been determined, scripts are assembled for each character with each line to be replaced. Once the ADR scripts are complete, the sound recording sessions need to be prepared for ADR. This includes creating recording tracks, assembling the playback tracks of the production recording of the lines to be replaced, and the adding and placing of the *beep tracks* that are used to cue the actors.

Beep tracks are tracks that contain audio recordings of three beeps that are cued just prior to the line of dialogue to be rerecorded. The actors will closely watch their lips on-screen and listen to the beeps to cue the start of their performance. The fourth "imaginary" beep is the start of the line to be recorded. Just preparing these sessions for recording can be quite time-consuming. Multiply this process by every scene, every character, and every line to be rerecorded and you can see that this is not an inconsequential process.

Once the sessions have been properly set up, the actor is scheduled to come into the recording studio to rerecord the lines in sync with the original performance. Depending on the budget and contracts on the specific movie, this may also mean additional compensation for the actor. The actors must recreate the emotional quality of the scene, interacting not with actors, sets, and props but alone in a recording booth with a TV monitor. Bear in mind that this recording happens usually months after the actual shooting of the scene. The process can sometimes be a terrific challenge in and of itself for the performer and for the director.

Once all of the takes have been recorded, the ADR mixer and the director audition each and every take of each and every line of rerecorded dialogue to determine which takes have the emotional quality acceptable to the director. The ADR mixer must also determine whether any take chosen by the director will be able to be edited to match the lip movements of the actor on-screen. Often there are ten takes or more for each line of rerecorded dialogue. In feature-length films there can be thousands of takes that must be auditioned and chosen!

Once the takes have been deemed the final choices, they are then placed in the new sound edit. Room tone must be added to massage them into the mix as well as whatever additional sound processes are required to make them sound similar to the original takes. Then these tracks are edited to best match the sync of the original recording. This process is done for each and every line to be replaced.

As you can see, this is not an insignificant task! Once filmmakers have been involved with some extensive ADR situations they begin to appreciate the role of the location recordist and the need for proper on-set recording.

So what exactly is "on-set ADR recording"? The ideal situation for recording on-set ADR is a re-creation of the actual scene on the same set with the same equipment and following the same action. The actors will not be lip-syncing to picture, of course; they will redo the scene with the audio being rerecorded on-set. If there were problems in recordings of some lines of the dialogue, this is a simple fix.

Editing affords filmmakers a great deal of latitude in capturing the best audio. The lines that have recording issues can easily be replaced using the on-set ADR, allowing a seamless insert of the new, better recordings. The sonic quality will match well, and often these new lines can also be easily "cut to sync" because the actor's inflections, tempo, and cadences will be so similar.

It is not always possible to recapture performances in this situation, but if it is possible, it can't be recommended highly enough. As the location recordist, you will know exactly which lines of dialogue have problems. Encourage the producer and director to rerecord those lines on the set.

The postproduction ADR recording stage is far removed from the excitement of the set and the action. ADR sessions are about the syncing of lip movements as much as they are about the actor's performance. When recapturing problematic recordings on the set, the replacement performances are generally of a much higher quality because the actors are still in "performance mode." They are still "in character." They are more excited, their pitch tends to be higher than the more relaxed ADR recordings, and they are investing more in their performance. Strike while the iron is hot!

Capturing Wild Audio

Wild audio is a term used to describe sounds, dialogue, or effects that are typically not in sync with the picture but are a good idea to get "just in case." Wild audio is typically not scripted material. It is not the same as on-set ADR, since that is exclusively scripted material that is re-created when audio problems occurred during the camera takes.

Have the script with you everywhere and be sure to always be on the lookout for sounds that could enhance the story. It is imperative to know the story that is being told. With that knowledge and with keen perception you may find some sounds that are completely unrelated to the actual shooting script but may prove useful in editing. Here is when your attention to detail will really shine.

Perhaps there is a particular machine that makes a unique sound; a strange birdcall that can be manipulated later for eerie effect; or perhaps even yells, laughs, screams, or other verbal but nondialogue elements that can help clarify a scene or a moment. Always be on the lookout for these things and, within reason, offer these ideas during production meetings for their possible capture. Don't waste what may truly be a once-in-a-lifetime opportunity.

On-Set Foley Recording

Foley is the process of re-creating and recording human sounds in sync with cut picture. What does this include? It can include everything from footsteps to clothing movement to the handling of properties as well as kissing and even breathing! Foley is a fascinating, highly skilled craft that requires, at a bare minimum, the Foley artist and the Foley recordist.

In general, Foley is recorded after the picture has reached the final edit. Foley is necessary for a number of reasons, and we will go into Foley in extensive detail in a later chapter. Right now, we will be focusing on Foley that is recorded on-set. In this section we will discuss

- Understanding the Story and the Edit Possibilities
- Unique Props Make Unique Sounds
- Unique Locations Make Unique Sounds
- Crowd Scenes—Don't Just Get the Dialogue

Understanding the Story and the Edit Possibilities

Motion pictures tell stories. The writer has created the story, and the director and the crews bring it to life. Always have a full copy of the script on hand as well as the individual script pages for and during each shooting day. Keep the script handy so you can decipher, understand, and capture the sonic world of the story. Make copies of the individual pages for yourself for each shooting day's coverage so that you can keep notes directly on the script. Compile these pages as the shoot continues and refer to them. Make lists of anything that should get recorded that hasn't.

For instance, you are shooting a movie about professional skateboarders. Among the signature sounds of the film will be the sounds of moving skateboards. Since skateboarders do tricks off of pavement, railings, ledges and the like, there is a great opportunity for capturing some amazing recordings. During the coverage of the script pages as you are shooting, you will likely be capturing the sounds of skateboards in action while recording the dialogue of the story. There may be some scenes of just skateboards in a chase sequence, but mostly the recordings of the skateboards will be determined by the action of the dialogue scenes.

The actors are likely to be pretty good skateboarders. Record wild audio of them doing tricks. Record them wild falling. Record them wild in groups and record them wild solo. Here is a golden opportunity to record these sounds in the actual locations, the way the actual skateboarders ride. The sound of the skateboards echoing off of the trees in location and the grunts and falls of the skateboard riders in action will be priceless. It will also be an intense assignment to try to create later because of the many layers of sound that will be required for each skateboarding moment.

The nature of DIY filmmaking has evolved in such a way that "getting the shot" has become so much the focus that amazing sound opportunities such as this don't merit the proper attention. While everyone marvels over the beautiful scenery or amazing locations, the sonic features of the location or the action are missed.

In the skateboarding example described, what typically happens is that when the project reaches sound editing there is a determination to Foley the various skateboarding scenes in the final picture edit. So a Foley artist or two will faithfully re-create, in a recording booth, the on-screen moves of the actors skateboarding. If the wild sounds had been captured during the shoot, the editor and sound editors would have been able to use these recordings for the soundtrack and minimize the Foley required.

I have the highest regard for Foley artists and Foley mixers, but with proper on-set wild coverage their task on the Foley stage could be simplified. If the budget doesn't allow for Foley sessions, then the lack of these location recordings can be a devastating blow to the quality of the final soundtrack. You will not be able to satisfactorily assemble skateboard sound effects from a commercial sound effects library. This example is where the limitations of sound effects libraries become clear. You may find a skateboard hit or two, but to realistically create professional skateboarding after the fact you will need a talented Foley artist, a talented Foley recordist, as well as plenty of time and money.

There are as many location Foley possibilities as there are stories and films. This is why understanding the whole script is so important and why understanding the uniqueness of the location is important. If you are shooting on a boat, get boat Foley. You should record people walking on the deck, raising the sail, or winding the winches. You should record the sound of water sloshing against the side of the boat. You should record the way the water sounds as you move through it, above the deck as well as below the deck. Remember, if these things do not get recorded by you during the shoot, they will have to be re-created later, recorded later, or at least found in a library later.

Unique Props Make Unique Sounds

Movie stories often depict extraordinary things. Special weaponry or unique vehicles, gruesome murders in bizarre manners, breakthroughs in high-tech laboratories, and airships rocketing through the skies are just a few of the many experiences to be created on a movie set. Very unique and special places and items that produce the sounds of these experiences are generally available only for a limited amount of time.

Exotic locations or special vehicles can be costly, so there may not be much time to capture what is needed. If a Model-T automobile has been rented and there are shots of it starting and moving down the street, see if you can capture clean recordings of it. The editors will be ecstatic to get great location recordings of authentic door slams, engine sputters, and the creak of the old shocks as this vintage car moves down the road. It is a very unique sound, and if you use sounds from effects libraries they just may not work.

The sounds of a Model-T are quite a bit different from the sounds of today's cars, which are what you are likely to find in a sound library. Always listen for things that may prove useful for the telling of the story. Be aware of the scenes that are being shot above and beyond the written dialogue and try to capture the action of the scenes without the dialogue for key moments.

Recording location Foley can be a bit different from recording voices. It is important to use perspective. Recording on-set Foley can be a really fun and rewarding experience. Since the sounds are being recorded wild, you don't have to worry about getting the boom in the shot! Without the camera, it is simply the microphone and the sound.

Think of the way things have been shot and the way they may be edited and get those unique location Foley recordings while the opportunity exists. Don't forget that what you are recording is the Foley only. There should be no talking, laughing, off-mic whispering, cell phones, and so on; record only what is to be used as Foley for the sound edit. In this regard it is no different than any other location recording, whether the camera is rolling or not.

Unique Locations Make Unique Sounds

Is the idea of this chapter becoming clear? There are so many wonderful opportunities that are presented when recording movies. You might find yourself speeding alongside a fleet of helicopters, riding camels into the horizon, standing on a remote mountaintop, or being chased in a field by a crop-dusting plane. With amazing locations come amazing opportunities to capture unique locations and all of their unique sonic attributes.

Don't forget that these locations also sound different at different times of the year. The weather can play an important part in the sounds of the locations. Some places get heavy rains during the winter months or have storms and strong winds. Other places attract unique wildlife for only small parts of the year. There are so many variables in the sounds of places, people, and things. Don't miss these opportunities to make your movie sound as amazing, unique, and different as it can. Using your skills of critical listening, you will uncover all of the rich sounds that may only exist in that place, at that time. Keep your ears open!

Crowd Sounds—Don't Just Get the Dialogue

Many movies have scenes with large crowds and groups of people. Although the location may be filled with *extras*, often all that is recorded are the lines of dialogue in the script. Extras are actors who perform in the background of scenes. For instance, if a scene is a couple arguing in a crowded restaurant, the extras are all of the people who are in the restaurant but have nothing to do with the characters or the plot, such as the patrons at other tables and the waiters walking by.

Many times, the extras in scenes are photographed and recorded pantomiming and mouthing *as if* they are talking and laughing. The reason for this is that it may be difficult later in editing to match shots that have lots of random speaking in it, and of course we want the scripted dialogue to be recorded well. The idea is create the image of a large space filled with people, but the actual shot or take is recorded with only the lines of the main characters speaking.

Encourage the director to find time to record the sounds of the extras in this location. The director and producer are in charge of the shoot. They will determine whether they think these additional recordings are justified. Encourage them to take the opportunity by suggesting that you record several minutes of the extras talking among themselves. Record several minutes of an escalating altercation, or have them directed to suddenly go silent as if the headmaster just arrived. This is an instance where you, as the location recordist, must understand the needs of a particular scene and a particular movie. Be specific to the needs of the scene and also the needs of the story.

If there is a scene where something happens to one particular character, perhaps there can be some murmuring with the key characters' names uttered sparsely throughout. Those recordings can be artfully edited by a sound editor to fit in subtlety within the context of the scene. Be creative and don't lose these opportunities. You will never find the sounds in an effects library with the specific character of the space or the particular cast that is right in front of you on location.

This idea can be applied in many different situations. If the scene is a busy restaurant and it is filled with extras, have them do a similar exercise. Have them laugh, murmur, or do whatever might possibly be used later in editing. These recordings will be invaluable for the sound editors who are creating the sonic world of the motion picture. And since the recordings will be from the same set, recorded with the same gear, they will blend nicely with the other sound elements in the edit. Don't miss these rare opportunities!

Use these cast member recordings to create emotional moments of the film. Creative sound editors can reuse such elements at will. Since these moments are not synchronous sound, they can be used in any number of ways. If enough different sorts of crowd moments are recorded, the uses can be edited in various scenes and in various ways.

These moments are like a butterfly landing on a fingertip. They are fleeting and in some cases will be a once-in-a-lifetime event. Make the filmmakers aware that these sounds can't be easily created later. Impress on them the importance of getting things while still on-set and in the location. Once the heat of location filming is complete, it will matter. You will be asked, "Why didn't we get those sounds then?" Create a library of sounds specific to your project. It will make the project better, and it will make a big difference in the final edited movie.

Summary

Shooting movies on location offers many opportunities to capture unique sounds and ambiences. Be sure to properly record and log all of the room tones for each location. Every room is unique, so be sure to capture it. When you begin the editing process, the need for the room tone will become paramount.

Always have an ear out for action, ambience, or props that sound interesting. You or the crew may not visit these exotic props or locations again. Try to record as much of the project's environment as you can. Capture the ambience of the location and use the script as your guide. Carry the script with you and let it inspire your imagination as you move from location to location. Find sounds that will help tell the story.

Capture wild lines from the performers as well as any needed on-set ADR. If there is a fistfight, get the wild sounds of grunting, exertion, and breathing. Capture the on-set Foley as you hear and see it around you. Be sure to capture the creaky floors or doors, the sound of the footsteps in the gravel, or any Foley sounds that can be used by the editors later.

When shooting large groups, make sure to capture their wild sounds with a clear understanding of the story being told. You are the expert on sound, and your input and expertise goes beyond just recording the dialogue well. Be sure to capture the sonic universe of your locations and your sets. Always keep the story ideas in mind as you listen to and record the locations and the scenes. Record more audio than just "the shot."

Review Questions

Questions like these are likely to appear on exams to test how well you understood and retained the information in this chapter.

1. What is room tone and what is its use? How is room tone properly recorded?
2. What are the key reasons for recording ADR on-set?
3. What is wild audio? How is wild audio different from ADR?
4. What is coverage, and how is the concept useful for location audio recording?
5. Why is it useful to record on-set Foley, unique props and vehicles, wild lines, and ambience?

Discussion/Essay Questions

Your instructor may assign you one or more of the following questions for discussion in class or as the subject of a paper.

1. Discuss several reasons why a location recordist should understand the story and the script beyond just recording the lines of dialogue.
2. Discuss the ADR process. Explain why there are advantages to recording ADR on-set.

Applying What You've Learned

Research/Lab/Fieldwork Projects

The following lab exercises will give you practice capturing additional recordings.

1. Make a list of ten location effects that you'd like to record. Use your story and the scene and the particular location to make the list. Take the production recorder around the location. Seek out unique sounds from the location to record. Try different microphone positions to record the action for different effects. For instance, if you are in an old house location and characters use the doors and windows during shots, get clean recordings of those doors and windows opening and closing. These should be short recordings of on-set Foley from around the location.

2. Make a list of three ambiences to record. Use your story and the scene and the particular location to make the list. Take the production recorder around the location. Seek out unique ambient sounds to record. For instance, if the noise of the city is a requirement of the story, record it—morning, noon, or night, whatever is appropriate to the project. Each ambience recording should be three minutes in length.

3. Take the production recorder around the location. Seek out unique sounds to record. Make a list of three room tones specific to the location. Follow the instructions for proper room tone recording. These should be one-minute recordings of room tones.

4. During shooting, work out a schedule with the production for ten to fifteen minutes with the extras to record wild crowd sounds. Make a list of ten specific items to record from groups of people. It can be from just a few people or large crowds or both, whatever is appropriate for your story. For instance, if your project takes place in high school, you might capture the sounds of large groups of kids eating and talking in a cafeteria. You might also record hallway sounds of students, smaller groups of laughing and yelling, or the mass exodus at the final bell and all the sound that accompanies it. Get it while you can!

Resources

The following resources have more information on the topics covered in this chapter.

FilmSound.org, "Walter Murch Articles" (http://www.filmsound. org/murch/murch.htm). There are many to places to visit while at this amazing website. Starting with Walter Murch is an excellent idea because he understands the importance of sound in the film experience as a sound designer and as a picture editor. He has developed theories and techniques about film sound use and its effect on storytelling.

John Coffey, et al., "An Open Letter from Your Sound Department" (http://www.filmsound.org/production-sound/openletter.htm). This letter was written by key members of the professional sound community to producers and filmmakers. It is a wonderful manifesto from those who provide the services to those who may require them. It should be required reading for anyone who is serious about crafting professional motion pictures.

CHAPTER 5

PREPARING AUDIO FOR EDITING

OVERVIEW AND LEARNING OBJECTIVES

In this chapter, you will learn about:
- Capturing and digitizing audio
- Cataloging the sound recordings
- Creating a filing system
- Planning for the final edit

Capturing the Set Recordings for Editing

The difficult task of production is complete and so now the recordings must be entered into a new state for proper sound editing. In today's world of *nonlinear editing* systems (NLE)s, the most common access point for the material is a computer. NLE is a computer-based type of editing system that provides random access to all of the media files to be edited. This means no more fast-forwarding or rewinding as with tapes. These sophisticated systems can provide advanced editing functions and are the standard for video editing today.

What used to be a very labor-intensive process of editing, and splicing by hand, sound that was recorded onto magnetic film, is now a relatively painless process with computers and hard drives. In this section we will learn about

- Digitizing the Audio into the System
- Cataloging the Sound Recordings

- Signal Flow and Gain Staging
- Levels, Levels, Levels

Digitizing the Audio into the System

Digitizing is a term that means taking some sort of material—audio, video, photos—and changing their state into that of a digital file. Modern digital equipment makes digitizing a simple process.

Standards

Digitizing is the first step in digital postproduction, so the key is to create a standard for the project and to stick to it. Then, as you digitize, convert all media to be edited to the specified standard that you've chosen for the project. Material that is already in digital form is already digitized. However, you still may need to move it from one media source to a hard drive for your editing. Already digitized material is considered to be *captured*, or *ingested*, into the system.

For instance, using a format established from a camera system, it is determined that a project's edit settings will be set to a frame rate of 24 frames per second (fps), and the audio will be set at a bit depth of 16 bits and a sample rate of 48 Kilohertz (KHz). In this example let's say that you need to convert audio CD files, which are standardized at a sample rate of 44.1 KHz, into a digital video editing system. After converting the CD files, create a new folder and place the files in there. Label the new folder accordingly.

Today most computer users are well versed in converting and capturing audio CD files. On some computer systems you may need a separate program to do the work. On some systems, such as a Macintosh computer, the disk simply shows up as a drive and the audio files can be dragged onto a hard drive inside the computer. Check with your particular computer system to determine how to add and convert audio files from CD.

There may be other material that will be digitized that will need to be converted to the standard. If you are digitizing from a VHS tape, for instance, be sure to make the settings of the new digital file match the standards you've created for the project. In this case you would want to be sure that the audio is being digitized at the 48 KHz sample rate as well as to the specified picture standards.

If the edit material is already digital, then moving it is as simple as creating a new copy on another media type, usually a hard drive. If the material is on tapes, even digital tapes such as digital video (DV), it will need to be captured for use inside an NLE system.

Connections

The major types of digital connections and *protocols* for digital transfer are called *firewire*, *AES/EBU*, and *S/PDIF*. Computer protocols are agreed-upon standards for computers to communicate with one another. It is the connector and the "language" the computer manufacturers have created for users to interconnect different systems together. Not all protocols have a hardware component. One of the most commonly used protocols is the *hypertext transfer protocol*, also known as HTTP. HTTP is a key method for addressing sites on the World Wide Web.

AES/EBU and S/PDIF use connectors that will already seem familiar, but note that the cabling is not exactly the same. S/PDIF stands for Sony Philips Digital Interface. Figure 5.1 shows an S/PDIF connector, which, as you can see, looks very much like an RCA connector.

AES/EBU stands for Audio Engineering Society/European Broadcast Union. Figure 5.2 shows an AES/EBU connector, which, as you can see, looks very much like an XLR connector.

Although these connectors and cables look similar to their analog counterparts, as mentioned, they use a different cabling to pass the digital signals. This is important because, as a general rule, you do not want to use

FIGURE 5.1 Although S/PDIF cables are terminated in RCA, they are made with a 75 OHM coaxial cable

FIGURE 5.2 An AES/EBU cable is terminated in XLR connectors

standard RCA cables for an S/PDIF connection or standard microphone XLR cables for an AES/EBU connection, although the connectors will actually fit. For proper digital transmission through cables, be sure to use the exact cables that are specified to be used for digital transfers.

Firewire is a relatively new, advanced protocol that can carry picture and/or audio information. It can also send control information to decks or cameras to remotely fast-forward, rewind, set in and out points, and play their tapes to capture them. Firewire connections are a widely used protocol for the DIY filmmaker. At the same time that digital video reached the consumer market, advances with computer technology, drive technology, and the invention of firewire made transfers and capturing a breeze. Figure 5.3 shows a firewire connector.

Getting from Here to There

If you have material like cassettes, VHS tapes, or other nondigital recordings, then they will have to be played through computer hardware that can take the analog signal and turn it into digital media. There are many types of computer interfaces that can digitize this kind of media. Some computers have these capabilities built in, others do not. You'll have to check your individual computer to determine your particular systems capabilities.

Typically, you would take the output of a device, for instance a VHS deck, and then input that into the digitizing device, which is

FIGURE 5.3 The cable on the left is Firewire 400, and the cable on the right is Firewire 800. Firewire is a computer connector that does *not* come standard with all computer types

connected to the computer. Depending on the device and the computer, there may be some simple software involved as well.

Some NLEs use the firewire protocol for a powerful implementation of ingesting. Final Cut Express , for example, has an importing feature that allows for digitizing with the firewire protocol. By plugging a camera or deck with a firewire connector into a computer with a firewire connector, a new world of capturing will be made available. You'll have a chance to set in and out points, name clips and tapes or media, and even specify only the capture of audio if needed.

In addition, the camera or deck will be controlled by Final Cut Express. You will see controls similar to those on a deck that will allow for fast-forwarding, rewinding, and the like. You will also be allowed to name, label, and notate each piece of media being digitized. Firewire has made the art and craft of digital filmmaking much more accessible for everyone.

Cataloging the Sound Recordings

If the recordings were done dual-system, with the camera recording to one media and the audio recording to another media, then all of the takes will need to have the audio recordings and the video recordings synced up. As mentioned in an earlier chapter, that means finding the audio of the clapper and matching the clack with the visual image. If all of the takes were done with the recordings through the camera, then the syncing is already complete.

As the material is digitized, be sure to create or have created a document that catalogs the additional sounds that were captured on the set. These would include room tones, wild lines, wild crowd sounds, on-set Foley, and so on. All of these items must be assembled and logged for later retrieval. Often an assistant picture editor does dual-system sound syncing and the ingesting of digital media, and since that person's domain is image, these additional audio elements may be disregarded.

Create a folder for all of the additional audio elements. Items other than sync takes that match the lines in the shooting script should be placed in this folder. The folder will be filled with many other folders, so be sure to keep things in good order. Create folders per audio type, such as Foley folder, wild dialogue folder, ADR folder, room tone folder, and so on.

Inside each of these folders the organization depends on the project and the shooting. Perhaps it is better to create subfolders by date, by scene number, or whatever method is most logical to your way of working. This folder will be shared with the picture editor, and a copy of this folder should be given to the sound editor. Create a document that lists the folders, the subfolders, and the contents of each, so everything is accessible for viewing in document form. Figure 5.4 is an example of a folder hierarchy.

Make sure everything is labeled clearly. Often, in the rush of production, tapes get inserted, used, and ejected, and the process starts again without accurate labels. If this is the case, then the time to fix that is now. If tapes were used, then be sure to write-protect the tape by adjusting the lock tab. If the media is on drives, memory sticks, or other magnetic media, be sure to make copies and label everything accordingly.

This part of the process can be tedious and time-consuming. Take the time needed to properly organize and log the material. This blueprint will dictate the rest of the postproduction process, and getting it right now will pay dividends later. Everyone from the picture editor to the sound editor to the colorist and the on-line editor will need to know where and what everything is. There is no bigger time waster than mislabeled or misplaced files. Spelling counts!

Signal Flow and Gain Staging

This section is intended for those who are transferring audio data from analog sources. It is important to keep these ideas in mind so

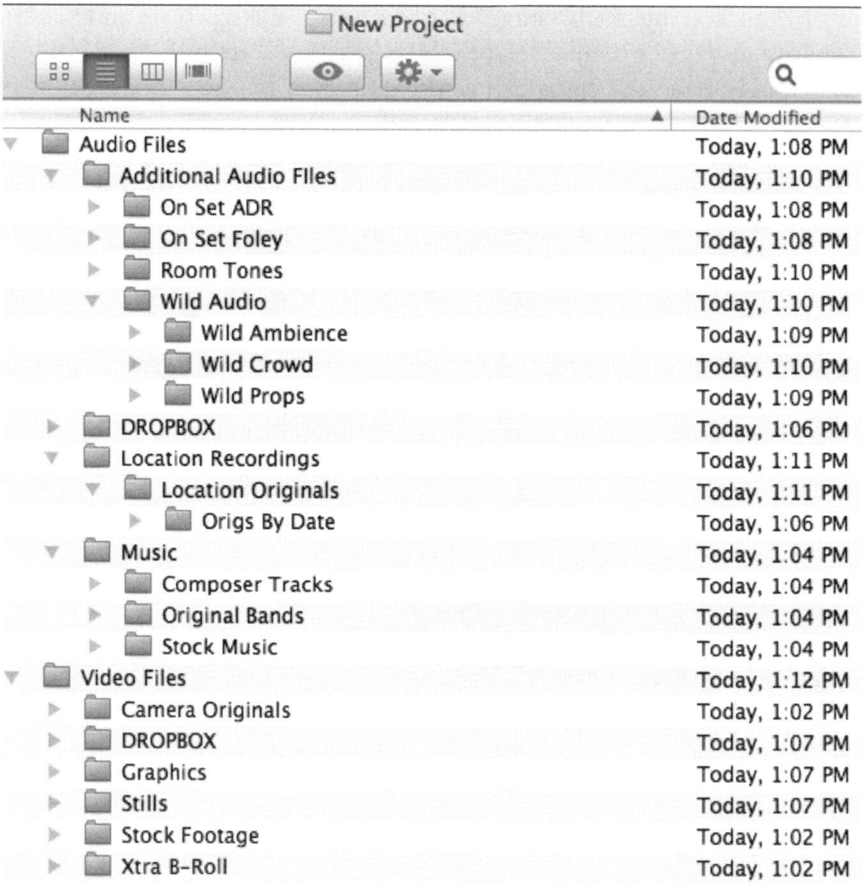

FIGURE 5.4 Every folder hierarchy will be unique to the particular project; use this example as a starting point for your own folder setup

that the signal that gets digitized is at a proper level and is as free from noise and *distortion* as is possible. Distortion goes by many names: overmodulation, clipping, saturation, and peaking, among others, but in the simplest terms it is an overload of electrical signal. It is too much gain applied or too much signal for the recording or digitizing device to handle—for example, a really loud horn placed too close to a microphone. Since distortion obscures the actual, original signal, distortion is generally unfixable; there is no magic filter or process to apply to eliminate distortion.

Distortion is analogous to an extremely blurry photo. No matter how good the software, no matter how fast the computer, no program will be able to get that blurry picture into crisp focus. Distortion sounds bad, and for our purposes, it must be avoided at all costs.

In gain staging, each "stage" can add noise or distortion, and meters may not always be available at each stage to indicate it. In the simplest terms, play back the signal, raise the gain to a maximum level that is still below distortion, watch the available meters, and listen closely. In gain staging you are essentially taking the output of an analog signal and putting it into a mixer to add or reduce gain. You may be using other devices in the chain that can further alter the signal, and at each stage of the signal flow you are changing the gain.

Most microphone levels are inherently low, and as such we add gain, or amplification, to make them useable for our purposes. At each new connection point—a mixer, an amplifier, or a recorder—the signal flow might need to add or reduce gain. *Gain staging* is the term that describes this signal flow moving through different stages of gain. The important idea in gain staging is that the signal is not reaching *distortion* as it moves through its path from point to point. Figure 5.5 shows a normal recorded waveform.

Distortion or clipping can be obvious in a signal's waveform. Figure 5.6 shows a distorted waveform.

Levels, Levels, Levels!

Level is a term for the measurement of the signal strength. Great recordings happen from a few key ingredients: excellent equipment

FIGURE 5.5 This is a view of a well-recorded waveform

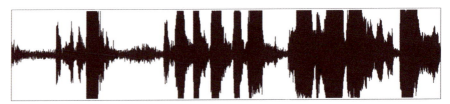

FIGURE 5.6 Notice the difference between this signal and that in figure 5.5. This signal has reached the limit of the device, creating this clipped waveform

used properly, microphone proximity and perspective, correct gain staging, and strong levels. Recording levels are the standards to which audio media are copied and outputted. Optimum recording levels are strong, clean signals that never reach clipping. You want to keep the *signal-to-noise ratio* appropriate.

Signal-to-noise ratio, abbreviated as S/N or SNR, is the ratio difference between the signal being recorded versus the noise that is also in the audio. You want to keep the signal well above the noise. Recording equipment and playback equipment all have an S/N associated with it.

All electronic devices create noise as they process sound. Electronic processes also by nature add noise during the process of recording or amplifying sound. The S/N is a measurement that quantifies the amount of noise inherent in any particular signal.

Prepping for the Final Output

Efficient postproduction requires standards. All of this hard work is going to culminate in a final *master*, which is an edit of the picture and sound married together into one final whole. The master will be used to create copies of the program for distribution. It is important to know the final master format to create the project's standards. The following ideas that will be explored in this section include

- Converting Audio for the Edit
- Frame Rates and Sample Rates
- Understanding the Final Master Format
- Stay Organized with All of the Raw Elements
- Communication with the Picture Editor (If It's Not You)

Converting Audio for the Edit

Personal computers have built-in software to play and convert audio files. The most common conversion is probably converting music or sound effect audio CDs from their native 44.1 KHz sample rate to the digital video sample rate of 48 KHz. Of course, CDs are not the only way to receive audio files any longer. Often files are copied from drive to drive or sent over the Internet and downloaded. Always check the file type. There are a number of different audio formats, and some of them are very low resolution. It is always best to start with the highest resolution audio file possible. Take a look at the box "Case Study: Audio File Formats."

CASE STUDY: AUDIO FILE FORMATS

The type of digital audio recordings that we have been discussing are called *PCM* recordings. PCM recording utilizes several different audio file formats to be played back on standard equipment. PCM files are *uncompressed*, which means that nothing has been changed from the original recording or the original file. There are several main PCM file types in widespread use today.

AIFF, or *AIF*, and *WAV*, or *WAVE*, are the most popular audio formats today and are widely used for sound in digital filmmaking. AIFF and WAV files are uncompressed and are of the proper resolution for postproduction editing and mixing. These files can be easily changed and modified to fit a project's standards without compromising their fidelity.

BWF is a newer file type, also a PCM recording, which is created from the WAV file type. BWFs have the ability to include metadata such as timecode information. BWF files are created by many of the current hard drive–based, multitrack location audio recorders.

MP3 is a compressed version of a PCM file such as a WAV. MP3 compression is called a *lossy compression*, since it throws away portions of the signal. This bears repeating—signal is lost when transferred into the MP3 format. MP3 is a great audio file for personal playback devices such as phones and iPods. But it is not suitable for professional moviemaking. So much signal has been lost that when played back at high volume through monitor speakers the "loss" can be quite apparent. If there simply is no other version of the file, then convert it to the project's standards and move on. However, typically MP3s are created from AIFFs or WAV files. It's a great idea to track down the originals for the conversion instead.

Windows computers ship standard with their *Windows Media Player* (WMP). WMP is software that can play many different types of audio and video files. It can also convert to and from many different file types. Go to the WMP preferences to set the conversion needed for your audio file standards. If you are converting from audio CD, you can change the "ripping" setting to match your project's audio standards. *Ripping* is how WMP defines digitizing from a CD into the computer's hard drive.

Macintosh computers ship standard with their *QuickTime Media Player*. QuickTime is used on Mac computers for video and for audio. If you use Final Cut Express or Final Cut Pro, then you will have already been upgraded to the pro version of QuickTime.

QuickTimePro is a powerful system for converting file types. Macs also ship with iTunes, which is their audio player. iTunes can be used in a number of useful ways for postproduction audio needs. One of the most common will be its ability to convert audio files. If you are converting from audio CD, you can change the "import" setting to match your project's audio standards. *Import* is how QuickTime defines digitizing from a CD into the computer's hard drive.

Frame Rates and Sample Rates

Frame rates are dictated by the camera system chosen by the production. There are many, many frame rates available today. For years there was only one standard frame rate, which was the frame rate of motion picture film, 24 fps. Due to the technology that was developed, several different television formats changed the frame rate from 24 fps.

NTSC television is the television format standard used in the United States, Japan, South America, and several other countries. NTSC standards include a frame rate of 29.97 fps. *PAL television* is the television format standard used in Europe, Scandinavia, Australia, and several other countries. PAL standards include a frame rate of 25 fps.

Digital filmmaking has opened up the options of many more frame rates due to various technological innovations in high-definition photography. Audio, however, has two main guiding standards, the sample rate and the bit depth. Material that was shot and recorded with differing frame rates may be a bit shorter or longer depending on the rate. *Pull up/pull down* is a term describing the method used to reconcile these speed/length differences prior to fast computers. In traditional pull up/pull down you would increase or decrease the rate of transfers from one machine to another machine.

For instance the pull up/pull down for film to television or vice versa is 0.1 percent. To transfer film sound to match NTSC video you would increase the speed of the film 0.1 percent to change the frame rate from 24 fps to 29.97 fps.

Fortunately, computers have made the work of conversion simpler than ever. Most audio programs designed for editing and mixing audio contain menus where you can specify a file and then specify the pull up/pull down changes, and it's done! No other machine is required and generally this happens faster than real time. So that means if a program is two hours long it won't take two hours plus to do the conversion.

Stay in contact with the director, the director of photography, and the picture editor. They will have the answers regarding the frame rates of the project. Get all of the standards in writing so there is no misunderstanding. Like many things in DIY filmmaking, one person may fill all these roles. The key standards needed are: the format of the camera shooting on location and the format the final master will be. Often these are not the same. If a project was shot on film, it may be destined for television. In that case, depending on the format, it may need to be changed from 24 fps to 29.97 fps or 25 fps. The sound editor will need to understand what frame rate the project was shot with and what it will be going to.

Check with the picture editor to determine the final master format. If conversions are necessary, do it at the beginning if feasible, there will be fewer distractions while editing. It is better to plan all of the technical aspects and get them all prepared first. This way, when doing the actual editing you can push further with the creative rather than be slowed down by the technical. And if technical questions or concerns are raised, you will have already accounted for them in your preparation. Match the camera system format standard to the standard you record on location; match the final editing standards as you edit toward the final master.

Understanding the Final Master Format

Not very long ago there were only a few common formats to be worried about when it came to creating a master. If it was a feature film to be theatrically released, you had a *printmaster*, which is the final film print of the movie, broken into *reels* because of the size and length required of feature film. Film reels typically hold fifteen to twenty minutes of film per reel, so longer projects had to consist of several reels.

High-definition (HD) photography has changed the technology of television and film production in several new ways. By definition, HD is of a higher resolution and quality than the TV that we all grew up with, which is called *standard definition* (SD). SD has been the standard since TV was invented. HD can accommodate just about any frame rate, and it can put that frame rate on a master known as *HDcam* or *HDcamSR*. These formats are the newest standards for finalizing a project to a master.

I won't go into all of the technical specifications here, but it is important to note that an HDcam master can play at 24 fps. This keeps the frame rate of a project shot on film the same all the way through finishing. With all of the types of deliverables required today, the accepted norm is to create a final high-quality HD master and create and convert the other versions from this final master.

Sometimes a particular edit workflow will make the conversion to the HD master the last item in the process. This is certainly the case if the source material was created in SD. The process known as *uprezzing* is used to create the new HD master. Uprezzing is the process of changing the SD file into an HD file.

Today this is most effectively done with hardware conversion machines. These sophisticated machines can "up the resolution" from SD to HD. Note that this conversion does not change or increase the quality of the SD signal. All things considered, if the program originated in HD and was finished in HD it would be of a greater resolution than if it started in SD. But this does allow an SD master to be finished in the highest quality, which is then used to create the various deliverables.

HD has a greater audio bit depth than SD. HD has a bit depth resolution of 24 bits, so it has a significantly higher audio resolution than SD, which is 16 bits. Depending on the complexity of the editing and the processing for final mixing, it is sometimes better to change the whole edit to 24 bits if it originated in 16 bits. This way, all of the new processing to the original files during editing and mixing happens at the higher resolution. This is a relatively easy process when using digital audio software.

Although HD is a format of today as well as a good archival medium for the foreseeable future, many programs are still created and finished in SD. Often DIY filmmaking is shot on DV, which is an SD medium. If the show was photographed in DV using the audio inputs for the sound, it is conceivable that the whole edit from start to finish was done with little or no converting. In this case that SD DV master may be uprezzed into an HD format for duplication and archival.

Stay Organized with All of the Raw Elements

One of the key elements in editing is the preparation of all of the raw elements. During the process of editing, files will be imported, modified, edited, deleted, and more. It is important to create a file system to organize the various media that will be edited to create the final master.

Have another look at Figure 5.4 for setting up a folder hierarchy on a hard drive. The idea is to create large categories such as "Video" and

"Audio" and then within them make smaller and smaller categories. I like to think of this as my "editing library," where I will browse for material, add and delete material, and backup and restore the project easily if the need arises.

This example indicates one possible starting point for a project. For instance, "Music" is a main folder inside of the "Audio" folder. Within music there are several more folders that define the type of music. One folder contains the score recordings contributed by the composer, another folder contains library music tracks, and another folder contains songs contributed by local bands.

Every project is different and has different elements, different requirements, and different standards. Each project, however, will use video, audio, and probably some photos and some music as well. Most projects add material to the edit as the editing process continues. The file system will always be changing, with files being added or changed regularly. It's a good idea to start with a project-specific template that can be easily changed or modified at will.

Your specific template could be modified to include many folders different from those in the example shown. One large category/folder might be ADR, inside of which there might be folders categorized by character, group, or wild. Depending on the complexity of the sound design, there could be an Effects folder. That folder could be subdivided by categories such as Ambience, Location Effects, Hard Effects, and whatever else was specific to your particular project.

When you are in the heat of creativity, nothing stops things faster than not finding a particular sound, line of dialogue, or song. The art of editing is a highly creative act and demands spontaneity and impulse. By taking the time to work this way, you make it easier on yourself to stay creative and not get sidetracked or bogged down when inspiration hits.

Making movies takes time. The shooting itself can happen in fits and starts. Sometimes editing will begin only to find out later that more footage will be needed. Then crews are reassembled and new location shooting happens. Sometimes projects, particularly DIY projects where just a few people are performing the functions of many, can last months and longer.

There are times when a project is put aside for whatever reason and continued at a later date. Having a well-organized approach will be beneficial in such cases because it will be easier to take stock of the project upon resumption if the media has been properly organized and labeled. If items were simply copied onto drives and across multiple drives, it will be quite a challenge to sort through files and try to decipher what files are what and which files are where.

TIP

Create a dropbox inside any folder that files are regularly added to. A dropbox is a folder that is used as temporary storage until it can be filed in the proper folder later. Dropboxes are handy when things are moving fast and furious during editing and you simply don't feel like you have the time to properly file all of the files that you are importing at that moment. It's a useful idea. It helps contain and maintain the file structure you have already created. When you are being creative and spontaneous with your editing, you want to keep moving no matter

There is one other note to make regarding organization. When the files are neatly organized and labeled it makes backing the material up a snap. Do not forget to back all of the media up. Since hard drives have become so inexpensive they are an ideal storage place for a backup of the entire editing library you've created. Drives that are external to your editing computer can hold copies of the material and then be stored remotely in a safe place. Be sure to update the backups as the editing progresses. Systems fail, hard drives crash, and files get corrupted. You must always have backups so that if something catastrophic happens to a drive or to other media, there is a copy to take its place.

Communication with the Picture Editor (If It's Not You)

Oftentimes in digital filmmaking the picture editor is also the sound editor. If this is the case, then you will already know what the format of the shooting was and at least have an idea of what the final edited master will be. You will also have made decisions on your own and in collaboration with the filmmakers regarding the audio's needs and desires. You'll know if there is a need for ADR or additional Foley, what sound effects are needed, as well as what elements comprise the musical score for the project. If you are not the picture editor, then it is important to establish and maintain good communication with that person.

The picture editor is often also the *postproduction supervisor* on a project. The postproduction supervisor, also referred to as the *post super*, plans, budgets, updates, and maintains the entire postproduction workflow. This person creates the postproduction schedule, hires and supervises the personnel required for the editing process, and sees the project through to the final edited master. The postproduction supervisor is in charge of all of the deliverables for audio and video, including duplicate copies, contracts, and alternate versions of the master for other broadcasting markets (NTSC Television Master, PAL Television Master, Film Printmaster etc.). Accordingly, the editor and the sound editor will be making decisions based on the final master requirements.

Since NLEs and computers are so sophisticated today, many of these standards conversions are simply created with the click of a mouse. However, without a clear understanding of the standards, more work is created in the short term and quality loss is a possibility in the long term. Understand what the specifications are for the audio output and how the final mix will be synced with the final master picture file.

TIP *(continued)*

what detours must be taken to get there. When not editing, you can go back to your editing library and properly file the miscellaneous things you've added to the dropbox. Schedule a regular appointment and stick to it; for instance, first thing every Friday morning, each dropbox is opened, sorted, and emptied.

The picture editor, or his or her assistant, will create the files that are needed to start the sound-editing process. Sometimes this process is called the *audio turn over*. The materials are "turned over" to audio to begin sound editing and mixing. Items would include the audio elements, the location audio edited to the picture, music tracks, and a movie file or a tape of the final version of the picture edit.

It is a good idea for the movie file to have timecode displayed as a part of the picture. Final Cut Express and other NLEs can superimpose the timecode onto the picture. This will assure the sound editor that they are editing the movie in a *frame-accurate* manner. Being frame accurate means that the editing matches frame by frame exactly. It is important to stay frame accurate particularly with sync dialogue tracks. When you are even two or three frames off, the lip sync will not match the image on screen. Be sure to have the timecode superimposed in the lower or upper part of the screen so as not to obscure faces or lips. The actors will need to be able to see their performance to match sync, so keep the timecode discreet.

Another important consideration is to have a *leader* played at the start of the movie file. A leader is a motion picture file that is a sync audio and video countdown timed in seconds and indicated with numbers from 10 to 2. Each number is flashed on-screen in a single frame. At the single-frame image of the number 2, a simultaneous one-frame pop of tone is played.

Sometimes the leader is merely a single-frame image that says "Picture Start" with a corresponding one-frame pop in audio. The one-frame image and the one-frame audio pop are dragged to match up in the timeline in the editing program to sync the separate audio and video files. The corresponding flash frame and single frame of audio pop are can also be called a *head pop*, *tail pop*, or *two-pop*, depending on its placement in the edit timeline.

The leader allows for a verification of frame-accurate syncing of the audio and the picture files. Leader files are often included as extras with NLEs. Leader files are relatively easy to create and are available over the Internet. It is also a good idea to add a *tail pop*. A tail pop is a one-frame audio pop with a corresponding one-frame video image sometimes a white flash, sometimes the word *end* played two seconds after the last frame of picture.

A leader can be used as a source for a tail pop. What is ideal about having both a head pop and a tail pop is that the editor can import the movie file and the sound file and line the pops up and immediately determine if there is a sync problem. If the pops line up at the head but not at the end, there is definitely some sort of issue that will need to be determined and worked out. It can be a real timesaver to know, before any serious work is done, that there is a looming sync issue that must be rectified.

Verify all files that are turned over from the picture editor. Make a checklist and a log of all original materials. Once you have taken what you need from any borrowed originals, give them back to the filmmakers. Let them be in charge of the original recordings. You need to be on top of the edit you are creating and back up that edit after each working day.

Summary

There are many elements required for a successful sound edit of a program. It is important to properly digitize or capture those elements from analog and digital sources. Once all of the media has been assembled, it should be properly organized by type, by date, or by usefulness. A document of the media and its hierarchy will need to be created that matches the editing library.

A dropbox should be utilized where files added to an edit are sorted, organized, and properly filed later. Communication must be clear with the postproduction supervisor and at least the picture editor if that is not you. The standards of the project and the final master must be determined and adhered to.

Check to see if the media needs to be converted to the chosen project standard. When material is turned over from picture editorial to sound editorial it should have a leader with a head pop and tail pop, and the movie file should have a timecode discreetly superimposed over the image.

Review Questions

Questions like these are likely to appear on exams to test how well you understood and retained the information in this chapter.

1. What is distortion and why should it be avoided?
2. Why is it important to understand the standards for an editing project?
3. What is a head pop and a tail pop, and why are they useful?
4. Why would it be useful to create an editing library hierarchy?
5. What is a dropbox, and why and how would you use one?

Discussion/Essay Questions

Your instructor may assign you one or more of the following questions for discussion in class or as the subject of a paper.

1. Describe and list the shooting standards for your project and describe and list your final master standards. What steps would you need to take if the standards do not match?

2. Discuss creating an editing library specific to your project. Discuss the editing library, the hierarchy, and the categories that are relevant to your project.

Applying What You've Learned

Research/Lab/Fieldwork Projects

The following lab exercises will give you practice importing sound to your NLE.

1. If you have been recording the audio in digital video with the picture, capture using the firewire protocol.

2. Digitize, copy, or transfer the additional recordings into separate folders on the working edit hard drive. Log all room tones, wild lines, alternate takes, and on-set dialogue replacement.

3. If you have been recording to a hard drive, memory sticks, or digital audiotape, import those materials into the working edit hard drive. Log all room tones, wild lines, alternate takes, and on-set dialogue replacement.

NOTE

Students who have ongoing projects may elect to use their own source material, such as video clips, with the instructor's permission.

Resources

The following resources have more information on the topics covered in this chapter.

"Final Cut Express Tutorials" (http://www.apple.com/finalcutexpress/tutorials/). Here you will find many useful articles and tutorials on Apple's NLE program Final Cut Express, including editing basics and workflow methods. Spend a bit of time here; these simple tutorials pack a lot of information.

YouTube (http://www.youtube.com/). Do a search on this popular video site for "Final Cut Express" and find many video tutorials on just about any aspect of editing in Final Cut Pro.

CHAPTER 6

ORGANIZING AND EDITING SOUND WITH FINAL CUT EXPRESS

OVERVIEW AND LEARNING OBJECTIVES

In this chapter, you will:

- Learn about audio with Final Cut Express
- Learn to stay organized with the sound while cutting picture
- Learn how to organize the audio tracks
- Learn about various types of audio edits

Audio with Final Cut Express

Final Cut Express is a powerful system for editing video and audio. Since this text is exclusively devoted to audio, we won't go into any detail on the video portion of the Final Cut Express timeline. This chapter will highlight some of the features that are necessary for importing, editing, and mixing sound in Final Cut Express.

Final Cut Express is a sophisticated and complex program that is capable of many different types of editing functions. As such, we will be only touching on some of its capabilities. I strongly suggest searching the Apple website and the Internet for a deeper understanding of this amazing software.

There are four major windows in the Final Cut Express application that are the main working areas of the program. Let's have a look at each one. The *browser* window is the place where you access the media used within the edit. This is where all of the imported clips and audio files are kept. You can create folders inside of the browser window called *bins*. Bins are folders that you define for each type of media or file. Bins are extremely useful for keeping large amounts of material organized. Figure 6.1 is an example of a browser window in Final Cut Express.

There are two playback windows, and each serves a very different purpose. One window is the *viewer*. The viewer is where you can watch or listen to audio and video clips. The other important playback window is the *canvas*. When you drag a media file onto the canvas, it goes onto the edit timeline. Figure 6.2 is an example of the viewer and canvas windows.

The final main window in the program is the *timeline*. The timeline is where you place all of the video, audio, and stills and is the main place to complete the bulk of the editing work. The timeline has many useful features that we will detail in this section. Figure 6.3 is a

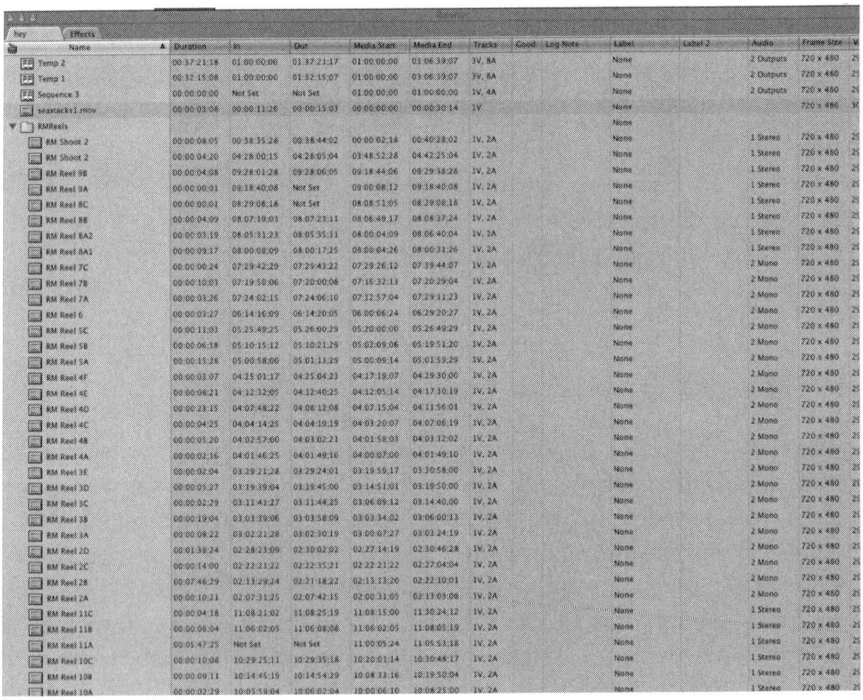

FIGURE 6.1 The browser window is customizable with many useful category choices

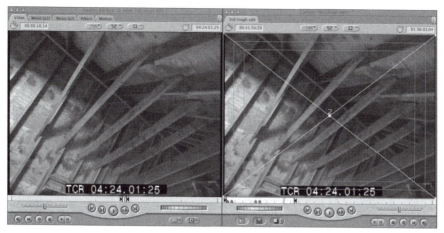

FIGURE 6.2 In this image the viewer window is on the left and the canvas window is on the right

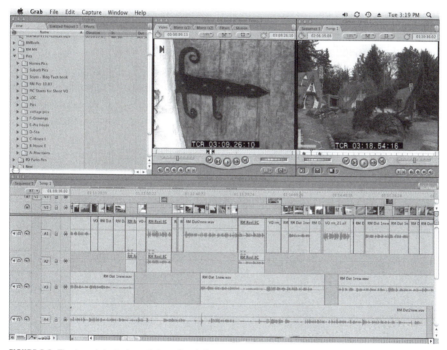

FIGURE 6.3 The is a default view of the edit windows

snapshot of the four windows as normally seen when editing in Final Cut Express.

In this section we will explore

- The Timeline
- Bins and Importing

- Automation, Keyframes, and the Pen Tool
- The Viewer
- Settings

The Timeline

The timeline is the main center for editing projects in Final Cut Express. This is where you will place audio files, add their keyframes, adjust their levels, and edit them. Figure 6.4 shows a standard view of the timeline.

You can see a dark double line in the timeline. This double line separates the video tracks, which reside in the top portion, from the audio, which resides in the lower section. Since we are just talking about audio, we'll be focusing on the lower portion of the timeline. Figure 6.5 shows some of the key components relevant to this discussion.

The buttons at the left define the on or off status of the track. If the button is green, then the track is on and active. If the green light is not lit, then the track is in an inactive state and will not play as you play back the sequence.

Just to the left of the green buttons in the audio portion of the timeline you can see two icons. On the left is a speaker icon and to its right is a headphone icon. The speaker icon is a *solo* button. The

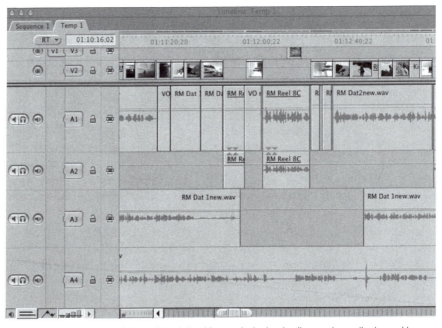

FIGURE 6.4 The view sizes of the audio and the video tracks in the timeline can be easily changed by grabbing and pulling them

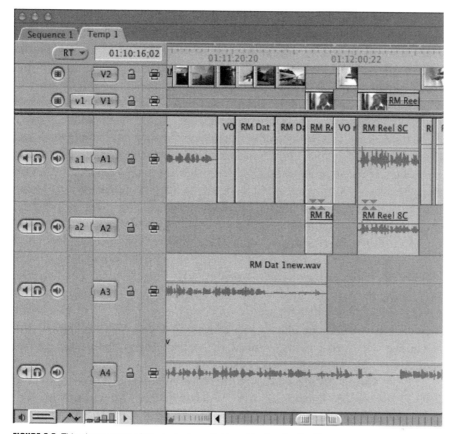

FIGURE 6.5 This shows some of the controls available on the timeline itself

solo button allows you to listen to only that one track of audio. The headphone icon is a *mute* button. The mute button allows you to turn off the sound for that one track. These buttons come in handy when you need to check the edit, the content, the placement, or the level of the audio tracks. In the far left bottom of Figure 6.5 is the *audio controls* button. Activating this button toggles the viewing of the solo button. Click once and the solo button appears; click it again and the solo button hides.

To the right of the green buttons are the *source* buttons, which are also called the targets. The source buttons tell the program where to place the media that you are adding to the timeline. There is one video source button and two audio source buttons. These handy buttons allow you to determine which tracks you are adding media to or determine the tracks used for stacking multiple audio and video tracks in the timeline. In Figure 6.5 you can see the targets are A1, A2, and V1, which indicate that if you drag media into the canvas window the video will go onto track V1 and the audio will go to tracks A1 and A2.

The source buttons are next to the *track names*. In this example you can see that the names for the tracks are V1 and V2 for the video track and A1, A2, A3, and A4 for the audio tracks. There is no way to change the names of the tracks in Final Cut Express. To the right of the track names is a *lock*. The lock does just what the name implies; it will lock the track and all the media on it. On a locked track you will not be able to edit, move, or in any way change the media.

There are a few more things to discuss about the timeline. A red line at the top of the timeline indicates that the sequence will need to be *rendered* in order to play back. Rendering is a process in an NLE that creates special files, called render files, to allow for real-time playback of many complicated edits, effects, and processes shaping the media of the edit. Complicated processes such as filters, speed changes, or different media types sharing one timeline will require rendering.

Computers are fast, but NLEs require a lot of processing ability to play complicated sequences back in real time. Render files help the NLE accomplish this. In Final Cut Express, when the audio has not been rendered, it will beep. You will be able to play the audio in the viewer, but it may not play back fully or properly if it is unrendered. Whenever this red line appears at the top of the timeline, be sure to render the file for proper playback.

Have a look at the media in the timeline itself. You will see red lines in the audio. Those red lines are for adjusting the volume level of the audio. The ability to toggle the red lines on and off from viewing is located on the bottom left of Figure 6.5. It is located to the right of the audio controls button and it is called the *clip overlay* button.

As you can see, the timeline is a key aspect of editing in the Final Cut Express program. It also has many of the frequently needed tools built right in. Like most programs as sophisticated as this, there is more than one way to get something done. Final Cut Express has been designed to make the essentials available in the four windows described.

Bins and Importing

Bins are where you sort and organize the media imported into the browser of Final Cut Express. The media really exists on your hard drives or computer, but the bins are a convenient way of keeping track of all of the imported media in your edit. Why not just call them folders? Well there is a bit of film editing history regarding the use of the term *bins*.

Back in the days when editors actually cut up little pieces of film, they had to store all of those snippets somewhere. A system was developed of large canvas sacks on wheels that had small hooks at the top to hang perforated film from. These rolling contraptions were called bins. Figure 6.6 is a photo of a film sound editor's editing station before computers and editing software completely changed the physical act of "cutting" film.

If you have been focused on staying organized with your media, you'll find that importing is a snap in Final Cut Express. Final Cut Express gives you a choice each time you import new material into the edit. You can choose to import any individual files into the browser, or you can also import whole folders from the hard drive into the browser. It will even import all of the folders within a folder! So if you were to import the additional audio files folder, it would import each subfolder, that is, the room tone folder, the on-set ADR folder, and so on. You will have prearranged a lot of the bins already with this approach.

This makes it easy to hit the ground running with your project. Since you don't have to start over importing all of the elements one item or one folder at a time, you will know precisely where all of the media is. In creating the organization of media in a clear and concise manner, you've made the preparation simple.

To import media into your Final Cut Express project, go to the File menu. Scroll through the File menu to the Import menu. Under the Import menu item, you'll see that there are options for importing files, importing folders, as well as a couple of other file formats. Choose the

FIGURE 6.6 Photo of the author when splicing and gluing bits of film together was the only way to edit sound

file or folder you want to import and then navigate to the particular file or folder you want. It will appear in the browser window. After importing, the material that is listed in the browser is available for immediate editing.

Automation, Keyframes, and the Pen Tool

Automation is the process of writing processing into the NLE that it then recalls and plays back exactly the same way each time until you change it. For example, audio can be automated to fade in and fade out or to continually change the volume levels. As with most functions in NLEs, *keyframes* play a major role in the automation of sound mixing and panning.

Keyframes are a mechanism for automating parameters in an NLE. For instance, one keyframe may be the start of a fade in, another key frame may be the end of that same fade. Keyframes will be used extensively in your work manipulating the sound within the Final Cut Express timeline. For audio purposes, sometimes keyframing is also called *rubber banding*.

All of the controls for audio playback within the Final Cut Express timeline can be controlled with keyframes. Keyframes can delineate the start and the stop of various commands to the audio. Panning, volume automation, muting, and filter parameters can all be controlled with the use of keyframes.

Panning is the action of taking signals and placing them it in a multichannel playback environment. For instance, in a stereo pan the controls can move the sound from the far left, playing only in the left channel, to the far right, only playing in the right channel. Panning controls help the sound mix mimic the action on screen. If a car passes from the left to the right of the screen, a sound mixer can follow the action of the car with the panner control, creating an illusion of movement. Figure 6.7 is an example of keyframes automating the volume of an audio clip.

Tracks A1 and A2 in the audio portion of the timeline are mono tracks, and they can be individually automated for volume level. The keyframes increase the volume level of A1 as the keyframes lower the level of A2. Tracks A3 and A4 are a stereo music track. The keyframes are linked together so that the volume levels change together.

There are a number of ways to add keyframes to particular parameters. One way is by using a special tool called the pen tool. Figure 6.8 shows the various tools available.

By clicking the pen tool on the volume automation line in a clip in the timeline or in the viewer window you will create a new keyframe.

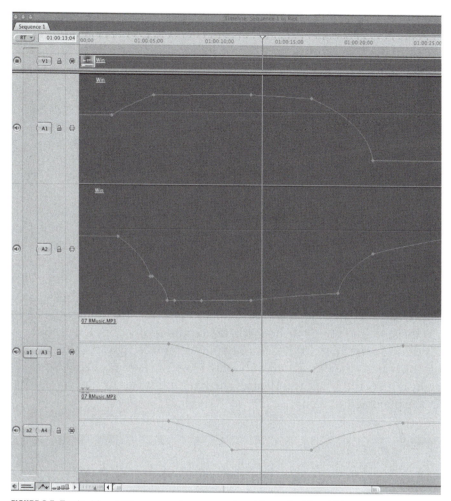

FIGURE 6.8 This is the tool palette of Final Cut Express. Note the pen tool located at the bottom

FIGURE 6.7 Tracks A1 and A2 are separate mono tracks, while tracks A3 and A4 are a stereo track; note the difference in the keyframing

Once the keyframes have been properly added to the volume line, you can easily move them to change the volume keyframe position with the pen tool or with the arrow tool. A handy part of Final Cut Express is that when you move to any particular keyframe the volume level in decibels appears next to the cursor. You can precisely change or move volume or any keyframe automation with a click of the mouse.

The Viewer

The viewer window is an area where you can perform a number of different actions including change volume with keyframe automation, add and change filters, or simply audition sounds for the edit. Figure 6.9 is a closer look at the viewer window.

In this window you can position a keyframe to a precise portion of the audio waveform for very accurate level or panning adjustments. Here's a brief tour of some of the features that are useful for sound editors in the viewer window. If you look to the top left of the window you can see the *tabs*. There are several tabs including: the *Video* tab, to watch video; the *Sound* tabs, which can be mono or stereo tabs; the *Filters* tab, where you will add and change filters; and the *Motion* tab, which deals with video matters. The tabs allow you to choose what aspect of the clip you would like to work with.

In the center top of the viewer window are several very important items. As noted earlier, in sophisticated programs such as Final Cut Express, many functions and commands can be done in several ways. You'll notice there are two sliders stacked on top of one another. The top slider is the volume slider. This will control the overall volume of a clip or follow the volume of the clip as it changes by keyframes. There is a small box next to the slider, which indicates the volume level in decibels. Below that is a slider for the panning of a clip. If the slider is all the way to the right, it will only play from the right speaker; if it is all the way to the left, it will only play from the left speaker. Also to its right is a small box that indicates the panning status at any given time in the playback of a clip.

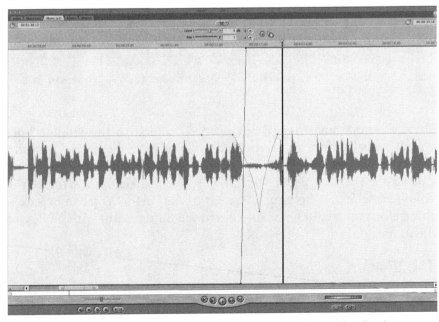

FIGURE 6.9 In this example, keyframes are used to create a dip in the volume at the edit point

Just to the right of these controls are keyframing buttons. You'll see that the buttons have arrows to the left and right. To create a keyframe, simply press the button and it will create a keyframe for volume or for panning, depending on which button you click. The arrows will navigate through the keyframes in increments of one. So one click of the triangle to the left of the volume keyframe button takes you to the first keyframe to the left of the current keyframe. The button will erase keyframes as well. Park the cursor directly on top of a keyframe, click the button, and it will disappear.

You can also see navigation controls on the light gray bar near the bottom. To the left is a slider that can scan forward or back; in the center are play, stop, rewind, and forward buttons; and to the right of that is a thumbwheel that allows for more precise scanning forward or back.

Settings

Final Cut Express is a complex program capable of professional-level work. As such, it has many deep settings that can accommodate many different functions. For our purposes, we will stick to a couple of items that are most important for the audio.

One key concept to know about Final Cut Express is the *sequence settings*. The sequence settings define what the media is that will be used in the edit. For instance, the settings may be DV for the video, and set to 48 KHz and 16 bits for the audio. When you import an audio CD track to this, it will not match these sequence settings. Since an audio CD has a sample rate of 44.1 KHz you will have to render it to be played back in the sequence. Or if the sequence has been set at 44.1 KHz then every clip of DV will need its audio rendered since it has a sample rate of 48 KHz.

This is why the concept of standards is so important. The best approach is to set the sequence to the appropriate *video* settings and ideally the settings that the project will be output to. It takes much longer to render video than it does to render audio. If you know the standards of your edit already, then before you start importing materials, set the sequence to those settings.

Once the settings have been squared away, have a look at the *audio/video settings* in the File menu. The audio/video settings menu item has several tabs. Look through the tabs and you will see that there are options for the playback of video and audio. If you are primarily using the computer, be sure to check the correct box so the audio will play through the computer. If you are using other devices, then toggle those devices for playback. If you are experiencing audio or video playback problems the place to check is here in the audio/video settings menu item.

Know Your Story and Your Source Materials

Making movies takes time, skill, patience, luck, and plenty of organization. During the preparation stage everything should be nicely organized, labeled, and ready to go. It is always a great idea to keep things that way. In the heat of editing it is quite easy to move files among drives, pull new sounds in, export rough edits, and so on. It is imperative to keep all of these new files organized. Create appropriate folders for new items, change folders if need be, but be sure to keep all of the media available and clearly labeled.

There are a few suggestions I would make before starting the edit process. Be sure that the picture edit is complete. The final edited picture is sometimes called the *locked picture* cut. A locked picture means that the picture edit is finished and now the audio post will begin. Once the picture changes, then all of the sync and frame counts from the sound edit will change. Thus, it is always best to begin a sound edit with a locked picture.

Watch the locked picture edit and listen. Go through your additional audio files folder and discover and understand the world of sounds at your disposal to create a new sonic universe. Reread the script, think about your arsenal of new sound elements, and contemplate the edit. The ideas explored in this section will include

- Great Picture Editors Cut Great Sound
- Using Alternate Takes of the Audio to Better Tell the Story
- Using Your Library of On-Set Additional Recordings

Great Picture Editors Cut Great Sound

There are several types of picture editors. Many talented, experienced picture editors are detail oriented and make every frame count. That will also include the audio, not just the picture. There are also some picture editors who claim that they "don't do sound." In my experience, I have found that if a piece is tightly edited with creativity and skill, the audio edit will be equally impressive. Excellent picture editors understand that sound completes the movie experience. Good picture editors spend extraordinary amounts of time on the soundtrack as well as the picture.

Excellent editors are also excellent filmmakers. They understand the limits of the shot footage, the limits of the location recordings, and the scope of the story, and they find creative ways to tell the story within those limitations. Picture editors are the holders of all of the recorded material, video and audio. They know and understand the alternate takes available for any particular scene and use them if need be to maximize the audio quality. They have, or their assistants have, logged and digitized the room tones, the wild lines, the on-set Foley, and ADR.

It is very rare that a picture editor will be a sound editor and a sound mixer as well. One notable example is the innovative, extremely gifted filmmaker Walter Murch. He is an innovator in picture editing and sound editing and has developed several theories and techniques on sound editing and mixing. He has also been nominated and won Academy Awards for both his sound editing and mixing as well as for his picture editing. There are numerous books about Mr. Murch available, as well as his own excellent book, *In the Blink of an Eye*. Search for him on the Internet, as many of his articles and interviews are available online.

Using Alternate Takes of the Audio to Better Tell the Story

It is a rare thing that a director does not call for additional takes of a particular scene. The only director I've heard of who "moved on" after first takes was the master filmmaker John Huston—and he even moved on from filmed *rehearsals*. Often these unused takes can be a gold mine of audio for the intrepid editor. As we will see in a later chapter, ADR is a difficult and time-consuming skill, and the extensive use of alternate takes can help minimize the need for ADR.

The picture editor, who is cutting both sound and image, may find acceptable edits around production tracks with serious sound issues. However, sound professionals are often not involved in the process until the picture is locked. In this case, the opportunity to cut around scenes is not an option.

The picture editor should critically listen to the production tracks and then go back to the location source tapes to look for alternate takes to replace the bad audio. Some picture editors do not feel that this level of audio editing is part of their job. If this is the case, it is then going to be the task of the postproduction sound department to see what, if any, alternate takes can fix the problems. If there are no solutions to be found in the alternate takes, then the last resort will be ADR.

If you were not the on-set recordist, be sure to check all of the logs and the lined script for alternate takes. Also be sure to check the logs for wild lines and for on-set ADR. Often, as noted previously, these items do not get digitized or properly set aside for turnover to audio post. Check with the audio logs to see if there is additional material to be found on the original source tapes. If you are mixing the project as well, you'll find that using location recordings to replace the problematic audio is less of a challenge than dialogue replacement. Of course, all projects are different, but in general, the location recordings will better match in sound quality and in the actor's performance level.

So you've found a line of dialogue that has a few issues. Perhaps there is a bump in the middle of a word from when the boom operator had to change position. Maybe there is also a clank on another word later in the same sentence when a wrench was dropped on the floor during a take. Issues such as this are prime candidates for the use of alternate takes. Search through the alternate takes and find this line of dialogue. Lay the take underneath the bad audio on another track in the audio timeline. See if the speed of the line matches. You will be surprised to learn that in some cases the recordings may be close to identical. Actors have an uncanny way of matching their own performances. Now find the offending words in the original edited take. Snip out the same words from the clean take and replace the offending words. Play the line and look closely for any sync issues. If it looks in sync, great! You have just used an alternate take to replace bad audio, saving yourself and the actor from ADR. This process is to be repeated throughout each scene, replacing all of the extraneous noises or problems that happen during location recording.

Typically, in audio post, the type of work that is being discussed is the domain of the dialogue editor. Dialogue editors are highly experienced editing professionals. They are masters of alternate takes, room tone, and sync. An entire chapter of this text will be devoted to the craft of dialogue editing. In many lower-budget and DIY projects, the dialogue editor is also the sound designer, effects editor, and mixer.

Top Hollywood dialogue editors are very much in demand. Since the dialogue track is the key element in the overall soundtrack, this specialized position is highly regarded. The dialogue editor will clean the production tracks, create effects tracks from the location recordings, use room tone to fill for ADR scenes, and cut the dialogue track into a seamless edit. It is the work of highly organized, detail-oriented individuals.

Why go to so much trouble finding these replacements by searching through camera tapes and DATs when it could all be replaced with ADR? ADR is a very collaborative effort that requires a high skill level for the recordist, the mixer, and for the talent. *Talent* is an entertainment industry term that refers to the performers. If union talent is being used, there will also be the matter of payment and schedules.

Even if it is an ultra-low-budget movie, the actors could still be unavailable or involved in other projects during the same time you may need them. These performers get paid for their time in ADR. If you multiply this process by several working actors, the coordination and the expense can be prohibitive. Since audio is often an underbudgeted line item, this can become a real issue during post. The first order of business should be to seek out every way possible to use the location recordings to complete the dialogue edit before resorting to dialogue replacement.

Using Your Library of On-Set Additional Recordings

Here is when the magic of the sound editing begins. The picture edit is complete and has many places that need to be filled with the proper sounds for the auditory illusions of time, space, and action. The wonderful sound library that has been created expressly for your project is now ready to be utilized.

If you have not already browsed and become acquainted with the contents of this folder, now is the time. Be sure to look for all the unique prop sounds, the atmospheres and backgrounds, and any particular or specific sounds recorded from the locations, such as creaky doors and floors.

This part of the edit can be called part of the *sound design* of the project. The sound design is the process of adding sound elements to embellish and heighten the experience of the locked picture edit. It creates the sonic world envisioned by the director and by the picture editor. The murmuring of crowds in the large group scenes, the odd roar of the old car one of the characters drives, the eerie wind whistling through the house, all of these small touches are subliminal but add to the motion picture experience.

Be sure to have a *spotting session* with the director to discuss the needs of the soundtrack. A spotting session is where the sound editor watches the final edit of the picture with the director to discuss the sound in very specific terms. The director may discuss certain sounds that he or she feels are necessary to a particular scene or moment.

Discussions about ADR, Foley, and other additional recording needs are all outlined during the spotting session. You, as the sound designer, might offer ideas on things that you think could help better tell the story, or mixing approaches that can better simulate a particular moment or scene. The spotting session is where finally everyone is talking about one thing, the sound.

Although not absolutely essential at the spotting session, it is good to have at least a temporary music track in place. It is important for the sound editor and the rerecording mixer to have an understanding of where the music will be placed (or *spotted*) and the way the music will be mixed in the soundtrack so that complicated and time-consuming sound designing does not get thrown out in favor of the music. Without proper communication a lot of hard work can be quickly eliminated with a stroke of the delete key. If you are creating an action adventure and the director is favoring music during the fight scenes, it is important to understand that. Otherwise all the intense editing of hits, crashes, and grunts will go unused in favor of the musical score.

Take good and meaningful notes during the spotting session. This may be the only time this part of team will be in the same room collaborating. If there is more than one sound editor on the project, try to get the others to the spotting session too. This is the one chance to be sure that the whole sound team is on the same page as the director and editor.

Be sure to take the time to watch and listen to the final picture edit of the show by yourself prior to the spotting session. Make your own notes about ways that you think the sound edit can enhance the experience of the movie and enhance the storytelling. Know and understand all of the sound elements that you have available beyond the recorded dialogue tracks. Have a good working knowledge of all of the media before the spotting session. Feel free to advise, offer opinions and options, and bring up limitations so that you and your team are working on the same goals and "vision" that the director has for the final project.

Organize the Audio Tracks

Organization is a key skill for any editor. It has come up in every chapter in this text so far. There are so many elements to motion picture sound that without organization things will quickly get lost, misplaced, and forgotten altogether. Organizing the audio tracks is another part of the organizing process. This is very important because this is the beginning of the end of post on the project. All of the elements in the audio timeline are there for specific reasons. Picture editors typically have a good deal of time to complete their edit. They can take many weeks or months to finish their work. Sound does not have this luxury, so it is imperative to create systems that make for an efficient use of the media and of your time. The ideas we'll explore in this section include

- Keep Tracks Separate
- Stay Consistent with the Track Assignments
- Document the Sound Edit

Keep Tracks Separate

Editing is an intuitive process that often throws discipline out the door. In the heat and rush of a fast edit it is easy to forget about organization just to get things done. Go with your gut. Editing is a highly creative act, and in the middle of inspiration it might not be easy to check exactly where things are placed in the timeline.

Of course there are also many times where the inspiration is slow to come and time wasters such as the Internet seem like a good idea. It is at those moments when cleaning up the tracks is a better idea. It forces you to have a good look at the timeline and the organization of the edit, and in the process it keeps your hand deep in the edit. It is through this labor of moving things to their proper places and sorting out audio files and bins where inspiration often strikes. No matter what process you arrive at for editing, always allow for some time at the end of each edit to review the work and to continue the organization of the imports, media, and timeline.

Keep all of the different elements separate from one another. Since the dialogue tracks are paramount to the final mix it's probably a good idea to allocate the top few tracks to dialogue only. Dialogue tracks are generally mono tracks, so be sure to have them all panned to the center or mono. There are specific approaches to dialogue editing that we will be discussing in detail later. For now, try to keep all of the dialogue elements on their own tracks.

Music tracks for the most part are stereo tracks. Be sure to assign two tracks for each music cue. Often it is a good idea to take four tracks total or more for the music tracks. This way, you have at least two stereo pairs that the music can be placed on. Often music tracks overlap or fade in and out over each other. With two discrete stereo music tracks you can alternate music cues from one cue to the other for that sort of fading automation. Some programs, including Final Cut Express, allow for *linking* of tracks. Linking is a process of telling the NLE that those tracks will automate together. Two channels are often linked together to create a stereo pair. One track is panned right and one track is panned left. They automate in sync with each other, so if, for instance, the volume rises or lowers on one track, it happens on both tracks.

Sound effects tracks can be a bit tricky because sound effects can be both mono and stereo. A good strategy is to assign a few tracks for mono effects and a few linked pairs for the stereo effects. This is most important because of the panning. For instance, if you have two tracks for the effects and they are panned as a stereo pair, one is left and one is right, then when mono effects are placed on them they will be panned either right or left depending on which track you put it on. In some cases that may be OK, but if a crash happens on screen left and the sound is panned hard right, it will pull the audience out of their experience. Make specific tracks for the mono effects and the stereo effects.

Stay Consistent with the Track Assignments

As mentioned previously, Final Cut Express does not allow you to individually name the tracks. They will simply be labeled A1, A2, A3, and so on. Assign each track a particular function. For instance, you can have tracks A1 to A4 be for dialogue tracks only. Then have tracks A5 to A8 be for sound effects only. Then have tracks A9 to A12 be for music only. Keeping similar audio elements on their own tracks makes things much easier as you build the edit.

A *track list* is the documentation of what audio element is being assigned to what tracks. Once the track assignments have been determined, create a track list and keep it up to date as things change.

Document the Sound Edit

It's a good idea to have a text document of the location and breakdown of all of the media files, all of the exports, all of the completed edit sequences, and all of the backups. Chances are that you have media in separate places and on separate drives or disks. Hard drives fail and sometimes get erased. Having a text document can help pinpoint dates, backups, and the extent of lost files if a crash happens to a drive.

An excellent approach to creating this documentation would be to have one document per media type. For instance, if one external hard drive is the main working drive for the sound edit, create one document for that drive. If you also have some media or maybe render files in your working computer drive, create a document for that. Wherever you've put the backups for the material, create documents for them. Also be sure to create documentation about the original files; when you have DAT tape or DV tape originals from the location recordings, create a document for those as well.

The document can be as simple as a handwritten sheet or as detailed as a spreadsheet. One simple way to document what's in all the folders is to take a snapshot of your computer screen while you have the folders open in view.

Print out all of these documents and create a binder that is specific to the project. This binder can be a very useful resource. You won't need to mount drives, start up computers, or insert disks to determine what media is where. You can open up the binder, have a quick look, and know immediately where to find the materials you need. A project-specific binder such as this is even more important when there is a team of sound editors collaborating on a project. There are times when someone else may have the media you need or you need to go back to an earlier edit that might be archived elsewhere. The binder would be a map showing where everything is.

I would also suggest a sign-out sheet for the tapes, drives, and backups. If there is more than one person accessing the material, media can get misplaced or even lost. If a sound editor needs to go back to the original camera tapes or make a copy from a backup, it should be logged and signed for. These media files are very important and should be securely maintained. A sign-out sheet will keep a log of everyone who has been accessing and may still have the media.

Additional Documentation

All of the media and documents should be put under the responsibility of one individual. This person can maintain the media and be in charge of all of the documentation. A post supervisor would typically fill that role. If a post supervisor is not involved, then generally the responsibility will go, at least temporarily, to the picture editor.

There are a few other pieces of documentation that are useful during the sound-editing process. Some already exist and some need to be created. In the following section we will discuss these important documents

- The Script Conformed to Match the Final Edit
- The Sound Logs
- The Lined Script

The Script Conformed to Match the Final Edit

Movies change as they are created. Scenes come and go, characters change names or identities, and most of the dialogue changes in one way or another. Often when the script has been filmed and that film has been edited, the final movie does not match the script.

It will need to be the responsibility of someone to watch the movie and create a script that reflects the final edit. This final, conformed script is important to many different departments. The distributor will require one. The legal department will require one. The sound department will require one.

Creating this final script is not typically the responsibility of the audio team. This generally falls under a producer function. I am mentioning this script because it can be very important for the sound editors, particularly the ADR recordist. Scripts will need to be compiled for each actor performing ADR.

Often the script does not match the scene in which the audio is being replaced. ADR is a difficult enough situation, so it is imperative to have a proper script prepared for an actor. Ask for a copy of the script when you are preparing for ADR. If the text and the edited scenes don't match or need extensive rework it's a good idea to inform the producer and the director of the situation.

The Sound Logs

The sound logs are also an important source of information. All of the strategies and approaches that I've outlined are ideals. In the heat of the edit some of these concepts may fall by the wayside. The original sound logs will be an important place to seek out sounds that were never properly sorted, labeled, or digitized.

The sound logs, along with the lined script, will help you locate the alternate takes of dialogue or the room tone recordings or anything that was captured on-set. If sounds are found on the original tapes, be sure to update the additional audio files folder as well as the documentation binder with whatever new items are being digitized or captured.

The Lined Script

Along with the original location tapes you will need the lined script. You may recall from chapter 2 that the lined script is a version of the shooting script that has been drawn with vertical lines notated with the take names of scenes that have been shot in that part of the script. It is a map to determine which takes correspond to scenes and dialogue in the edit. This script along with the sound logs will show you on which tapes or drives particular recordings are located. You'll need this information if you are searching for alternate takes or other location recordings.

The truth is that DIY filmmaking often doesn't have a script supervisor to create a lined script. With so many crew members wearing so many "hats," a lined script may seem like a luxury. If no lined script is available, then you will have to decipher where to find takes from the sound logs.

Summary

Final Cut Express is a powerful tool for sound editing. Using the main four windows, the browser, the viewer, and canvas windows, and the timeline, you can properly import, organize, and add all of the media to the edit. Keyframes are useful and precise tools to instruct Final Cut Express to make certain things happen at specific frames. Keyframes allow Final Cut Express to automate processes over time; however, some processes will need to be rendered to play fully in real-time playback.

As the sound designer, it is imperative that you watch the locked picture edit and know all of the additional materials that you have on hand, available for editing, prior to the spotting session. Once the picture has been spotted with the director, you are free to create the sound design of the movie. Use elements from the additional audio folder to enrich and enhance the story. Be consistent with your track assignments as you build the new sound edit. All of the extra effort in organization will pay large dividends as the edit progresses.

Review Questions

Questions like these are likely to appear on exams to test how well you understood and retained the information in this chapter.

1. What are the main working windows in Final Cut Express?
2. What is rendering and why is it important?
3. What is a locked picture and why is it important to sound editorial?
4. What are keyframes? What are two ways to add keyframes to your edit in Final Cut Express?
5. What is a spotting session and who should attend?

Discussion/Essay Questions

Your instructor may assign you one or more of the following questions for discussion in class or as the subject of a paper.

1. Why are good picture editors usually good sound editors as well?
2. How is cutting sound digitally different than it was before computers and NLEs?

Applying What You've Learned

Research/Lab/Fieldwork Projects

The following lab exercises will give you practice importing sound in Final Cut Express.

1. Import your additional audio files folder into the browser of Final Cut Express. Organize the material and create bins as needed.
2. In Final Cut Express, assign particular tracks to specific elements. For example assign tracks 1–4 to dialogue only, assign

tracks 5–8 for sound effects only, and assign tracks 9–12 for music only. Document the assignments with a track list.

3. In your edit timeline find a troublesome line of dialogue. Search the lined script or sound logs to find the alternate takes of the line. Replace the dialogue in your timeline with the alternate take of the same line.

Resources

The following resources have more information on the topics covered in this chapter.

"Final Cut Express" (http://www.apple.com/support/finalcutexpress). Apple's online support and tutorials for Final Cut Express can be accessed here. This site is filled with plenty of editing information.

Lynda.com (http://www.lynda.com). This is not a free resource but the value is truly outstanding. For a yearly fee you have online access 24/7 to tutorials, demonstration projects, and tips, and tricks for video and audio editing. It is an excellent way to learn the fine points of Final Cut Express as well as other audio-specific programs, such as Apple's other main video software Final Cut Pro.

CHAPTER 7

SOUND EDITING IN DIGITAL AUDIO WORKSTATIONS

OVERVIEW AND LEARNING OBJECTIVES

In this chapter, you will:
- Learn about digital audio workstations
- Understand OMF files
- Learn how to sync audio and video files
- Learn about the additional audio files folder

What Is a DAW?

A *digital audio workstation* (DAW) is a computer-based audio recording, editing, and mixing system. There are many types of DAWs but most consist of a computer, software that is audio specific, and usually some sort of hardware device beyond the computer. The hardware can be a simple stereo input and output sound card that operates inside the computer. Or it can be as sophisticated as a network of digital devices that can digitize, edit, and mix complex, multichannel audio soundtracks.

For many editors Final Cut Express or other video programs are sufficient for their sound-editing requirements. For more demanding sound-editing and designing needs, DAWs have considerably more powerful audio tools. If you plan on pursuing audio in a more professional environment, DAWs will be the next logical step for you to take. This chapter will highlight some of the additional functions of these sound-editing workstations.

DAWs are built for sound. They allow for precise control of many audio parameters at one time. They allow for highly customized, automated mixer configurations. DAWs offer high-quality filtering, processing and noise reduction, automation, and signal-routing capabilities. Many of the DAW systems can add additional hardware and software to increase these abilities. There are also software emulations of vintage equipment used inside of a DAW that are as good as their hardware inspirations at a fraction of the cost. DAWs are powerful tools that record, edit, mix, and master the soundtracks of digital filmmaking. In this section we will investigate

- Pro Tools and Other Audio Computer Workstations
- Hardware and Software DAW Packages
- Hardware Controllers

Pro Tools and Other Audio Computer Workstations

One of the major DAWs on the market today is called Pro Tools. As its name implies, it is a professional system that is used extensively to produce music for major-label musical recording acts and to edit and mix the sound for major Hollywood films. It can be safely said that the vast majority of audio postproduction is created with Pro Tools.

Digidesign, the maker of Pro Tools, was acquired by leading video-editing company Avid Technologies with the purpose of creating a seamless integration with its flagship video-editing software, Avid. Both of these products are mainstays in professional motion picture postproduction. When DAWs such as Pro Tools first entered the market they were quite expensive and limited in what they could do. With the advances in computer technology and computer chip speeds, the DAWs of today are quite powerful.

There are several levels of Pro Tools systems. The flagship system is called a TDM system that consists of an *input/output* (I/O) interface, the Pro Tools software, and a computer. This system gives you the most flexibility and options for postproduction audio work. It also allows for connection to additional devices for integration with video and audio decks as well as integrated hardware controller devices. The TDM system allows for multiple hardware devices for many types of I/O. They can be analog or digital and typically run in series of eight in and eight out.

Digidesign has also developed a line of less expensive systems that are called LE, which is a rack-mounted hardware box that attaches to a computer and runs the Pro Tools software or a small USB key that allows for very limited (I/O). Although the LE systems have much of the same functionality, they do have certain limitations, such as a limited track count, but they are quite cost effective when compared to their much more expensive big brother TDM. It is similar in principle to the difference between Final Cut Express and Final Cut Pro.

Digidesign's Pro Tools is by no means the only DAW available today. There are quite a few systems that are used in the professional and hobbyist domains. Some DAWs excel at music production, such as Apple's Logic Audio or Steinberg's Cubase. These can also be used for audio post. Like any tool, whichever one you use should always be the right fit for the job. Each program offers advantages and disadvantages and research must be made to find the right tools for your specific job.

Although we discussed sound editing in the Final Cut Express chapter, DAWs are specific tools for audio, and they excel at audio the same way that Final Cut Express excels at picture editing. To truly take your audio to the next level, serious consideration must be given to a DAW for audio mastering and finishing.

Apple's Final Cut Pro Studio suite of software includes a program called Soundtrack Pro. Soundtrack Pro is a DAW that has a convenient integration with Final Cut Pro. It offers many of the same sorts of sound-editing functions of most DAWs, such as advanced editing and mixing tool sets. It runs from the Apple computer without the need for additional hardware and is an excellent way to transition into sound editing with a DAW. Adobe Audition is also a software-based DAW and has a tight integration with its video-editing brother, Adobe Premiere Pro.

Besides personal computer–based systems, there are also *stand-alone DAWs* by various manufacturers. A stand-alone DAW has no additional computer and contains almost everything you need for the DAW in one hardware box. These include multitrack systems from Korg, Roland, and other high-quality audio manufacturers. One of the key aspects for a DAW in audio postproduction is its integration with viewing video images. It is important to be able to look at, scroll through, and easily move forward and backward in the video as you edit the sound.

Hardware and Software Packages

Some DAWs can operate with just a personal computer and others require additional hardware to operate properly. Not so long ago even the most advanced DAWs were quite limited in the amount of tracks that they could handle at one time and in their capacity for video playback. Advances in computer technology have eliminated many of those original limitations. However, for professional use, additional hardware is typically needed beyond the computer to achieve the required results.

Feature films can have a hundred tracks or more of audio. These tracks can be going through any number of processes to alter their original state. Computers today are fast, but they still need additional hardware to be reliable in playing back, processing, mixing, and outputting large audio track counts and video.

Professional DAW systems have deck control capability, high track counts, and superior signal processing. Many of the DAW makers have also developed simpler systems that offer much of the same functionality. A great solution is to sound-edit the bulk of the program on the smaller, scaled-down systems until the more advanced functions are needed. When the project is at a logical point, the entire sound edit can be brought into a larger DAW system for making final adjustments and creating the final mixed soundtrack outputs. This helps contain costs while still providing a professional outcome.

The Pro Tools TDM system is a professional DAW used worldwide. Pro Tools TDM can run on Windows or Apple computers. The core system consists of the Pro Tools DAW software, hardware cards that are designed to fit inside of the computer case itself, and a *digital-to-analog and analog-to-digital* (DA/AD) *converter* box that is attached by a cable to the hardware cards inside of the computer. Each hardware card contains computer chips that are dedicated to Pro Tools and its capabilities. More hardware cards will mean that there is more audio-specific processing power available to the program.

Digital-to-analog and analog-to-digital converter boxes do exactly what their name implies, they convert audio from digital to analog and back again. Generally these boxes do more than just convert audio. They can also be input/output (I/O) devices that can get audio to and from the DAW. Be aware that not all of these boxes are alike. They vary in quality and can directly affect the audio's excellence. The converters that come as part of a DAW software/hardware package are usually of a high quality.

Pro Tools standard TDM systems offer one, two, and three hardware card systems with the ability to add many more if needed. The program will automatically determine how many cards are present in the system. Major feature films may use more than one Pro Tools system linked together to handle the complicated audio processes required to do the job.

There are additional devices that are also used in professional audio settings including a device called a *synchronization box*, or a sync box. A sync box's main purpose is to sync devices, most often video and audio decks, together with the DAW. Today a popular method is to deliver the final mixed audio files on a data disk or hard drive. Final audio mixes, however, are delivered in a number of ways.

For example, you may need to record your final edit and mix from the DAW onto the master videotape. That would mean that the DAW and a deck would need to sync together. That is where the sync box is required. The sync box sends matching timecode information to the deck and to the DAW. The sync box will align the tape deck and the DAW into perfect sync to allow for a frame-accurate recording of the audio onto the tape.

There is one more essential device needed for this level of professional audio, and that is a *digital clock*. The digital clock creates and sends *word clock* information to each digital device and serves as the master clocking device. Word clock is the term for the digital clocking information that is sent through cables from device to device. For digital devices to properly interface, one device acts as the word clock master and all of the other devices act as word clock slaves. In larger audio post facilities there is a *master clock*, sometimes called the *house clock*, which serves as the master source of word clock for all of the facility's digital devices.

High-quality digital clocks are required if recordings or transfers are made between digital audio devices. Simple or less complicated audio editing and mixing may not require these devices. It is possible with today's technology, to record, edit, and mix inside most of the major NLE applications. However, as the complexities of the projects rise, or if there is a need to sync a device such as a deck, then these items become a necessity.

Hardware Controllers

Hardware controllers are devices that look like mixing consoles but offer other features beyond a standard mixing board. Hardware controllers operate the DAW software. They have faders like a mixing console, but they also offer start and stop, play, and record and may also include a system for monitoring the sound. They offer almost complete automation for the functions of the DAW software. All of the actions from muting, to volume automation to panning and effects are recalled for the next playback.

There are many different types of hardware controllers on the market. No two models are alike, and no two offer the same functionality. Some hardware controllers are DAW-software specific and they will only operate with particular designated software.

Hardware controllers activate the software program to perform various functions. For instance, if you move the faders on a hardware controller the faders that are on the on-screen mixer in the DAW program you are using will also move. You can think of a hardware controller as a ten-button mouse. By using a hardware controller you can push five or more faders up or down at a time, making the experience of mixing easier and faster than when you are working with a mouse. And an added benefit is that you will always have the mouse available for precise parameter adjustments.

Several manufactures of hardware controllers offer models that contain audio components as well. Many of these devices offer microphone inputs, have extensive monitoring capabilities, and offer DA/AD conversions. Their cost is reflected in their feature sets. Hardware controllers are an excellent option for you to expand the functionality of the DAW software.

The OMF File

DAWs require a reliable way to exchange edit information with NLEs and other DAWs. One solution is the *Open Media File Interchange Format* (OMF), a file type that was expressly created for moving audio and video from NLEs to DAWs. OMF files are standard files used extensively in audio postproduction. In this section we will explore

- What Is an OMF?
- How to Export OMFs
- OMF Limitations
- Best Practices with OMFs

What Is an OMF?

Editing audio in NLEs can often be time-consuming and counterintuitive. This is not surprising, since they are created and optimized for editing picture. Because DAWs are specifically geared for editing and mixing audio, there needs to be a good way to get the sound out of the NLE and into a DAW. Avid Technology invented the OMF file type as a convenient way to move the audio and video from one program to another.

An OMF file contains all of the audio clips or audio media, edited exactly as it is edited in your NLE audio timeline. It will include crossfades on the audio if they are there, the panning of the audio clips, as well as the *volume automation*.

Volume automation is the process of changing and saving the volume levels of audio clips in NLEs and DAWs. By using volume automation, the levels that are used during a mix are stored as information within the program and are available until changed later. Until volume automation was invented, there was no way to save all of the fader moves while mixing. This made re-creating and repeating an exact mix close to impossible.

The OMF file has revolutionized digital audio procedures. The picture editor will complete his picture edit and sound edit with a sound mix. If the editor wants to have a sound editor mix and master the sound on a DAW, then the audio timeline can be exported as an OMF.

The picture editor's sound mix will include location audio tracks and perhaps narration and music tracks as well. The OMF file that the editor exports allows the sound edit to be opened in a DAW in the exact same state. If, for example, the picture editor cut in a tire screech at 1 minute and 10 seconds and 10 frames, the OMF will reflect that. A sound editor working in a DAW will open the OMF to see the exact tire screech sound effects file, at the exact timecode and with its volume automation and name. This, of course, will be true with all of the audio clips within the OMF.

Figure 7.1 shows the audio timeline as edited within Final Cut Pro.

Figure 7.2 shows the audio after it was converted to an OMF and opened in Pro Tools.

FIGURE 7.1 A close-up view of a sound edit within Final Cut Pro

FIGURE 7.2 This is an expanded view of the OMF export from Final Cut Pro now in a Pro Tools file

The Pro Tools file contains the same number of audio tracks and audio files and mimics the audio timeline from Final Cut Pro completely. Pro Tools can now use these files to further edit, mix, and process the audio to create a final mix of the project.

An important note if you are a user of Final Cut Express: Final Cut Express does not allow for the exporting of OMF files. Since Final Cut Express offers fewer features than the more expensive Final Cut Pro, OMF exporting is one of the features left out of the program. The good news is that Final Cut Express edit sequences can be opened in Final Cut Pro. So all of the editing can be done in Final Cut Express and opened in Final Cut Pro for an OMF export later. Check with your particular NLE software to determine if OMFs are an available export.

OMF files are not a new file type, and they have not been updated for quite some time. There are several things that would be useful in OMFs that are not currently included. Some of those things include any type of plug-in or filter, track names, or even stereo files. At the moment, however, OMFs are still a powerful and useful way to move audio material in such a precise manner. There are not many other ways of doing it so that things will stay perfectly in sync from timeline to timeline.

How to Export OMFs

Fortunately, exporting OMF files is a snap. I will explain the process from within Final Cut Pro, but most of the NLEs do it in a similar manner. Figure 7.3 is an example of the timeline in Final Cut Pro.

The in and out points tell the OMF where to start and where to stop. The video portion of the movie should be created from the same points. This way the movie file and the OMF will be frame-accurate with one another.

This type of OMF is referred to as an *embedded OMF*. Embedded OMFs contain all of the metadata and the digital audio files in one file. After the export is complete, an embedded OMF file would be, for example, MyProject.omf, and it would include the entire audio timeline of audio clips, panning, volume automation, and so on from in point to out point.

Typically you would want to include any options that are available to include when exporting an OMF. Options can include, panning, volume automation, bit depth, and sample size. Figure 7.4 shows the options for exporting the OMF.

One important consideration when exporting OMFs is the *handle* length. Handles in digital audio and video editing refer to the media before and after an edit point. For instance, a media file is two minutes

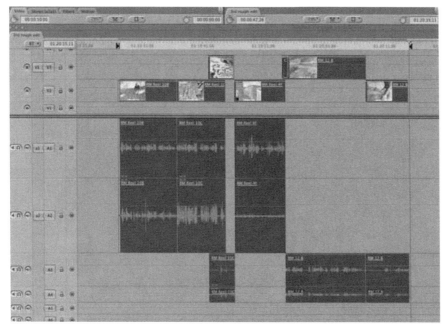

FIGURE 7.3 The highlighted area in this example is the media between the in and out points

long but only one minute is used in the edit. The remaining media are handles on either side of the edit that make up the unused other minute.

The default handle length of most programs is one second. Depending on the frame rate, that one second will be twenty-four frames, thirty frames or more. Longer handles are generally more useful to sound editors. Five-second handles are a good compromise between useful material and file size. Five-second handles provide a good number of frames for a sound editor to work with.

Of course, if a clip is fifteen seconds long and all fifteen seconds are used there will be no handles. OMFs are smart enough to know that. They use the number that you choose as the "ideal" handle length if the media length supports it. Once you've determined the appropriate handle length, then under the File menu under "Export" one of the options will be to export "audio to OMF." Click that to begin the OMF export.

A note regarding OMF files: If you are exporting an OMF file from an Avid editing program, there are a few more options available when exporting. Avid also allows for "linked or non-embedded OMFs" as well as "embedded OMFs." If you create a non-embedded OMF file, you create a small file "MyProject.omf" that links to a media folder. The media folder contains all of the actual audio files, and when the OMF file is opened it asks for the media folder so that it can open the OMF.

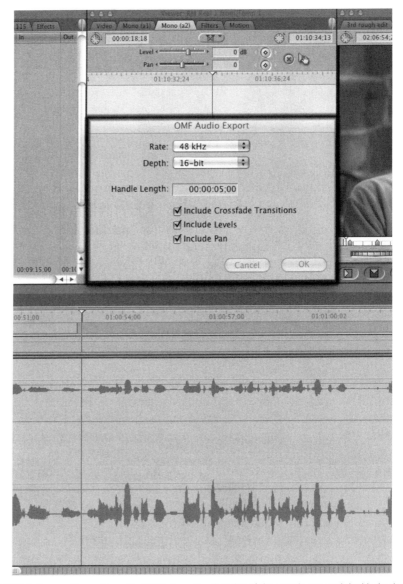

FIGURE 7.4 Among other options, the OMF allows the changing of the sample rate and the bit depth of the edit

There is a way to create a non-embedded OMF file from Final Cut Pro using software from a vendor called Automatic Duck.

The reason it could be advantageous to do non-embedded OMFs is because the media folder could be quite large but the OMF file would be tiny in comparison since it would not contain any of the media but only the editing session's metadata. Some operating systems, such as Apple's OS X, have a 2-gigabyte limitation on any single file size. If projects are large, sometimes several embedded OMFs will need to be created. They would each be 2 gigabytes or less in size. If you have an extremely large project, exporting an OMF as a non-embedded OMF allows for a small OMF file for a project that spans more than 2 gigabytes of media.

OMF Limitations

OMFs will do the job that needs to get done, but like many things, it could use a bit of dusting off and an upgrade. OMF files are a handy way to move large chunks of audio from system to system. However, they are a fairly old file type for computers and software that upgrade constantly. None of these limitations are deal breakers, and considering the masterful way it does what it does, it may seem like nitpicking; however, these items are important to note.

There is no track-naming convention in an OMF. (That's true for Final Cut Express as well.) All of the tracks will simply be labeled "Audio 1," "Audio 2," "Audio 3," and so on. As long as you have a clear picture of how you edited and laid out the tracks, it will be simple enough to write the track names in the DAW.

All files will be imported as mono files. If there are stereo files in your edit, they will be broken into two mono files. When the OMF opens and the files are imported into a new program, be sure to properly pan any of the stereo elements back into their proper place. All tracks that are mono tracks will be panned to the center. If there are stereo tracks that got split into two mono files, then check that stereo left is panned to the left and stereo right is panned to the right.

Filters added to your audio clips will not be translated by the OMF. This is more of an issue when files are being transported from DAW to DAW. Since many of the filters and effects can be inside of several different DAWs, it is important to note that any filters or any keyframing of filtering will not translate in the OMF. This is the case even if both DAWs have access to the same filter set. Filters are not included in OMF exports.

Best Practices with OMFs

OMFs are most useful and provide the best results when some important standards are followed. OMFs start with the sound edit in your NLE project. Since the OMF is an exact replica of your sound edit, it is important to organize and make things logical. One of the amazing things about NLEs is their ability to handle up to ninety-nine audio tracks at one time. I've never met a picture editor who has used ninety-nine tracks of audio (thankfully!) but there is no reason to cram all of the audio files onto just two or three tracks.

The OMF will create the exact timeline from your picture edit session. Keep things organized by track. Keep the main location audio from lavaliere recordings on one track, keep the main location audio from the boom recordings on another track. Keep sound effects on their own tracks, and keep the music on its own tracks. When the exported OMF is imported into a DAW, the tracks and the audio files will load this exact way. It makes the job for the sound editors easier because they can clearly see where everything is.

On no-budget projects this may seem inconsequential, but on larger projects this sort of file keeping is essential. If you are paying a sound editor to locate, sort, and rearrange audio files, it will cost you time and money. These are certainly duties in a sound editor's job description, but better use of the time and money is sound editing and mixing.

Sync Pops and Video Files

Now that the complete audio edit has made it to the DAW, it's time to import the movie file. Since the advent of sound for films there has always been two parts to movies—the picture portion and the sound portion. You will need a way to sync the two together in a reliable manner. In this section we will discuss

- Head Pops and Tail Pops
- Movies with Burn-In Timecode
- OMFs and Movie Files

Head Pops and Tail Pops

Head pops and tail pops are simple and effective ways to sync picture and audio files with one another. Head pops and tail pops, as described in chapter 5, are simply one frame of audio and one frame of video that line up with one another. When played back there is a one-frame flash that plays with the one-frame beep. A countdown file, often used at the start of movie files, contains a head pop that is commonly used for syncing. They play prior to the picture start as well as after the picture end, hence the terms head and tail.

Head pops and tail pops are available online or as additional files from your NLE install. It is a simple matter to create your own. Since tone is such a common audio source, it is easy to find and use for the audible "pop." If the leader is black prior to picture start, then a *flash frame* can be inserted as the picture "pop." A flash frame is usually a frame of video that is pure white. It is edited into black and when played in sequence will "flash." A flash frame is an excellent choice to use if you are creating a head pop or tail pop, since it will be clearly different from the black it is edited with. Place the one frame of tone under the one flash frame and you have just created a head pop or tail pop.

A very common placement for the head pop is two seconds prior to the picture start. If the picture start timecode is at one hour or 01:00:00:00 then the head pop can be placed at timecode 00:59:58:00, which is exactly two seconds prior to picture start. A head pop placed here is also called the *two-pop*. Two-pops are standard in postproduction. That same two-pop can also be placed at the tail of the project, but this time it is located at two seconds after the picture ends. These pops allow for easy syncing of the movie file and help identify sync problems. If the head pop lines up and the tail pop does not, then you have immediately determined that there is some sort of sync error.

Movies with Burn-In Timecode

The main determination of absolute sync is with the project's timecode. Timecode is one of those things that make novice filmmakers duck and cover. Timecode is merely the counting of frames. When working with picture and audio, it is imperative to make sure that the timecodes between the video and the audio match up frame accurate. Superimposing a timecode over the picture file is known as *burn-in timecode*. With burn-in timecode, a sound editor can check that the timecode on the picture and the timecode within the DAW are exactly the same.

Most NLEs provide some way to burn-in timecode to the picture file. Final Cut Express has a timecode generator that creates a timecode that can be superimposed onto the picture file. If you are creating a picture file from a tape, most decks have the capability to superimpose the timecode onto the picture when outputting.

If you are creating an OMF and a movie file from an NLE timeline, it is a good idea to use the same in and out points to create them. It is also an excellent idea to provide long handles before and after the actual picture edit. If, for example, your show begins at time code 01:00:00:00, you may want to have the movie file start at 00:59:30:00. This will give you a good thirty seconds prior to the picture start. You would want to do the same at the end. Why would you do this? The main reason is that if and when the time comes to lay the session back to tape or some other device, the extra time allows for everything to get up to proper speed before the actual program begins. You would certainly have to place the in point prior to the two-pop so that it is included in both the OMF and movie file.

Is burn-in timecode absolutely necessary? No it's not. But it assures sound editors that at every point in the program they are frame accurate. It also allows for more precise communication if there are problems. If there is a problem, the sound editor can pinpoint, to the frame, exactly where the problem is. Timecode is useful for the other post sound team members for the same reason. You can use exact timecodes for ADR preparation or sound design or dialogue editing and notes. No one in the audience will care about frame rates, timecode, or two-pops, but they will certainly care if dialogue or sound effects are out of sync.

OMFs and Movie Files

As you can now clearly see, in the world of DAWs and audio post the OMF file and a digital movie file are the stock in trade. The DAW will import both of these files. The OMF will recreate all of the individual audio files and their respective tracks and the movie file will play in a special video track that will be output to a monitor to watch the picture.

These two files will need to be synced together to edit the project. In the DAW you should be able to spot the movie file to the burn-in timecode on-screen. Spotting, as used here, is the process of defining the exact timecode at which any one particular element is placed. Many DAWS offer a "spot" command that allows the user to enter an exact timecode for an event to occur.

For instance, the movie file is showing you a frame of 00:59:50:00. Then activate the spotting command, type in the exact timecode, and the movie file will move or spot to that timecode.

Another method to sync these files would be to use the head and tail pops. Once both the OMF and the movie file have been imported into the DAW, then find the flash frame or reference video frame for the two-pop and move the frame to line up exactly with the one frame of tone in the audio timeline. Once you have lined up the head pop, then go to the end of the movie file in the timeline and check that the tail pop also lines up. After verifying that, then park the play head in the middle of the project and hit play. Watch the actors' mouths closely to be sure that everything is in perfect sync.

Check the burn-in timecode to be sure that the timecode that is indicated within the DAW matches the picture file. Sometimes when the head and tail pops line up, the project plays in perfect sync and yet the timecodes do not match. Sometimes the head and tail pops line up and the movie plays out of sync.

There are a number of reasons these things can happen. A sequence setting could be improperly set when the OMF was exported or the DAW had the wrong timecode selected or any number of things. If there is a problem, now, before the sound edit has begun, is the time to

NOTE

DVDs are an amazing invention. They have allowed filmmakers to squeeze extremely large files onto a single small disk. The technology that has allowed this uses compression—a very smart, very good-looking compression, but compression nonetheless. Sometimes DVDs, which are used as a source material as the video portion for sound editing, can randomly skip or repeat frames of video. This can be a problem when, as you're editing, you see that the burn-in does not match the timecode of the DAW. Due to the nature of compression in DVDs and this occasional problem, it is recommended that the picture editor generate a digital movie file from the NLE or output a tape, which can be captured, rather than use video from a DVD file as your movie file for the edit.

fix it. There are so many "moving parts" in postproduction it is easy for something small to throw a big wrench in the works. Each part of the post process leads to the next, so figuring out exactly where things went wrong and fixing them is imperative.

The Additional Audio Files Folder

The additional audio files folder is something that has been discussed throughout this text. Let's take a moment to see what it looks like from the postproduction perspective. In this section we will explore

- Unedited Music Tracks
- B-Roll Audio
- On-Set Dialogue Replacement
- On-Set Foley
- Room Tones

Unedited Music Tracks

Music editing is a skill that requires having a sense of rhythm, timing, and understanding of how the music impacts the emotional moments on-screen. Sometimes movies have extensive music editing built in from the picture edit, sometimes there is no music and the project is awaiting the score tracks from the composer. There is no one way that projects are completed, edited, or posted.

For instance, some television programs are completely edited with their sound, their music, and even their sound effects prior to audio postproduction. Some very talented television picture editors are also very talented music editors. Many editors get music tracks from *commercial music libraries*. Commercial music libraries offer many types of fully produced professional music tracks and license their use at reasonable rates. The music tracks can be auditioned online and downloaded for immediate use. Most of these libraries structure their music tracks in a long version of the song, maybe three minutes in length, and then several shorter versions as well.

The OMF does not contain an entire track or version of any of the music. Since, during the export of the OMF, the handles have been defined at, let's say, 150 frames' worth, what comes across in the opened timeline are only the bits of edited music tracks with their respective handles. This is generally not a problem—until things need to change.

Often, there can be a request for a different edit of a piece of music. It's a good idea to have a complete version of each track of the music in case you are required to do music editing.

Ask the picture editor to supply, outside of the OMF, the full tracks of any music that was used in the edit if you don't already have it. Be sure that all of the music tracks are of the highest resolution possible. No MP3s if it can be avoided!

B-Roll Audio

The folder of B-roll audio is a very important folder of sounds for the sound design of the movie. This folder will contain the atmospheres, special sounds, and unique sonics to the movie. Know the contents of this folder; this is a "go-to" folder for a sound editor. Before getting too far into the edit, be sure that this folder is clearly labeled and organized. You will want to refer to this folder often to try new ideas, so understanding what's in there is important. Look back to Figure 5.4 in chapter 5 for organizational ideas.

If you've recorded and captured great ambient backgrounds, lay them in under the appropriate scenes. You might mute them before you get into any serious editing or designing, but if they are already placed in the timeline, then they are available for immediate use. When a picture editor is starting the edit, he or she will watch all of the relevant clips for each moment to determine what parts will work best for the edit. Think of this folder as being full of the entire pertinent source files that you need for your sound edit. There will most likely be numerous occasions where the contents of this folder will help smooth difficult parts of the edit as well as contribute to the final sound universe of the movie.

On-Set Dialogue Replacement

This folder is essential when it comes time to properly edit the dialogue portion of the sound. Labeling and organization is the key to the best use of the contents of this folder. When you are seriously determining the needs of the dialogue edit, the contents of this folder will be paramount. This will allow you one more opportunity to keep the ADR to a minimum.

We will be discussing the dialogue edit in detail in a later chapter. At that point this folder will be playing a prominent role in the editing process. For now, however, be sure that the material is properly labeled; easy to find; and, of course, backed up.

On-Set Foley

This folder should be regarded with the same reverence as the B-roll audio subfolder and on-set ADR folder. A good sound editor needs to understand all of the tools, or in this case sounds, that are available to them. These on-set Foley sounds are very important to creating a realistic edit of key moments like fight scenes, or of unique props or unique features of sets and locations.

These on-set Foley sounds are also an important element in the creation of the production effects track (PFX). Remember that the PFX track is key for creating complete and useable music and effects (M&E) tracks.

Knowing and understanding what elements were captured for all of the various moments will be important as the sound edit develops. These bits of on-set Foley will help further the illusion of, for instance, fighting or explosions and will help enrich and expand the emotional impact of the images on the screen. You've tenaciously recorded all of these wonderful sonic additions; now is the time to understand what you've got and edit them in.

Room Tones

The importance of room tone cannot be overstated. It is the glue that holds together the location recordings and all of the additional elements that must be edited together to create the illusion of a seamless edit. All of those room tones should be properly labeled and stored in this folder.

As you edit, place the appropriate room tone for each scene, muted, on a track into the edit timeline. This way, as the location tracks are edited for the final mixing, all of the room tones are there and available as source material as you create the edit. You may not use every available room tone in every scene, but in all likelihood you will.

Excellent sound editing is required to create the final illusion that these captured moments happened at once, in real time. As filmmakers, we understand that the shots may have been done over a period of days and maybe even weeks or months. But the audience does not care about that. They want to get lost in the story and the characters, and room tone shifts or dropouts will pull the audience out of that illusion. They might not be able to verbalize or identify exactly what is wrong, but even the most unsophisticated viewer will be able to hear a problem that takes them out of the emotional moment of the scene. Room tone is the key ingredient in smoothing out the rough patches between edits.

Summary

DAWs are powerful tools for editing, manipulating, and mixing audio. There are many types of DAWs in use today, and they can be computer based, stand-alone, or a part of a network of digital devices. A key component for a DAW is a DA/AD converter that will get the audio into the digital state required by the DAW software.

Word clock and sync boxes are important to make sure that all of the devices are receiving the correct information for proper operation. You may also consider using hardware controllers to automate many audio parameters such as panning, muting, and volume automation without the use of a mouse.

OMF files can be used to transport the edits from system to system when the picture edit is complete. OMFs can include all of the digital audio files as well as the metadata such as the volume automation and the timecode placement of all of the files. Then by utilizing two-pops, the separate OMF audio and the movie file can be synced together. The head pops and tail pops as well as the burn-in timecode will ensure a frame-accurate transfer of the edit.

Once the picture edit is complete, it is time for the sound editing and design of the movie. This is when to make use of the additional audio files folder. Use those unique sounds to fill in the world of the movie. Adding the power of a DAW will create a professional soundtrack in a more user-friendly way and with greater sonic qualities than with an NLE.

Review Questions

Questions like these are likely to appear on exams to test how well you understood and retained the information in this chapter.

1. What is a DAW?
2. What is an OMF file? What contents and information can be inside of an OMF file?
3. What is a two-pop? What is the purpose of a two-pop?
4. What is word clock and why is it important?
5. What is the purpose of having a burn-in timecode?

Discussion/Essay Questions

Your instructor may assign you one or more of the following questions for discussion in class or as the subject of a paper.

1. What considerations should be made to properly transfer the audio edit from the NLE to a DAW? Discuss the process and requirements.
2. What are several strategies to ensure accurate syncing of picture and OMF audio?

Applying What You've Learned

Research/Lab/Fieldwork Projects

The following lab exercises will give you practice exporting movie files and importing OMFs into a DAW.

1. Place an in and out point on the timeline of your edit. In your NLE, export your audio timeline to OMF.
2. Use the same in and out point on the timeline of your edit. In your NLE, export the edited movie as a single, digital movie file.
3. Find a DAW that imports OMF files. Open the OMF and see how your edit translates to the audio workstation. Import the digital movie file into a DAW and sync it with the OMF.

NOTE
Students who have ongoing projects may elect to use their own source material, such as video clips, with the instructor's permission.

Resources

The following resources have more information on the topics covered in this chapter.

Designing Sound (http://designingsound.org). This blog is devoted to all types of audio. Be sure to check out their great section of video interviews with top Hollywood sound mixers.

Film Sound Daily (http://www.filmsounddaily.com). This is a blog devoted to postproduction audio on Hollywood features.

FIGURE 14.2

FIGURE 14.1

FIGURE 12.2

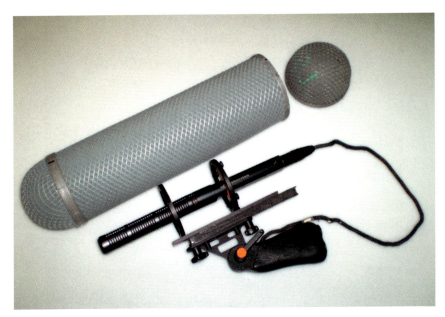

FIGURE 3.3

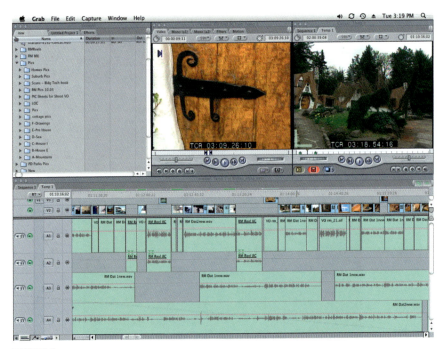

FIGURE 6.3

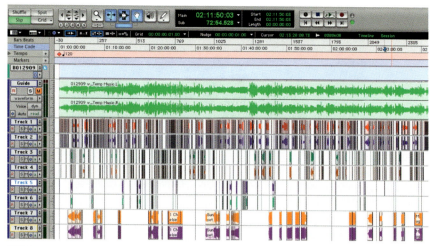

FIGURE 7.2

FIGURE 2.6

FIGURE 12.6

FIGURE 12.7

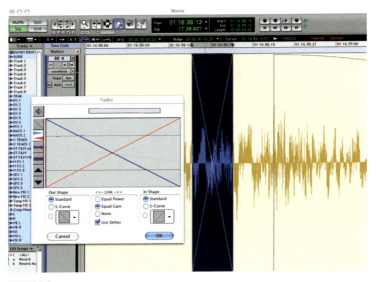

FIGURE 8.3

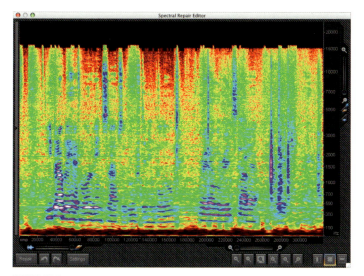

FIGURE 14.9

FIGURE 10.1

FIGURE 3.2

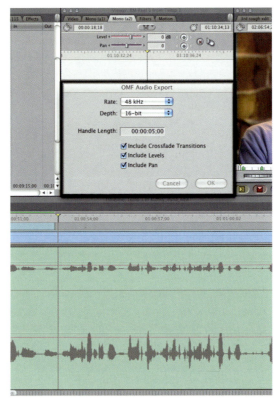

FIGURE 7.4

FIGURE 7.1

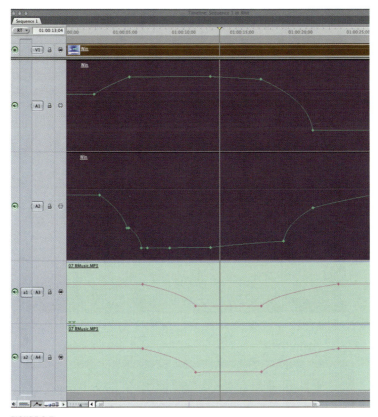

FIGURE 6.7

FIGURE 2.11

FIGURE 11.3

FIGURE 13.5

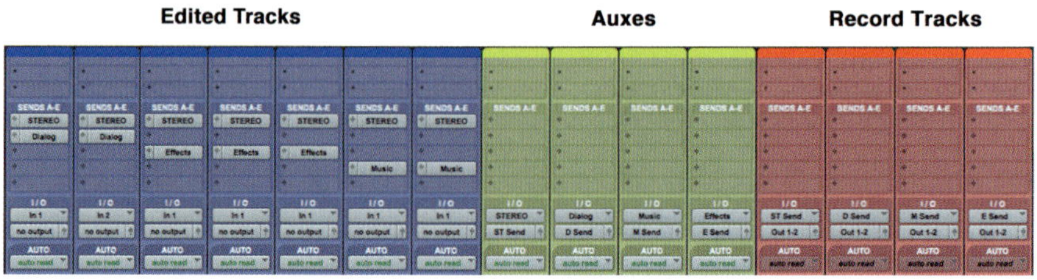

Edited Tracks   Auxes   Record Tracks

FIGURE 14.3

CHAPTER 8

THE DIALOGUE EDIT

OVERVIEW AND LEARNING OBJECTIVES

In this chapter, you will:
- Learn about the dialogue editing process
- Learn how to arrange the dialogue tracks
- Learn about special track assignments
- Learn how to tell the story

The Dialogue Editing Process

Dialogue editing is an exacting craft. The dialogue track is the one source of audio that will be playing almost the entire length of the film or program. Audiences need to clearly hear what the characters are saying and doing. Be aware, too, that audiences excel at spotting out-of-sync dialogue and hearing abrupt audio shifts. They may never have ever heard of room tone, but they will hear it if it is missing or wrong.

The dialogue edit is completely dependent on the quality of the location recording tracks. The dialogue editing process is where the project's dialogue issues and needs are determined. This is where the final determination is made on the exact lines that will be needed for ADR. This is where it is determined if narration, crowd, or group recordings will need to be made. This is where it is determined if Foley is required and to what extent. No matter what genre or type of movie your particular project is, during the dialogue edit many of the sound track requirements are uncovered. This section will discuss

- Postproduction Sound Mixing and the Dialogue Edit
- Room Tone and Crossfades
- Assigning and Editing Tracks by Character or Recorded Perspective

Postproduction Sound Mixing and the Dialogue Edit

An understanding of how sound is mixed for motion pictures is required to properly order, edit, and assign the location audio clips to tracks for the dialogue edit. Dialogue editing has several purposes, including: cleaning up the audio, assigning tracks, and separating and ordering the audio clips for final mixing. When mixing, certain processes affect an entire track of audio, and certain audio elements need to be separated from others for proper signal routing and outputting of the mix.

Inserts are access points in the mixing console that allow for software or hardware devices to pass between the signal playing from a track into the final mixing track. Examples of insert devices are equalization (EQ), compression, and limiting. Inserts are added to an entire track so, for instance, an EQ setting can affect all of the audio playing through a particular track, not on just one clip of that track.

Inserts are very useful for *rerecording mixers* to add devices to make different sounding recordings sound similar. A rerecording mixer, also called a postproduction audio mixer, is the person who mixes the audio of the final soundtrack. Rerecording mixers are in charge of creating a professional sounding mix from the final sound edit sessions, applying whatever processes are required for the mix and for outputting that mix into the specific deliverables for the project. The dialogue editor will create the appropriate track assignments that are best for mixing.

Dialogue editors use the final sound edit from the NLE timeline of the picture editor to begin the dialogue edit. After they receive the sound edit from the picture editor, the dialogue editor will typically remove any filters or volume automation on any of the audio clips or tracks in order to hear the quality of the actual recordings. The dialogue editor understands that the work of the rerecording mixer is to process the audio tracks for a seamless illusion of sound. Dialogue editors listen closely to the audio quality of the clips and assign similar-sounding clips to the same track. They often work wearing headphones to hear the subtle detail of the location recordings.

In many ways, the dialogue editor is starting from scratch. He or she takes the original sound edit and moves, adds, or deletes audio, doing whatever it takes to make the tracks sound as clean and consistent as possible. Every step of the way during sound editing the dialogue editor is heading to the goal of the final mix. The picture editor's final sound edit will be deconstructed and reedited to route, design, effect, and properly output the soundtrack. Since all of the elements of the picture editor's sound will be changed, it is important to always have a reference of that first sound mix available.

This track is called the *guide track*, which is the basis for the decision making regarding the editing of the audio clips and the track assignments. The guide track is the final temporary mix that was created when the movie file was exported. Exported movie files from NLEs are, typically, a picture file married to a stereo track of all of the audio tracks mixed together. The dialogue editor will strip the audio from the exported movie file, sync it back to the movie file, and then add it to the sound edit timeline as its own track. Figure 8.1 shows an example of a guide track.

The picture editor is, of course, mixing the project's audio as he or she edits the picture. Although during the picture edit the emphasis is on the images, attention nonetheless is paid to the sound. It may be a perfunctory sound mix, perhaps just making sure that all of the dialogue is being heard. Nevertheless, many choices were made during

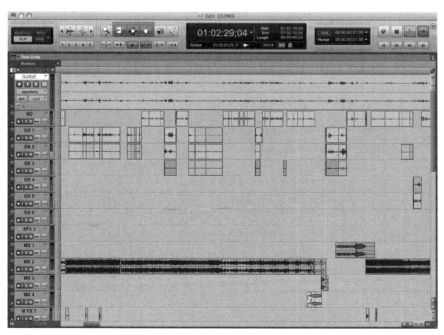

FIGURE 8.1 The guide track is at the top of the session file, muted but available for reference at any time

picture editing regarding the audio, and these will be expected to be a part of the new sound edit when reviewed by the picture editor and the director.

Since dialogue editors strip automation and volume from the audio clips as they prepare the new edit, the guide track will serve as the master guide as to the intent of the picture editor regarding the soundtrack. Some audio, until properly mixed, may seem misplaced or improperly edited into the audio timeline. It is then that the dialogue editor will check the guide track to understand the intent of the editor and will adjust the sound edit accordingly. To the dialogue editor, and to the rerecording mixer, the guide track is the main reference for the new sound edit and mix. See the accompanying sidebar: "Case Study: Interview with a Hollywood Dialogue Editor."

CASE STUDY: INTERVIEW WITH A HOLLYWOOD DIALOGUE EDITOR

Jacquelyn Johnson is a Hollywood dialogue editor who has edited the dialogue tracks of many feature films, documentaries, and television programs. Jackie is also a pianist who has played music all of her life and was trained classically at Northwestern University. Her skill and extraordinary jazz voicings led her to a ten-year stint as a pianist and bandleader. Figure 8.2 is a photo of Jackie hard at work.

Today Jackie splits her time between her dialogue editing career and playing music professionally. I discussed dialogue editing with Jackie, and here's a part of that conversation:

Woody: What are the essential tools for the dialogue editor?

Jackie: The most essential part of my toolkit is a disk full of room tones that I've created and assembled from prior films. Good monitor speakers and headphones are very important as well. A good working knowledge of post sound mixing and basic inserts to alter the tone of recordings also comes in handy.

Woody: What are good traits for a dialogue editor to have?

Jackie: A dialogue editor should be a perfectionist and should find enjoyment in problem solving, solitude, and detail. Most importantly they should be able to stay focused for long periods of time.

Woody: What is *backfilling*?

Jackie: Backfilling is creating or adding room tone to wherever audio has been removed so the result is seamless, as if the missing audio were never there. For instance, in the case of backfilling for ADR, you have to find a way to take away the words while leaving the room tone.

Woody: Can you describe your relationship with the rerecording mixer?

Jackie: The dialogue editor's job is all about making things easier for the rerecording mixer. The most common questions I ask the mixer or sound supervisor are either about layout and placement of audio on tracks, or about whether they think that recordings can be saved in the mixing process or whether they will need to be replaced.

Woody: What makes dialogue editing a great career choice?

Jackie: What's great about being a dialogue editor is that you're a part of a team, yet you're autonomous; and, you get the chance to create something clean and simple out of something that was previously unformed, like sculpting or chiseling.

FIGURE 8.2 Jackie Johnson editing dialogue for a feature film at Allied Post Audio

Room Tone and Crossfades

Filtering, effects, and volume automation are not parts of the dialogue editor's tool kit. The key to excellent dialogue editing is room tone and *crossfading*. Crossfading is the process of one audio clip fading in while simultaneously another audio clip is fading out. In the center of that interchange, the fades will cross. Crossfades and crossfading are essential for creating a seamless illusion of continuous sound. As filmmakers, we know that scenes were shot over a period of hours and days. However, a scene of events occurring between characters on-screen must trick the audience into believing the events are happening in real time. Figure 8.3 is an example of a crossfade on a dialogue edit session in a Pro Tools DAW.

Crossfading in this example is of two regions into one another. Sometimes it is preferable to have the audio to be crossfaded on separate tracks. You can create the same effect as a crossfade by having the same two regions on separate tracks and then fading one track out as the other track fades in. Figure 8.4 is an example of this type of crossfade.

So what is being crossfaded anyway? Location recordings and room tone are crossfaded for smooth transitions. Room tone, as has been discussed, is a key element in dialogue editing. Room tone allows for a seemingly continuous playback of the location recordings. Human

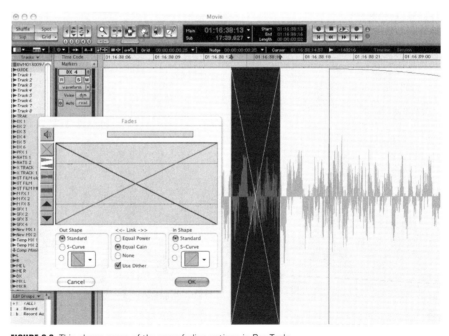

FIGURE 8.3 This shows some of the crossfading options in Pro Tools

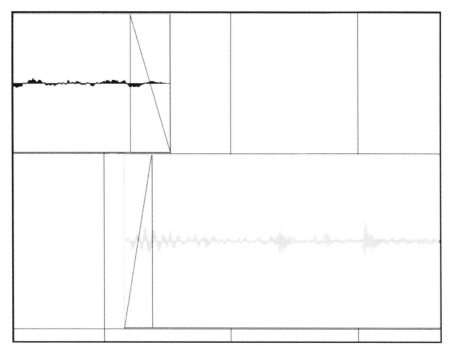

FIGURE 8.4 In this example the top track is fading out as the bottom track fades in

ears are quick to discern abrupt shifts and changes. Crossfades allow for more gradual transitions between audio clips. These crossfades of varying types and lengths make the room tone shifts much more difficult to hear.

Assigning and Editing Tracks by Character or Recorded Perspective

One of the first things done during dialogue editing is choosing track assignments for all of the speaking characters. On a scene-by-scene basis, the dialogue editor will listen to all of the location audio and begin to make track assignment choices. If it is a two-character scene, it might make sense to assign one track to one character and another track to the other character. If both of the sources sound similar, that approach might make sense. However, if there are different angles of the scene, and the microphone placement is also different, then separating tracks by the recorded perspective might be the way to go.

It is always a good idea for the dialogue editor and the rerecording mixer to be in constant discussions regarding the edit. The rerecording mixer understands the process that the tracks will need to be put through for a proper mix. It never hurts to check and see exactly how the mixer wants the tracks laid out before you get too deep into the editing. If you are the mixer as well, then your proper preparation of these tracks will assist you greatly when you are mixing.

Often, location recordings are not of the highest quality. Due to any number of reasons that have been discussed in earlier chapters, problems can arise during production. It could be that there is a hum in the recordings, but perhaps, only during the close-up shots of a particular scene. Or maybe there was a miking issue where the boom operator could not get close enough during the wide shots.

Figure 8.5 is a depiction of a dialogue edit, by microphone perspective. As you can see, it alternates from shot to shot. This choice was made because of the sonic character of the location recordings. By breaking up the clips to separate tracks the rerecording mixer was able to process the tracks individually for a better sounding mix.

If the quality and perspective of the recordings are similar to one another, then another approach can be used to create track assignments. You can also assign audio to tracks by character only. In this editing approach, any dialogue spoken by a main character is always on its own discrete track. Audio recorded on controlled sets usually works best when cutting dialogue for character. These recordings tend to sound more consistent, since studios are managed environments.

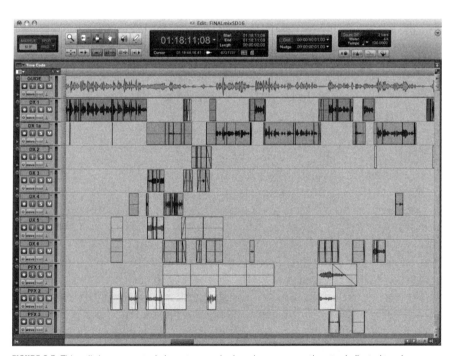

FIGURE 8.5 This edit has separated characters and microphone perspectives to dedicated tracks

Choosing Takes

Picture editors understand that they don't have the necessary tools to make definitive choices regarding the quality of the location recordings. What may seem to be a particularly bad piece of audio to the picture editor can, in the hands of a dialogue editor, be a simple fix. For that reason, picture editors include all of the audio from the location recordings.

For instance, there may be a sit-down interview with someone who was wearing a lavaliere microphone. One recording track may be the lavaliere, while the other track may be a seemingly unusable recording from the camera microphone. When the final edit is transferred over to a sound editor, both of those tracks will be in the timeline. The picture editor will not delete any audio that was recorded for any given shot.

Picture editors understand that although they think that the audio might be unusable, a good sound engineer may be able to find use for it. This section will discuss

- Creating an Edit for a Mix
- The Lavaliere Track and the Boom Track
- Alternate Takes and Wild Lines

Creating an Edit for a Mix

The dialogue editor is a key assistant to the rerecording mixer. Although they do not work side by side, the contributions of the dialogue editor directly affect the work of the rerecording mixer.

The dialogue editing process has several steps. It begins with listening and auditioning each clip of audio. Then the decisions are made to cut by character or by camera angle on a scene-by-scene basis. Then the quality of the audio is evaluated. If there are two sources and one sounds good and one sounds bad, the dialogue editor will cut in the good one and mute the bad one.

Dialogue editing takes away all of the unnecessary elements and reorders what is needed to make the session simpler for the rerecording mixer to create the mix. It is a slow process of peeling away all of the layers until only what is absolutely needed is left in the edit timeline. This preliminary work should be done in consultation with the rerecording mixer.

As the dialogue editor creates track assignments, they are auditioning each clip of audio in the timeline. Some clips will sound better than others. Some clips may be duplicates of each other. Some clips may be silent or just hum, static, or noise. The dialogue editor is entrusted with deciding what pieces of audio are valuable and what is excess or just plain bad.

Typically, the dialogue editor will not discard any audio from the timeline until there has been a consultation with the rerecording mixer. If the choice is made to keep the "bad" audio, for whatever reason, it may edited to new tracks, muted, and then hidden. This way, the audio is out of sight but still a part of the session if needed. This audio may eventually end up on other specific tracks that will be detailed in a later section of this chapter.

After the tracks have been arranged and the best audio is cut in place, room tone and crossfades are put into action. Typically, this sort of work is done wearing headphones for critical listening of room tone shifts and other sound issues. Room tones will be added to smoothly transition the sound from clip to clip and from track to track. Depending on the edit, the required choices will be made for the crossfade type and the crossfade length.

The creation of the production effects track (PFX) is a major task in dialogue editing. The PFX track, as previously discussed, is all of the action recorded on-set that is in-between the lines of spoken dialogue. PFX is any on-set, recorded sync action, such as the sounds of eating dinner, to running in the rain, to tapping a finger on a desk, and just about anything similar. Don't forget that the PFX track will need room tone and crossfades as well.

The Lavaliere Track and the Boom Track

The key to great sounding audio is consistency. Whether that consistency is real or manufactured doesn't matter, but the sound must flow smoothly from clip to clip. The reason that dialogue editors remove the automation and filtering is to create clean audio just by editing. If the audio sounds clean and consistent without mixing and filtering, then it can really shine when given to an excellent rerecording mixer. One of the deliverables will be a mix of only the dialogue track playing. A dialogue editor makes sure that dialogue track plays seamlessly without the effects and music tracks.

Often scenes are shot with both a lavaliere and a boom microphone. These tracks will sound different from one another. The boom track will have some "room" in it due to the nature of the recording procedure and equipment. The lavaliere track will be a closer sounding recording, maybe a bit more "dry" than the boom track.

A dry lavaliere track can be processed to better match the ambience of the boom track. That is because the sound can be processed to add "room" to the final sound. The reverse is not true. You cannot remove the "room" from recordings. This is one of the main reasons why location recordings should not originate from the camera microphone.

If the camera was shooting from across the room, there will be no way to "move the actor closer" to the microphone, after the fact.

As a general rule, rerecording mixers prefer the sound of the boom microphone. Every situation is different because, of course, every movie and every recording is different. There are no hard and fast rules for making these choices. These things can vary on a scene-by-scene basis. It always comes down to one thing: what sounds best.

The key is in understanding the quality of the audio and the mixing process. If you created, for instance, one track, called it "dialogue," and put all of the useable audio there, you would be creating quite a tough job for the mixer. It is your job as dialogue editor to find the very best audio and remove extraneous or useless pieces of audio from the timeline. You are expected to have the tracks arranged to better serve the mixing process. If you are the rerecording mixer as well as the dialogue editor, you will thank yourself for all of the good dialogue editing you've done!

Alternate Takes and Wild Lines

There is an enormous amount of detail involved in proper dialogue editing. The edit from the picture editor is only the starting place for the new sound edit. As noted earlier, some picture editors excel at audio editing. They will place proper room tone, they will search for alternate takes and check the location recordings for wild lines or on-set ADR.

Good dialogue editors take pride in their work. They will create a great-sounding edit on the strength of the location recordings alone. They will fuss and finesse each clip of audio until it sounds clear and crisp, whether it's PFX, or a mumbling performer's dialogue.

This level of commitment takes effort and time. During the process of auditioning each clip of dialogue, the dialogue editor is making choices regarding the audio quality as well as the performances. He or she doesn't have the authority—and in the case of sync audio, the ability—to drastically change a performance. But often a performance can be improved substantially with some simple adjustments.

Dialogue editors are the keenest audience a movie will ever have. They will hear and remove lip smacks, odd vocal noises or ticks, they will seek alternate takes for poor diction, and they will generally do everything in their power to enrich and enhance the dialogue of the movie. If a key word is mumbled or if the actor's action has obscured their mouth and dialogue during an important line, they will find an alternate take to replace it.

I have witnessed dialogue editors pouring over lined scripts, with boxes of tapes, and with sound logs askew, all in pursuit of the perfect edit. This sort of work is part of the dialogue editor's job description. A good dialogue editor can save whole scenes from ADR with careful trimming, alternate takes, and room tone.

I can offer an excellent, personal example of this. A feature film had an issue with the location recordings. The movie was shot on film, and the camera was making a noise because the film-reel magazine that held the film running through the camera was slightly bent. A rhythmical scraping noise could be heard throughout a very quiet and intense performance. An excellent dialogue editor was hired to solve the problem by creating a very precise editing of room tone that was inserted throughout the dialogue tracks each time the scraping was heard. And each bit of recorded dialogue that had the scraping noise on top of it was replaced by an alternate take that didn't have the scrape on the word. It took some time and very careful editing, but when the scene was complete there was no longer a bent film magazine destroying the lead actor's performance. No one was the wiser, except the few of us who were involved.

This editing saved the actor from redoing the scene in a dry ADR booth. It saved the director the whole experience of rerecording a scene he loved and all of the time involved in choosing takes. It saved the rerecording mixer all of the time required to properly process the ADR to match the location recordings. It saved the producer and the production a substantial amount of money for all of the services just outlined that were no longer necessary. And it gave a supreme sense of satisfaction to a dedicated audio professional, that dialogue editor who knew full well the importance of a job well done.

Take a note from this consummate dialogue editing professional and make the effort for a great dialogue track. If there are alternate readings, on-set ADR lines, or wild line recordings that can add clarity to a scene, find them and use them. This may sound like tedious hard work, and it can be, but professional moviemaking is not an easy task. Doing it well requires time, skill, and effort. Give your movie the care it deserves.

Special Track Assignments

In all of this audio file sorting and ordering there are certain tracks that have a particular purpose. As discussed earlier, the PFX track is an essential track to create a meaningful music and effects (M&E) output for delivery, saving time and money in Foley. But there are other tracks as well that are important to different types of movie projects. This section will explore

- The Production Effects Tracks
- The "X" Tracks

- The "Futz" Tracks
- The Narration Track

The Production Effects Tracks

The simple truth is that not all projects require a PFX track. Many television programs and documentaries don't require a PFX track. Editing this track can be painstaking work, involving the editing of many tiny elements like door slams, tapping feet, and even breathing onto a special track, for each scene throughout the entire movie. But it is an important track that will keep the identity and sonic character of the original soundtrack intact for international audiences.

When movies are repurposed for foreign sales, one of the key audio deliveries is an M&E track. For a movie to be properly dubbed into another language, the original language's dialogue track must be removed for the new language's dialogue track to be added. It is not as simple as just muting the final mixed dialogue track and adding new voices. Without a PFX track, muting production dialogue tracks will make whole sections of the movie silent.

Here is an example of the importance of PFX. Imagine a two-character scene in a kitchen. A couple is arguing as they clean up the kitchen. During the occasional dialogue outburst, the water is running, plates are clanking and silverware is banging together as the action ensues. Now mute those character's dialogue tracks. What happens? The dialogue is now silent but so too is all of the action in the kitchen. When a PFX track is properly edited, much, if not all of the audio of the action, will remain a part of the scene when the characters' dialogue track is muted.

A great PFX track can minimize the need for Foley. Perhaps whole scenes can be passed over by the Foley team because of the PFX. If PFX cannot be created, then Foley recording will cover all of the appropriate missing sounds. Foley is a wonderful, demanding, and creative craft. It is also time-consuming and, most important for the producer of the movie, expensive.

PFX being on its own track also helps during the final mixing to evaluate the location recording against the Foley. In some cases, it is decided that the Foley is a better recording or performance of a particular action. In such a case, that portion of the PFX track is muted and the Foley track is used in its place.

Dialogue editors are key members of the postproduction sound team. They are a producer's secret weapon for controlling audio postproduction costs. They can save money from a postproduction budget many times over. Their detailed work can eliminate the need for ADR with great alternate-take editing, and a great PFX track can reduce or eliminate Foley requirements. The dialogue editor is truly the unsung hero of the audio crew.

The "X" Tracks

The X *track* is an audio track where dialogue editors will place audio elements that may or may not be used in the final mix. It can contain extraneous bits of audio, location recordings of lines to be replaced by ADR, alternate edits of words or sections of dialogue, and anything where there is a question as to its final use.

It is a very useful track for a mixer to have available when changes are required during a mixing session. As final choices are being made, directors will want to audition ADR takes against the original production recordings. Being able to quickly mute and unmute these audio clips for evaluation is handy during a mix.

If there are some troublesome edits in the timeline, they may be represented on the X track as well. A dialogue editor may create a number of versions of an edit. This way the director, during sound mixing, can have a couple of choices for the problematic edit. The X track is a sort of catchall track for anything that may be useful through mixing. If you have a question about the usefulness or value of a piece of audio put it on the X track.

The "Futz" Tracks

A *futz track* is a track dedicated to audio that will be heavily filtered in some way. An example of futz tracks include filtering the dialogue to mimic telephone-quality sound. Another example would be futzing music so that it sounds like it's coming out of a car radio.

Many movies have scenes that can make use of futz tracks. There are countless scenes where characters talk on the phone and the audio quality shifts back and forth with each picture cut. Each time a character is "on the phone," place their dialogue on the telephone futz track. The rerecording mixer will be able to effect the futz track with whatever filter or effect works for that moment and that movie. Any audio that is placed on the futz track will be effected exactly the same way.

There are also separate futz tracks that can be created for music. Perhaps your movie has scenes inside and outside of a loud nightclub. Perhaps there are lots of people and the music is blasting. Maybe several scenes are intercut between the outside of the club and the inside of the club.

Futz tracks can be created for the music that was playing at the club. One futz track can be assigned for inside the club and another futz track can be assigned for outside the club. The loud music will sound very different outside of the club than it will inside. The futz tracks can make it easy on the mixer to effect each track properly to create the proper sound for the mix.

Futz tracks are versatile. They can be used for dialogue, music, or whatever is required depending on what the effect needs are for your project. Futz tracks are a simple way, through editing, to make complicated mixing processes simpler.

The Narration Track

The narration track is typically a voice-over track. Narration tracks are very common in motion pictures and television programming. Narration tracks will be the subject of the following chapter, "Voice-Over Recording."

Voice-overs are a key dialogue track; therefore they fall under the responsibility of the dialogue editor. The voice-over must be treated with the same care and editing as any other dialogue track. It must be scrubbed clean of odd noises, and mumbled or swallowed words should be replaced with alternate takes when available.

Tell the Story

The dialogue edit is the final chance at choosing the best recordings of the best performances of the dialogue and the action from the shoot. In the search for alternate takes from the original takes of the location recordings or just in the process of editing the location tracks the dialogue editor may discover interesting sound bits to help tell the story. The following section will discuss:

- Choosing the Best Performances
- Clarify the Storytelling

Choosing the Best Performances

Acting is a difficult craft, and sometimes editing the recordings of some performances can be a challenge. Whether it is removing odd lip smacks or breathing, choices will be made one way or another editing an actor's performance. All of these choices will impact the final performance of the actor.

Actors can sometimes mumble, have diction issues, or swallow words so that they are inaudible. Another task of the dialogue editor is to clean up these takes so that all of the dialogue is clear and audible. The dialogue track is a key track, so it is imperative that all of the dialogue is clearly understood.

In the world of DIY and digital filmmaking, often those involved cover the duties of several departments simultaneously. It is typically not the role of the dialogue editor to make artistic choices regarding the movie that they edit. This is one of the reasons that the guide track is so important to them.

On the other hand, your own participation in your movie may be a bit more complicated than that. Perhaps you are the picture editor and the sound editor. Or maybe you wrote it or directed it. If this is the case, then you probably have more influence than someone hired to be the dialogue editor as part of a post audio crew. Whatever your particular situation is, the dialogue editing period is the time when many final decisions are made regarding the soundtrack.

As you edit the dialogue track of your project, keep listening for any anomalies that can be fixed. Some things might be a simple fix with room tone. You may need to search the original recordings for alternate takes to find a fix for some things. Fortunately, swallowed words or mumbled lines can usually be replaced with the other takes. If the entire performance was mumbled, then it is up to the director to decide whether the performance will need to be rerecorded.

Clarify the Storytelling

The dialogue editor is the expert of the location recordings. He or she knows what's on the timeline and what is missing. Having searched the location recordings, digitized wild lines, on-set ADR, and on-set Foley, the dialogue editor knows what's there and also how to find it.

The dialogue editor is the point person for determining the final quality of the location recordings. This person is also intimately involved with the story and the storytelling. In the process of editing, he or she may find alternate takes that may help a performance or better tell the story.

The dialogue editor will also have the additional audio files folder that has the crowd recordings, the on-set ADR, and additional audio recordings. These materials were recorded to better tell the story that the filmmaker is creating. The dialogue editor should spend time with the dialogue elements in the additional audio folder and *sweeten* the edit with it. *Sweeten* is an audio term that describes adding audio elements to an edit to enhance the soundtrack. Adding additional audio elements to the edit to better tell the story is sweetening.

The dialogue editor has a key role in helping the filmmaker tell the story. There could be all sorts of wonderful sounds that were recorded on-set to be added to the edit. The sound effects editor can handle special sound design elements, but the dialogue editor should deal exclusively with all dialogue elements.

Being a great dialogue editor helps your filmmaking collaborators tell the story better. And all of the hard work in assigning tracks and auditioning each clip of audio to determine only the highest quality also helps the rerecording mixer create a great-sounding project. The importance of the dialogue editor and a great dialogue edit cannot be overstated.

Summary

The dialogue track is the one track that will play almost continuously through a film or a program. The dialogue editing process involves listening to the takes and choosing the best recordings and performances. All of those takes are then assigned tracks in consultation with the rerecording mixer. As the new sound edit is assembled, the guide track, created by the picture editor, is used as the main point of reference of the original sound edit and mix, created by the picture editor and the filmmaker.

Dialogue editors choose to edit the dialogue to tracks according to perspective or by character. The dialogue edit is when all of the audio clips are sorted to dialogue tracks, PFX tracks, futz tracks, and X tracks. Performances will be cleaned up and alternate takes will be found. Room tone and crossfades are the main tools of a dialogue editor. Room tone is used as fill for the ADR takes and to smoothly blend the dialogue, PFX, and other tracks. The dialogue edit is a complex and exacting skill, making the dialogue editor a key member of the sound-editing team.

Review Questions

Questions like these are likely to appear on exams to test how well you understood and retained the information in this chapter.

1. What are the role and responsibilities of the dialogue editor?
2. What are inserts and what might be an example of how they are used?
3. What is a guide track and why does a dialogue editor use it?
4. Give an example of why a dialogue editor would assign audio clips and tracks by scene angle instead of by character.
5. What is a PFX track and why is it used?

Discussion/Essay Questions

Your instructor may assign you one or more of the following questions for discussion in class or as the subject of a paper.

1. Discuss the differences between lavaliere tracks and boom recordings. Discuss how these differences will influence the dialogue edit and affect the final sound mixing.

2. Discuss the process of creating a dialogue edit from the picture editor's original sound edit. Discuss the various options and tracks in dialogue editing.

Applying What You've Learned

Research/Lab/Fieldwork Projects

NOTE
Students who have ongoing projects may elect to use their own source material, such as video clips, with the instructor's permission.

The following lab exercises will give you practice working with dialogue editing in Final Cut Express.

1. Find moments in the dialogue tracks where no one is speaking. Create a new track and place those "nondialogue" recordings to this new track. This new track will be your PFX or "production effects track."

2. Create an X track and place location audio that is being replaced and other bits of production audio there. Be sure to mute the recordings or mute the track.

Resources

The following resources have more information on the topics covered in this chapter.

Apple Computer (http://www.apple.com/support/finalcutpro). This site is filled with many wonderful articles and tutorials. Go to the Final Cut Pro 7 user manual and locate chapter 6. Inside this chapter you will find "Tips for Dialogue Editing," a good primer on using Final Cut Express or Final Cut Pro for dialogue editing.

Motion Picture Editors Guild (https://www.editorsguild.com). If you look under the "Magazine" link on this site, you'll find many great articles. Do a search on dialogue editing and you will find several excellent sources of additional information.

CHAPTER 9

VOICE-OVER RECORDING

OVERVIEW AND LEARNING OBJECTIVES

In this chapter, you will:
- Learn about voice-over recording
- Learn about timed voice-over recordings
- Learn how to get the performance
- Learn to edit the narration track

Considerations about Voice-Over Recording

Voice-over (VO) is spoken narration that moves the story, concepts, or ideas of the show forward. Many types of movie projects are driven by narration. There are serious motion pictures that feature VO, such as Martin Sheen's incredible performance in Francis Ford Coppola's *Apocalypse Now*. There are also many first-person documentary films, such as *Roger and Me* by filmmaker Michael Moore, that make use of voice-over narration. VO tracks are used in many different types of projects.

Television programs typically use a great deal of voice-over in a variety of ways. Sometimes it's with dedicated announcers, as in talk shows or game shows; sometimes it's with characters in reality TV shows; and sometimes it's the lead character of a sitcom that is telling the story of the program. Each of these types of programs has its own considerations with regard to the recording and use of voice-over narration. The ideas we will explore in this section are

- The Recording Space
- Microphone Choices and Setting Levels
- Marking the Script
- Wild Lines

The Recording Space

The truth is that there is no one place that will serve as the perfect VO recording space for every project out there. The key to a proper VO recording track is in understanding its use. Understanding the requirements of the final voice-over narration to the project is important in every aspect of the VO. From the text to the VO actor and his or her interpretation to the space the recording is made in, all of these decisions are relevant to the needs of the project itself.

For example, let's suppose that you are shooting a documentary film and have mostly been recording the VO on location. During the editing, it is determined that VO *pickups* will be required. A pickup in filmmaking terms is recording or filming additional material for the production. Pickups are often required for both the picture and the sound as the edit progresses.

In this documentary example, you would re-create the original recording scenario as best as possible if these recordings are going to be intercut with the original location recordings. Here the VO recording is more like dialogue replacement, since it should match the sonics of the original recording.

Room tone will be quite useful for VO editing. Depending on how different the pickup recordings are from the original VO, the room tone can add just enough ambience to create a seamless illusion from edit to edit. The room tone is edited underneath the pickup VO in the sound-editing timeline. Figure 9.1 shows a short sequence of VO and pickups edited in a timeline.

Sometimes, due to budget restrictions, VO is recorded in an editing bay, in an office, a closet, or maybe in a vacant room. This is not an ideal situation. There could be noise generating sources within the room itself as well as sound intrusions from the exterior. The recording area will also need to remain quiet for the length of the VO recording.

If there is no other way to record the VO than in a casual location, there are a few things to keep in mind. Do not record in a room with a computer running. The sound of the fan in the computer will reverberate in the small room and will be difficult to remove later in postproduction. Also, the sound quality of the room itself may prove

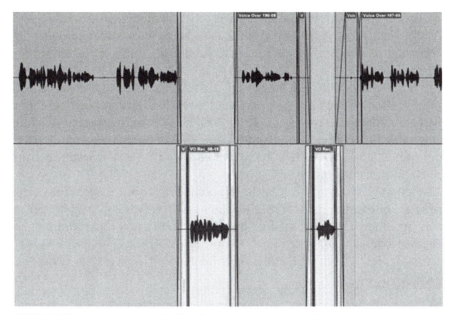

FIGURE 9.1 This is a close-up view of a VO edit from two separate recording sessions

problematic. Small rooms that are not treated for sound must be approached the same way that they would be during production. Be sure to use sound blankets and check for and find the best recording spot in any less-than-ideal place.

Unfortunately this type of recording situation, when not done at a recording studio, is often simply a microphone plugged into a computer in an editing bay. If the VO track is a major narrative to your project, the VO recording demands more attention than that setup.

Many feature films and television programs record their VO in a recording booth at a recording studio. The high-quality recordings that are made there are ideal for many VO needs. The vast majority of professional VO recordings take place in these types of settings.

Recording studios have booths that are built to be isolated from exterior sound intrusions as well as constructed in a way to minimize reverberations. They also will typically provide a high-quality condenser microphone and other professional gear to record the audio with. For VO-driven material where the VO was not recorded on location, this is the way VO should most appropriately be done.

Microphone Choices and Setting Levels

The microphone choice is dependent on the material that is being recorded and how it will be edited together with the existing recordings. There are projects that require new VO to match the VO recorded on location, and there are other projects whose entire VO track is replaced. If the entire track is to be replaced, then it is usually recorded in a way that matches the pace and timing of a temporary VO track.

If the new VO will be edited in with the old VO, then it will match best if similar gear is used for the new recordings. For instance, if much of the existing VO was done on location using the talent's lavaliere microphone, it may be best to match that equipment. Record a few tests to hear what sounds best for your particular situation.

When recording voices in a recording booth, generally the microphones and recording equipment are very professional. Since they produce high-quality, full-spectrum recordings, the audio can be easily processed to better match the other recordings.

Marking the Script

VO recording requires appropriate documentation for archival purposes as well as hand-off to the editing team. Figure 9.2 gives an example of a *marked script* for a VO session.

A marked script is a copy of the script being recorded that is marked with all of the appropriate take numbers next to each scripted line. There can be many recorded takes and re-auditioning, and each one can be a time-consuming task. The remedy is a system called *circle takes*. Circle takes are take numbers of recordings that have been circled to indicate that they are the preferred take for that line or recording.

This is a simple and excellent way of marking the preferred takes. VO scripts for features and television programs can be many pages long. The take list for a given VO script can go into the many hundreds. Circle takes make it easy to determine which takes are the preferred takes.

Imagine recording a thirty-page script, with each line getting three takes or more. The take count can get very high quickly. If you had to relisten to all of that material, it would take quite a bit of time. When a producer hears a take that they like during the VO recording session, they tell the engineer to "circle it" on the script. This helps cut through the maze of takes to spotlight the good ones.

Circle takes eliminate the need for someone to have to listen to all of the takes again. The editor can simply import all of the circle takes and begin the edit with those recordings. If there are odd noises, breaths, mouth clicks, or other anomalies, then they can be altered or fixed with an alternate take of the same line.

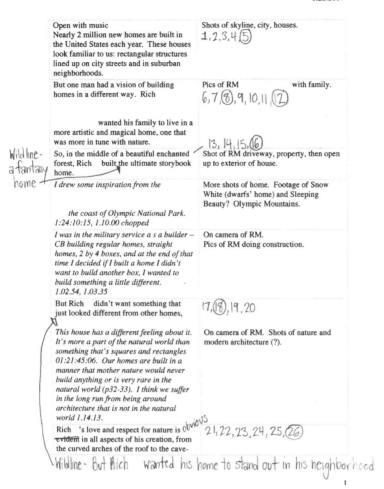

1.22.2007

Open with music Nearly 2 million new homes are built in the United States each year. These houses look familiar to us: rectangular structures lined up on city streets and in suburban neighborhoods.	Shots of skyline, city, houses. 1, 2, 3, 4 (5)
But one man had a vision of building homes in a different way. Rich	Pics of RM with family. 6, 7, (8), 9, 10, 11, (12)
wanted his family to live in a more artistic and magical home, one that was more in tune with nature.	13, 14, 15, (16)
Wild line – a fantasy home → So, in the middle of a beautiful enchanted forest, Rich built the ultimate storybook home.	Shot of RM driveway, property, then open up to exterior of house.
I drew some inspiration from the	More shots of home. Footage of Snow White (dwarfs' home) and Sleeping Beauty? Olympic Mountains.
the coast of Olympic National Park. *1:24:10:15, 1.10.00 chopped*	
I was in the military service a s a builder – CB building regular homes, straight homes, 2 by 4 boxes, and at the end of that time I decided if I built a home I didn't want to build another box, I wanted to build something a little different. *1.02.54, 1.03.35*	On camera of RM. Pics of RM doing construction.
But Rich didn't want something that just looked different from other homes,	17, (18), 19, 20
This house has a different feeling about it. It's more a part of the natural world than something that's squares and rectangles 01:21:45:06. Our homes are built in a manner that mother nature would never build anything or is very rare in the natural world (p32-33). I think we suffer in the long run from being around architecture that is not in the natural world 1.14.13.	On camera of RM. Shots of nature and modern architecture (?).
Rich 's love and respect for nature is *obvious* evident in all aspects of his creation, from the curved arches of the roof to the cave-	21, 22, 23, 24, 25, (26)

Wildline – But Rich wanted his home to stand out in his neighborhood

1

FIGURE 9.2 This is a marked script with changed lines and wild lines added

Many audio recording computer programs, such as DAWs, will name the recording with a number suffix. For instance, in Pro Tools if a track was named "VO Take," then the first take would be called "VO Take_1." Each subsequent take would be followed numerically. This makes keeping track of take names easy, and if the preferred takes are circled, then the marked script becomes a very useful document.

Be sure to mark any changes to the text accordingly. Many times during a VO recording session the talent or the producer may decide to change some wording or add lines. It is important that the new text is notated on the marked script and that the appropriate take numbers identify them.

Wild Lines

VO recording sessions are sometimes simple, straightforward sessions. Other times, however, substantial script changes are taking place and new lines are written on the fly. It is a good idea to keep a blank sheet of paper handy for new material that may not be on the script. These new wild lines should be clearly written out with their appropriate take numbers next to them.

The marked script is going to be the blueprint for the editor to determine which takes to use. It will be a text of the recording session as well as a document of which takes correspond to which lines in the script. The writing should be clear and legible. The numbers should accurately correspond to the text that they are written next to. Subtle text changes need to be reflected on the marked script so that the editor is choosing the correct material.

Often during VO sessions, it is decided that additional wild material should be recorded. These are, of course, program specific. If it is a television program, for instance, perhaps it is decided that different variations of "we'll be right back," "see you after the break," or "stay tuned, we'll be back for more after these messages" are needed. It is important to write these new lines down accurately and to mark them for take numbers as well as circle the preferred takes. Wild lines are a standard occurrence during a VO session.

> ### TIP
>
> Use a pencil when marking the script. It is always a good idea to be able to erase and change things. VO sessions can go fast and furious, and people do change their minds. Write clearly and legibly and make sure the pencil is sharp. A good approach is to draw lines from the text to your take numbers. Always try to mark the script in a clear, simple, and readable format. You will probably be able to rewrite some things after the session is over on the script. Since the sessions can move fast, take good notes so you can address them after the recordings have stopped.

Timed Narration Recordings

Many times the VO track is written, recorded, and edited prior to the final mixing of a feature or television program. This is often referred to as the temporary VO track. The temporary VO track allows the editor to precisely edit the picture with the narration.

These types of tracks are usually poorly recorded in less-than-ideal circumstances. Often picture editors voice the temporary VO tracks themselves. When the picture edit is complete and moves into the

■■■ AUDIO PRODUCTION AND POSTPRODUCTION

postproduction audio phase, the VO track is rerecorded in a recording studio with the VO talent. The new VO recording will be edited into the timeline replacing the temporary VO. This section will examine

- The Timed Script
- Making Things Fit
- Changing Text When Needed

The Timed Script

A *timed script* is a script that has each line of VO script notated with a timing of its duration in the temporary edit. Figure 9.3 is an example of a timed script. Each line of new VO must fit exactly into the editing timeline, so the timings need to be extremely accurate. For example, they might be listed as "5 seconds and 10 frames" or "2 seconds and 5 frames" so that the exact frame is indicated.

The timed VO script text should match the previous VO text exactly, with the timings placed next to each line to be rerecorded. Typically, the duty of creating the timed script falls to the producer's team. The producer or director will oversee the VO recording session as well.

During the recording session the VO recordist will keep the timings of each recording. Those timings should match the script timings with a buffer of several frames. Most NLEs and DAWs have the ability to accurately time the clips in the timeline. If you are the writer, picture editor, director, or producer, you'll be able to judge the recordings. If you are not, then the program's producer or director will direct the VO recording session. They will have a complete understanding of the timings of the edited material that these recordings are destined for.

It is often all right for the VO recordings to be longer than the timing indicated on the script. For example, imagine that you are recording the VO for a program about mountain climbing. The show has an extended sequence of footage of Mount Everest. Music plays throughout the edited scene, and there are occasional lines of VO explaining the landscape being shown.

Since there is a lot of time and not much narration, the timings of the recordings at this point in the program are not as critical. Each rerecorded take from the VO actor can be longer than the temporary VO track. The producer will have a good understanding of the material and can determine whether the longer VO will work for the program.

Not all material will require a timed script, of course. Sometimes filmmakers may write the script and then record the VO track first. They then use those VO recordings to edit with during the picture editing. Sometimes the VO requirements for a program are small and the VO track does not require such tight edit timings, so the VO track is recorded wild.

VIDEO	AUDIO	VO Timing
	SOT 24.12.15 // THANKS FOR TUNING IN TO *ENTERTAINMENT L.A.* I'M YOUR GIRL JESSIE. WE'VE GOT A GREAT SHOW FOR YOU TONIGHT. THERE'S A LOT GOING ON IN THE CITY //	
09.22.47 -B-ROLL 09:23.19 09.23.54	**SINGER, SONGWRITER LENNY SMITH IS WORKING ON A NEW ALBUM SCHEDULED TO COME OUT THIS FALL. HE TALKED TO US ABOUT HOW THE CITY OF L.A. HAS INPIRED HIM**	12:27
	SOT 8.24.08 // I'VE BEEN SPENDING A LOT OF TIME HERE IN L.A. THIS IS WHERE I GREW UP AND LIVED FOR THE FIRST HALF OF MY LIFE. THE MEMORIES OF ALL THE GOOD TIMES ARE SPARKING UP SOME SONGS. I'M EXCITED //	
12.00.53 -B-ROLL	**WE ALSO HUNG OUT WITH JACKIE JONES WHO JUST SIGNED ON TO STAR IN A SCI-FI THRILLER WITH THE LOVELY LUNA LEON.**	7:22
	SOT 03.44.15 // I'M REALLY EXCITED ABOUT THE PROJECT. LUNA AND I HAVE ALWAYS BEEN GOOD FRIENDS BUT WE HAVE NEVER WORKED TOGETHER. I'M SURE WE'LL HAVE FUN AND GET TO KNOW EACH OTHER BETTER, EITHER THAT OR WE'LL END UP HATING EACH OTHER (LAUGHS) //	
05.46.14 -B-ROLL	**THEN WE'LL GO BEHIND THE SCENES OF *GLORIA* THE HOTTEST SHOW ON BROADWAY**	4:18
	SOT 07.33.41 // WE'VE HAD A GREAT YEAR AND A LOT OF FUN //	
11.25.13	**AND FINALLY, WE'LL MEET UP WITH MARK WHO WILL REVEAL THE NOMINIES FOR THIS YEAR'S L.A. AWARDS**	6:04

FIGURE 9.3 In this example of a timed script the VO timing is in seconds and frames

Making Things Fit

In ADR recording, the performers will watch their performance on a screen or a monitor to sync their performance to the original recording. Typically, when recording VO, there is no video playback during the recordings. The timings reflected on the script are used as the reference for the edit.

■■■ AUDIO PRODUCTION AND POSTPRODUCTION

There are times when the temporary VO track is performed at a pace different from the new track. For example, a picture editor hurriedly records a temporary VO to complete the edit of the movie he is editing. Knowing that his performance is going to be replaced, he does not offer a performance of the script but simply reads it without emotion and too fast. When it comes time to create the actual VO, it is determined that the text cannot be read properly in the same amount of time. The edit moves too fast for an emotional reading of the script.

This is an excellent example of why a picture edit that is based on a temporary VO track needs that track to be performed in a manner similar to what the final VO will be. With a good temporary track, the picture editing team will be able to take into consideration the pacing, the length, and the emotional quality of the narrative as told through the VO track.

Changing Text When Needed

Many things can be discovered during a timed narration recording session. A problem could occur that is the opposite of the previous example with the VO pacing of the show. The new VO talent might read the script twice as fast as the timings indicated on the script. Some people don't take direction well, and some people don't know how to take direction. For example, the subject of a documentary or a reality television program may have never recorded a voice-over track before and may find the process difficult. Then there are times when the temporary track is just fine and the new VO performance is just fine, and yet the timings don't match. It could be a subtle thing where it is off by a second or two every couple of lines.

If your involvement does not extend to choices regarding the show's content, then these situations call for the director or producer to make a decision. Perhaps it's just the dropping of a word here or there. Sometimes whole sections need to be reworked. Be sure to write all of the new lines down, mark their take number, and circle any of the preferred takes.

Getting the Performance

There is nothing insignificant about the VO track. It might be the main dialogue track of the work. It can't just be somebody reading lines off of a page; it needs to have emotion and conviction. Not all VO performers are trained professionals. Documentaries and television programs may have the people who are the subjects of their shows provide the narration. This section will explore

- The Voice-Over Recording Session
- Working with the Voice-Over Talent
- Technical Considerations: Clicks, Pops, Breaths, and Pronunciations

The Voice-Over Recording Session

The VO recording session can happen in any number of ways. It is dependent on the needs of the particular program. If it is a branding element, various different readings may be required. For instance, if a line is something like "Leave the driving to us," it could be interpreted and spoken in a number of different ways. A producer might ask for it to be read three times, each with a different inflection.

Each session will have different demands. It is important to get the flow of the session right. There are a number of things that have to happen, and everyone must get in the swing of it. The recordist has to record-enable a recording track, hit record, and then cue the talent. The talent has to wait for their cue and then read the appropriate lines. The recordist must wait to be sure that the take is complete. Once complete, the recordist stops and marks the script. The recordist then times the take and compares it with the timing of the script. Then the producer or director offers notes or insights and the line is retaken or they move on to the next line of VO.

There are usually many takes, due to any number of factors. Perhaps the VO talent flubbed a line or took an odd breath or had the rhythm of the line wrong. Perhaps the reading is not to the director's liking and there are a number of retakes required until a satisfactory one is achieved. It is common practice, even when takes have been circled, to record a *safety take* just in case of any problems during the edit. A safety take is an additional take of the line that ensures that the line was recorded properly. Never only record one take, circle it, and move on. You may never have access to that particular VO talent again!

Sometimes directors like to record VO one line at a time. Sometimes directors like to do whole sections at a time. Once the style for the recording is established it is up to the recordist to see to it that things move along. Everyone might have a different way of working, so it is important to get everyone on the same page. It may take a few minutes to get the session running smoothly.

The key point for the recordist is to be sure to get all the takes. Sometimes the talent doesn't wait for a cue and starts before you are recording or starts another take just as you hit the stop button. Try to get a flow going where everyone is communicating well with one another. The recordist has to get the takes no matter what the situation is in the recording room.

Working with the Voice-Over Talent

The performance is very important for the final VO track. It will set the tone of the show and may possibly be the main narrative element. It is important that the VO performance matches the tone of the written text as well as the tone of the show.

In many instances, the talent performing the VO may not be used to the entire recording experience or may never have been in a recording booth before. People outside the industry may not have heard their voice recorded in such a fashion or in headphones. They might be shy, inhibited, or unable to take direction well.

The director must take the time that is needed to get the performance right. If it is your own project, then *you* must get the performance right. If the VO is dull and flat it will bring down the quality of the whole show. If it sounds like someone is just reading words off of the page, it won't have any emotional impact.

There are some things that can help when faced with an inexperienced speaker for the VO track. You should get the person comfortable immediately with speaking into the microphone and with wearing headphones. If picture is being referenced, then he or she will be looking at a screen as well. Get the speaker used to watching the picture and speaking the text simultaneously. Prepare him or her for whatever the session requires.

Have water on hand to sip during the session. There should be good lighting and something to put the script on, such as a music stand. Have extra pencils handy and a highlighter as well. Sometimes, if the talent is making a lot of clicks and mouth noises, a bite of an apple can help reduce those problems.

Technical Considerations: Clicks, Pops, Breaths, and Pronunciations

The recording of the VO track is just as important as the performance of the VO track. It should be well recorded and have low noise with a properly gained signal and no clipping. Care should be taken with the performer's movements, clothing rustle, slapping, tapping, or clapping during the recordings. The recording should only contain the voice.

Recording VO and performing VO are skilled tasks and can take a bit of practice to get comfortable with. Sometimes due to the script there are a lot of words with many *plosives* in them. Plosives are vocal sounds that are made with the consonants of words. Plosives are a burst of air aimed straight at the microphone. The plosives that affect voice recording in particular, are words that start with the letter *b*, *t*, and most particularly *p*. Plosives will clip the recording, and they are to be monitored at all times.

The recordist must be sure to position the mic in a way that provides an excellent recording but also minimizes the plosives. If it is a continuing problem, then moving the mic to a position that minimizes plosives may be the solution. A performer can learn to soften their plosives to get better recordings. Sometimes a slight tilt of the head during the recording can move the mouth away from creating plosives on the microphone.

Editing the New Narration Track

Now that the narration recording is complete it must be edited into the sound edit timeline. There are a number of considerations when editing in the new VO to the timeline. This section will discuss

- Replacing the Temporary Voice-Over
- Keeping in Time
- Cleaning Up the Recording

Replacing the Temporary Voice-Over

You will use the temporary VO as a guide track to create the new edit. If you did not do the recordings yourself, then get the marked script and the recordings from the session and import them into your editing program. If there is a way to see your recordings in the *waveform view* in your editing program, it should be set that way. Waveform view is one of a number of ways that NLEs and DAWs offer to view the audio recordings in a timeline. Figure 9.4 is a picture of a VO track in waveform view in Final Cut Express.

Once the guide track is in place and the recordings have been imported, then each circle take will be edited into the timeline on a

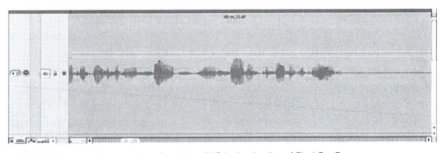

FIGURE 9.4 Here is a close-up view of one line of VO in the timeline of Final Cut Express

separate track. If you are editing in takes from a timed script, you'll find that the waveforms look very similar. Since they were timed to fit the space, there was not a lot of leeway in terms of how the words were spoken. It can be a relatively simple reedit, simply following the waveforms in the timeline. Figure 9.5 is an example of a Pro Tools session with a temporary VO track and a replacement VO track.

Keeping in Time

There are times when the timed script does not match the new recordings. They may be just a bit too long or just a bit too short. In many instances, a different reader will time the phrasing of words slightly differently than the temporary VO. One solution is to try and cut some words while keeping the intent of the script. This sort of work will need to be approved by the producer or director.

There are also special, advanced tools that are available in DAWs that can assist in this problem. Many DAWs and NLEs have a tool called *time compression expansion* (TC/E) that does exactly as its name implies. It will shorten or expand time on any particular audio clip. It will do this without changing the pitch of the audio, only changing its speed.

That is not to say that this process does not affect the audio quality. If you try to compress or expand with these tools for more

FIGURE 9.5 In this example the new VO's timing is slightly different from the temporary VO

than a 10 percent difference, you can hear it affect the quality of the recording. It can have *artifacts*. Artifacts are any effects that degrade the original signal. The artifact in this case is a tinny-sounding version of the original audio file. These tools can work wonders, but they need to be used sparingly and only when the editing is not providing the solution that is needed.

Cleaning Up the Recording

Once the track has been edited into place it needs to be evaluated just like any dialogue track. The performance should be strong and clear. If there are words that are mumbled or garbled, they should be replaced if possible by alternate takes. VO recording can be a strenuous affair for the performer. If there is a lot of text, the voice can get weak or change character, or the performer may have a tendency to rush or mumble text after extended periods of time.

Identify any lines that might need to be fixed or changed. Go back to the marked script and see if there are other takes that may offer a solution to a problem. Perhaps there is a swallowed word during the circle take read, perhaps that word can be replaced by one of the other takes.

Particular care must be given to recordings in the edit that have popped plosives. These can be problematic for a mixer. If they are particularly egregious, then seek out the alternate takes to see if there is a better take with no plosive. You may need to refer back to the marked script and look at the non-circle takes to see if you can edit in a solution from another take of the recording. The VO track must be edited with the same scrutiny and care that is given to any dialogue element.

Summary

Voice-over tracks are a major part of a wide cross-section of motion pictures and television programs. If the original VO track was recorded on location, it is important that the new narration is recorded in a similar fashion to properly edit into existing material. If there is a temporary VO track that is being replaced, then a timed script recording session will be required to fit the new VO into the existing edit timeline.

You need to be diligent with the naming and numbering of takes. The numbering should be a simple system that can be easily notated on the script. Takes that are considered the best are circled to reduce the time spent in editing with all of the newly recorded takes. Wild lines should be properly copied and marked with take numbers and circle takes. Any changes to the text of the script should be indicated on the marked script as well.

Care must be taken during the recording of the new VO track. It should be well recorded as well as performed in a manner that tells the story in a style appropriate to the material. The final edit of the track should be free of pops and clicks and any sort of vocal anomalies that can arise from a voice recording session. Make the effort to get this track right. It just may be the one single driving narrative of your entire project.

Review Questions

Questions like these are likely to appear on exams to test how well you understood and retained the information in this chapter.

1. How do you mark a script during a VO recording session?
2. What is a circle take and why is it useful?
3. What are plosives? What steps can be taken to minimize their effect?
4. What is a timed script and why would you need one?
5. Why wouldn't you record the VO in an editing bay or a closet?

Discussion/Essay Questions

Your instructor may assign you one or more of the following questions for discussion in class or as the subject of a paper.

1. Assume that a documentary has been filmed in various rainforests across the world and the lead filmmaker recorded the VO on location. After the program was complete, a new script was written and new VO needed to be recorded to add to the existing edit. Describe how this recording should be done and what tools will assist in the recording and in the editing.
2. Describe the process of how you edit the newly recorded takes into the timeline of the existing edit of a program.

Applying What You've Learned

Research/Lab/Fieldwork Projects

The following lab exercises will give you practice working narration scripts, recording voice-over, and editing voice-over.

1. Time out each section of the temporary narration track. Put those timings on the narration script.

NOTE
Students who have ongoing projects may elect to use their own source material, such as video clips, with the instructor's permission.

2. Record several passes of each narration "bite" to the timings indicated on the script.

3. Replace the old narration with the newly recorded narration.

Resources

The following resources have more information on the topics covered in this chapter

Ben Baxter, "Voice-Over/Podcast Recording Studio Equipment Reviews & Tips," BenBax.com (http://www.benbax.com/voice-over-studio. shtml). This site has some excellent articles, and in particular this article is a great round-up of many different types of microphones and their uses in VO recording.

Perry Anne Norton, "Recording the Spoken Word," *Electronic Musician* (http://emusician.com/tutorials/emusic_recording_spoken_word). This article published in the magazine *Electronic Musician* is an excellent resource to expand on the ideas from this chapter.

CHAPTER 10

RECORDING AND EDITING DIALOGUE REPLACEMENT

OVERVIEW AND LEARNING OBJECTIVES

In this chapter, you will:
- Learn how to prepare for dialogue replacement
- Learn how to keep track of your takes
- Get tips for believable dialogue replacement
- Understand the tools of the trade

Preparing for Dialogue Replacement

Automated dialogue replacement (ADR) is a unique skill for all of the personnel involved. The actors must be able to re-create their performances, in sync with edited picture. The recordist must try to capture the sonics of the location recordings to incorporate into the ADR recordings for the final mixing. The filmmakers must learn to love the new ADR recordings and performances as much as the original ones. They must also be sure to budget the time and resources to do ADR sessions. ADR is a skill for all of the parties involved. This section will discuss

- Understanding the Dynamics of Dialogue Replacement
- Beep Tracks

- Placing Beeps and Cues
- Organizing for Recording Efficiency

Understanding the Dynamics of Dialogue Replacement

ADR has been discussed at length already throughout this text. It can save an actor's performance, and in some cases it can save a movie, but it won't save any time and certainly won't save any money. There are a number of factors to consider about the ADR process. I will detail some of them.

Once the lines for ADR have been determined from the final picture edit, then the ADR preparation will begin. Recording sessions will be created in whatever program you will be recording in. The lines will be cued for the engineer to easily get from line to line in the recording session. Scripts will be created for each actor's ADR session. The recording space and equipment will be configured to best match the location recordings.

The recording session will create recordings of each line in however many takes are necessary to fulfill the demands of the scene. The director will review the recordings to choose the best performances. The final takes will be cut to sync to match the mouth movements of the actors. Room tone will be edited in under each line of ADR. The ADR will be processed and mixed to sound the same as the location recordings.

A critical aspect in the ADR recording process is that these recordings must sound similar to the location recordings. Often, ADR takes are edited together with takes from the on-set recordings. If the recordings don't sound similar, the different-sounding recordings alternating back and forth will make the scene unwatchable. Or at least the difference in the character of the recordings will jar the audience out of their enjoyment of the movie. Audiences can spot ADR a mile away. They may have never heard of ADR, but they know when they hear something that's not right. The ADR must seamlessly integrate with the location recordings or the illusion of continuity will be lost.

A simple thing to do that will greatly enhance the process is to use the same or quite similar equipment when recording the ADR. Every microphone and every preamplifier is different, and all of these things, including the ADR recording room, will add up to a different sound. You want to re-create the old sound. Equipment really does matter.

Another important aspect of ADR is the performance itself. The actors must be able to effectively re-create the same attitude, emotion, and quality of the original performance. This can be a difficult exercise in and of itself. In this scenario the actors are no longer reacting to one another and the imagined situation. The performers are acting in a booth with a microphone. They will need to mimic perfectly their original inspiration for the scene. For some actors this is an easy task; others will find it amazingly difficult. Figure 10.1 shows an actor in an ADR booth. The talent is in the booth and the filmmaker and the recordist are in the control room.

The filmmaker must oversee the ADR session to guide and inspire the talent. Actors may need encouragement and motivation to perform, and the filmmaker can help them get back to the emotional place they were in for any particular scene. Highly charged emotional scenes can take some time for the actor to prepare and perform.

There is another key component in the session that needs to be addressed. That component is lip sync. You may have the ideal recording setup for matching the location recordings. The director and the actor may have developed the performance to match the emotional quality exactly to where it was on the set. But none of that will matter if the actor can't also match the lip movements on the screen. If the sync cannot be matched, then all of the effort and time will not create the illusion that is needed. Audiences of all ages can spot sync issues of two or three frames easily. Even the most casual observers can spot these subtle problems.

The success of ADR falls squarely on the actor, first, in being able to reconnect with the original performance, and second, in being able to re-create that same performance lip-syncing to the picture. There is also one other small detail that can derail the entire process. Think

FIGURE 10.1 The actor watches her lips on the screen and tries to re-create her original performance

about how movies and TV shows are edited. The actor may have a long speech, but most likely the picture will not be just a close-up shot of his or her mouth. The mouth of the actor will not be seen clearly throughout any given scene of the movie. Perhaps the line starts off-screen, and then it is on-screen, off and on again. This makes things particularly difficult because the actor may not always have a reference of the mouth and may have to catch the lip movements when the scene cuts back to his or her face. This is not an insignificant task!

Beep Tracks

The main tools for cueing the talent are *beep tracks* in the timeline. Each beep track contains recordings of three evenly spaced beeps played in succession. Figure 10.2 shows a Pro Tools DAW timeline with beep tracks. These beep recordings are placed on the beep tracks under the location audio lines to be replaced.

The idea behind the beeps is simple. The beeps are spaced one second apart. The actor hears the beeps and listens to the rhythm that is created between the beeps and the lines. That rhythm is essential for the actor to be properly cued for the sync.

The beginning of the line the actor is to revoice falls on the fourth "imaginary" beep: Beep, beep, beep, line. Beep, beep, beep, line. Rehearse the actor by playing the beeps and the production guide track four or five times in a row. Then mute the location audio guide track and hit record. That recording will be take one. Just a few hundred more to go!

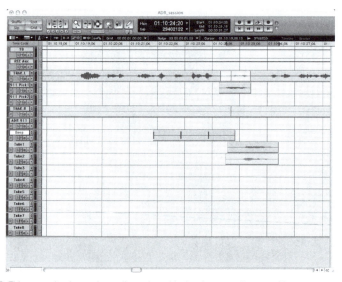

FIGURE 10.2 This example shows the audio region with the three evenly spaced beeps

The actors must get used to recording the ADR without playback of the guide track. If they do not, it will slow them down, since they will be a beat behind as they listen. Actors often want to hear the lines in the headphones, but this will directly affect the performance. It can also bleed from their headphones into the ADR recording, which can be a major problem and will render the take useless.

Hopefully the actor has a sense of rhythm! As a recordist running a session such as this you must create and maintain a loose but regular rhythm in the recording session. If you start missing takes or are not in sync with the actor, the session will be more difficult. Just like all recording tasks, you do not want to miss a take. Inevitably the one missed will be the one take the director and actor like the best. You do not want them to ask you to circle a take that you were not recording!

Make the beep recordings easily moveable on the beep track. Actors sometimes anticipate the cue and start early or wait a beat too long and miss the cue. In those instances, you must be flexible and move the beeps recording a frame one way or the other to accommodate the rhythm of the performer. Be sure to discuss the moving of the beep track. The actor may be just getting the hang of the original placement when you move to the new placement.

As the ADR recordist, you must stay focused on the picture as you listen to the performance. You will be the main insight for the filmmaker regarding the final sync. If it looks horribly out of sync, then you may want to keep retaking until the sync looks good. If the sync looks good and the director and performer are happy with the performance, then you can move on to another take. Do not, however, simply move on to another line if they love the performance but the sync is not accurate. It will not work in the final edit and mix, so they are depending on you as the ADR recordist to determine the sync quality of the line.

Placing Beeps and Cues

Placing the beeps for cueing is a critical task. If the beep tracks are not aligned in a repeatable and anticipated manner, it can make for a long session for everyone involved. The beep tracks are key for cueing the performer to sync to the picture.

Figure 10.3 shows an example of a complicated ADR beeping session in a Pro Tools DAW. You'll notice that the beep audio itself accounts for the imaginary beep that has been discussed. This is very useful in aligning the beeps to the production audio. By aligning the end of the beep audio to the start of the line to be replaced, as in this example, you are properly cueing the tracks.

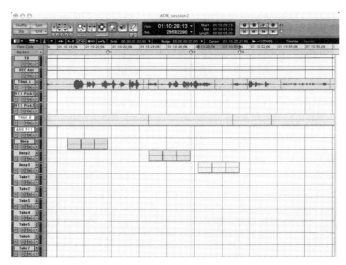

FIGURE 10.3 Pro Tools allows the addition of markers that can locate the recording position precisely for each recording

Preparing the sessions for ADR recording can be a bit tricky. Like all things in digital filmmaking, organization is very important. The following scenario has worked for me. Use a guide track that is free of music and effects. The simplest way to make things relatively easy is to use that track as a cue track for the performer.

The dialogue edit can be used, but there might be many tracks to deal with when working with that audio. The OMF audio can be used as well if the dialogue edit has begun, but the same problem remains, too many tracks. The guide track will be a single track of audio that will be more convenient for muting and unmuting.

Using the guide track frees you up to focus on the beep tracks and the new ADR recordings. There will be a certain rhythm that you, as the recordist, must get into as well. When you are in the thick of it with the director and the actor, you need to be as organized as possible. It's in the pressure of the situation that mistakes, miscues, and missed recordings can happen.

Figure 10.4 is an example of a Pro Tools session that has been prepared for ADR. You'll notice that there are several beep tracks. Since the cueing can get a bit complicated, by using several beep tracks the session will run smoother. The key is making sure to mute the additional beep tracks when going from cue to cue.

Figure 10.5 is an example of a Pro Tools session where ADR has already taken place. Here you can see tracks identified as the "pick" track. I use that track to place the recordings that I know the director selected as a circle take. It makes things easier to keep track of. I will create a "Pick 1" track and a "Pick 2" track so that there is an alternate

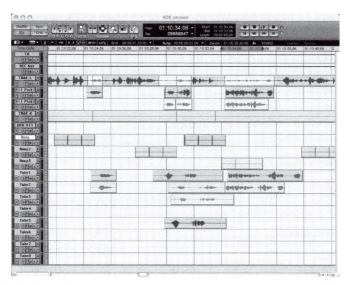

FIGURE 10.4 In this example several of the beep tracks will need to be muted to properly cue the actor

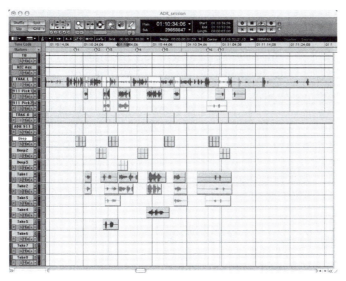

FIGURE 10.5 This example shows picks tracks, alternate takes, and the beep tracks

take available for whatever reason later on. *Picks* is an arbitrary term of course. You can call it whatever seems right for your project. You'll also notice that all of the additional takes are on tracks below the pick track.

By working this way everything is in reach for the director or talent to audition takes or the guide in the heat of the moment. Often they will want to hear one take or the other as well as the original production audio. By keeping everything handy in one session it's a simple matter of muting and unmuting to accomplish this.

TIP

If you are the recordist for the session, then you need to take the reins and steer. Until you've spent some time recording ADR, all of this is theory. When you sit in the hot seat, you'll understand the session rhythm I've spoken of as well as the need for organization. One idea to keep in mind is that you are running the session. Don't get bullied or intimidated by the situation. It takes time to cue the software, to mute and unmute tracks, and to notate the script. Sometimes the others involved have unrealistic expectations of how the session should go. It is imperative that you create and maintain a speed for the session that is to your liking. Don't allow yourself to get rushed because that is when mistakes will happen.

Create different recording sessions for each required ADR performance. All of the beeps and recordings can grow exponentially, so it is a good idea to keep it all separate. If you have a small number of ADR lines, it may work in one session, but as Figure 10.5 shows, just one person's ADR can be a substantial recording session. If you multiply that by several actors all in the same scene, then it can be difficult to keep everything in order.

Organize for Recording Efficiency

Since these sessions can become so large, it is important to create them in a manner that affords the best efficiency. You will want to minimize the chances for mistakes. And in this definition of mistakes, they are just that—missed takes. Try to not let that happen.

Create only as many beep tracks as needed. Checkerboard the beeps between two tracks or more if needed. Try to keep the beep tracks down to as few tracks as necessary. There is no one right way to do it, of course, since the demands of each session will be different. Using a single guide track as the ADR reference track keeps the location dialogue tracks to just one track.

It is important to create a simple system for yourself and the performer. You will need to be able to easily mute tracks and audition recordings on the fly for the director. When you are creating the sessions for each of the ADR recording sessions, try to standardize them. This way, once you are comfortable with the first session, you've made a predictable scenario. You will always know where the guide track is to mute, where the beep tracks are to mute, where the picks tracks are, and where all of the takes tracks are located. This consistency will help streamline your workflow during the recording sessions themselves.

Keeping Track of Your Takes

Similar to a VO recording session, the take count during ADR can get very high. For VO recordings, however, the takes are generally recorded wild. The circle takes from ADR recording need to be spotted, in sync, and available to view with the accompanying picture file. When changes are required or the filmmaker seeks other choices, you will need to be able to easily find alternate takes. The ideas explored in the following section are

- The ADR Script
- Takes Notation on the New Recordings
- Wild Lines, New Text, and Walla

The ADR Script

The ADR script will be the roadmap to guide the ADR editor to the proper take number for each line of ADR recorded. The script must be an exact representation of the lines that are spoken on-screen. Be aware that the shooting script may in fact be considerably different from the final edit of the project. Each word for the ADR script should be exactly what is said on-screen.

The smallest differences in text will throw the actor's performance off during the ADR recording. There is a rhythm that must be re-created and a lip sync that will have to match. It will not be good enough to get close to what is being said. It will have to be exact, no exceptions. You can imagine the frustration of an actor who has so many things going on during a session and now must also rewrite the script throughout the session because the text does not match the lines that need replacing.

ADR sessions can be intense and intimate situations. If you have not spent much time with actors, you'll discover that it is all about the performance. They each "get there" in different ways. It is a mysterious process but not a technical one. So be sure, as the recordist, to take care of all the technical aspects for them. That means the recording room, the beep timing, and the script need to be as good as they can be to free the actors to reach the level they need to be able to re-create the emotional quality of the scenes that they are recording.

Takes Notation on the New Recordings

All of the ADR takes must be clearly marked. Circle takes should be used for the chosen performances. Although the suggestion was made to place the preferred takes on a "pick" track, documentation will still be a necessity. In the heat of the moment, the filmmaker will choose whatever he or she thinks is the best take and the alternate. However, when it comes time, after the session, to listen to the "picks" again, some lines may have to be rechosen. You'll need the notated script to be able to find them.

Directors like to have the flexibility to change their mind. If you are using the system of picks tracks and spotted the other takes in the timeline below them, then why document the session at all? Because in general the take counts can get very high.

The editing of ADR can be tricky too. Sometimes directors like half of one take and half of another. Or they may ask you to use a word in one take but the rest of a different take for a line and so on. It is important to keep track of all of the takes and the changes of the choices of takes on paper as well as in the edit session.

Wild Lines, New Text, and Walla

One of the advantages of ADR is that it can allow the director to make changes to the script if they are desired. Not all ADR will be sync dialogue, and in those off-screen moments the director may decide to add words or phrases to better tell the story.

These new wild lines should be written out verbatim on the script. They should be numbered by take and circled if chosen as a preferred take. It is always a good idea to put a timecode reference next to the wild line as well; this makes it clear after the recording session where the lines are to be spotted.

There are also ADR sessions that are called group or *walla* recording. Walla is the background murmuring of actors in scenes. Walla is useful in many different types of scenes. Restaurant scenes, outdoor scenes, and any scenes where a lot of actors are located are prime uses for walla. Many times when recording walla the lines are all wild.

Traditionally, walla is indistinct words and murmuring. Legend has it that in the old days of radio, actors providing background voices would say, "walla, walla, walla." In European countries they use the term "rhubarb." Regardless of the sounds being said, the idea with walla is that it is an indistinct wash of human voices.

One issue to be aware of with walla is the requirements of actors' unions. The reason that walla is generally indistinct sounds is because if the actors are speaking lines of dialogue, that may change their status from being merely an extra performer to being an actor, who may need to be paid as a performer in the movie. Extras are paid on a very different scale than actors in the movie. It is important to be aware of this on a union motion picture or a television program.

I mention this because often during walla recording sessions directors might be rewriting their script for better storytelling. They may start offering specific lines that could be used in the final edit and mix. It's a bit of a gray area, but it is important to point out.

Tips for Believable Dialogue Replacement

As you can see, ADR is an intensive process. Preparation is always essential. The preparation will take some of the pressure off of you, the recordist, since you'll be able to anticipate the demands of the session. There are also some other tips that can be useful for more believable ADR. Ideas we will explore in this section include

- Microphone Proximity
- Headphones

- Getting the Right Performance
- How to Cut Sync

Microphone Proximity

Actors have a tendency when wearing headphones to speak too closely to the microphone. There is a term for this called the *proximity effect*. Proximity effect is an exaggeration of the low-end frequencies of the voice. It sounds "warmer," "richer," or "fatter," which can be pleasing to the actor. It is not, however, useful for ADR recording.

Location recordists try to get the boom microphone between three to six feet from the performer's mouth. Lavaliere microphones are hidden in clothing and are also generally at least a foot or two away from the mouth. Although these microphones are relatively close to the performer, there is still a significant distance.

Since the proximity effect is a pleasing sound, it is natural for a performer to put his or her mouth right up to the microphone. But ADR is not radio. ADR is a very specific recording technique that is intended to re-create the recordings from the set. Lines that are recorded close-miked with proximity effect will not edit together properly with the location recordings.

Encourage the actor to back away from the microphone. Be sure to gain the levels accordingly. Since you will be using the same or similar equipment as the location recordings, also mimic the microphone distance in the ADR booth if possible. Use an overhead boom stand for the microphone and have the actor stand in a position similar to on-set.

Danny Boyle, award-winning director of films such as *Trainspotting*, *28 Days Later*, and the worldwide hit *Slumdog Millionaire*, has strong ideas about ADR. Most great directors have a clear vision of how to get the performances that they need. Danny Boyle is no exception to that rule. Under difficult filming situations in India for *Slumdog Millionaire* he had his performers and ADR recordist mimic the action on-screen.

He feels strongly that the actors need to run if they are running on-screen, hop if they are hopping onscreen, and so on. He has the location recordist follow the actor in the ADR process. In a way, he is doing a sort of on-set ADR in an ADR recording studio. He believes the only way to recapture the quality of the performance and the quality of the ADR is in re-creating the scene as best as possible. This process does make for interesting lip-sync issues. Danny Boyle is always seeking new and unique ways to tell his powerful stories.

Headphones

Headphones are an important piece of equipment in all aspects of audio from location to post. For ADR it is essential for the talent to hear the beeps, to hear the production audio that they are replacing and also to hear the director who will probably be in another room offering guidance.

Actors have a tendency to keep the headphones' volume level a bit high. It is important for several reasons to keep the level as low as possible. I encourage actors to keep the level just loud enough to hear what they need to hear.

One major issue is that audio from the headphones could bleed or leak into the recording track. The headphones will be quite close to the microphone, and the microphone could pick up the playback. If the ADR recordings are not clean, it will make their editing more difficult.

Another issue, perhaps the biggest, is that headphones playing too loud will affect the performance of the actor. Sometimes you need to send playback of other characters' lines for them to react with, and the wrong playback level can affect their performance. Obviously for ADR, the desire is a re-creation of the original performance. If you are recording the ADR and hear the actor whispering or talking softly, then chances are the headphones are too loud.

Sometimes actors can be resistant to stepping away from the microphone or from turning down the headphones. You will need to fight this resistance to get the performance and the recording that you need. Enlist the director's support by telling him or her about proximity effect and how loud headphones can affect performances. What often happens is that the director will then take the reins and specifically remind the actor to step away from the microphone and turn down the headphones.

One technique that can be useful but is a bit trickier to pull off is to use a small speaker in place of the headphones. This approach frees actors from cable and headphones completely, giving them the freedom to move, and they tend to act more in accordance with the picture. They will also tend to back off of the microphone, since they no longer will be able to hear the proximity effect loudly in the ears.

There are a few pitfalls to this approach. One is a note in general about recording ADR. You must stay aware of any additional sounds that the actor is making while recording. In some cases it can be beneficial to the ADR; in others it will be distracting. For instance, take a scene where the actor has a lot of body movement. In some cases, if the movements are being recorded in the ADR, it can help the ADR sound more realistic. The movement will be a natural part of the recordings just like the location recording. In other scenes, any sort of movement during the recordings will be distracting.

It is important to keep on top of all of the characteristics of the recordings. There are many things for everyone to keep in mind. The director is looking for a great performance; the actor is re-creating the emotions and lip sync; and the recordist is listening for the quality of the recording, the accuracy of the lip sync, and the intrusions of any sounds that may mar the recording. As I've noted, ADR is a labor-intensive task for all involved.

Getting the Right Performance

You, as the recordist, cannot do the acting for them. There is a mysterious connection between the actor, the director, and the script. The job of the recordist is to provide the proper environment to allow a great performance to happen. You want to facilitate that mysterious bond to help re-create the magic of the performance.

Actors can be sensitive. Often they need to be coddled, cajoled, and coerced into the moment. Sometimes they'll sit in the recording room happily drinking coffee and chatting, prolonging the moment before the ADR starts. Sometimes they are ready to go and want to get rolling immediately. It is important to read their mental state and act accordingly. This situation is similar to location recording when dealing with miking the performers. You must respect them, give them their "space," and let them do their thing.

Once the flow and rhythm of the session has been established, try to keep it moving the same way. The actor will depend on that flow that has been created. The process can be complicated. You need to audition the location audio for them with the beeps. They rehearse. You then mute the location track and record the takes. Place the takes on the proper track, notate the script, and start the process again.

Actors are experts at pretending. Pay strict attention to the details of any particular scene. Be sure to get their breaths, coughs, lip smacks, anything that you hear in the location tracks. These ADR recordings need to be realistic and should faithfully reflect the performance.

How to Cut Sync

Once you've recorded all of the ADR, you will need to check the sync on all of the chosen takes for each line of dialogue. Verify with the director each preferred take for each scene. Once the director has firmly decided on at least most of the takes, it is time to cut the recordings to sync.

Cutting sync means that you are going to try to edit the ADR to match the original recording. With the power of NLEs and DAWs the ability exists to look at audio recordings in waveform view.

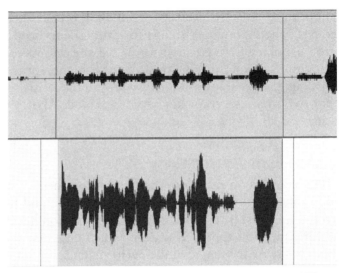

FIGURE 10.6 In this example the top track is the guide and the bottom track is the ADR

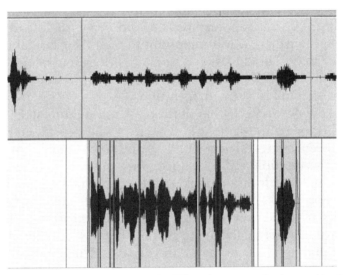

FIGURE 10.7 With some editing and crossfades the ADR track now more closely resembles the original recording

Figure 10.6 shows the original location recording and below it is a track of ADR. Notice that the recordings are similar but not exact. When cutting sync you want to match the ADR recording to the original. Zoom close into the waveforms and note their differences. You will try to edit the ADR track to better match the waveform from the location recording.

Figure 10.7 shows the same two tracks again, but this time the ADR track has been cut to sync. The waveforms are a better match, and the lip sync on-screen is a better match. Each ADR recording should be inspected like this against the location recording. As you learn to edit ADR takes, a few interesting things will become clear.

Not all ADR will need to be cut to sync. You will watch the take against picture and verify its sync. If it looks good, it's best to leave it alone. There is another interesting phenomenon. Even though two waveforms don't "line up" in the timeline and can look quite different, the ADR line can still, in some instances, work fine with no editing. You will also have to listen closely to all of the ADR that does get edited. Sometimes even though the edit looks perfect, in playback it sounds odd, off, or just plain wrong. Those will require additional editing or a look into alternate takes for the problematic part of sync.

Tools of the Trade

The final key to the ADR puzzle comes in the mixing of it. The ADR performance can be great. The lip sync can be spot-on. The perspective of the recording can be correct. But the tonal quality of the takes can clash when edited together with the location recordings. There are some tools that can help blend the audio quality during the mixing process. Specific tools utilized for mixing ADR addressed in this section are

- Equalizers
- Reverb

Equalizers

Equalizers (EQ) are audio filters that can alter the frequency characteristics of a recorded sound by cutting or boosting frequencies in a number of ways. Humans hear sound over a theoretical frequency range of 20 Hz to 20,000 Hz. In frequency ranges the lower the number, the lower the frequency; the higher the number, the higher the frequency. Adults will typically lose the ability to hear frequencies quite that high.

EQ is an essential tool in mixing audio. EQ was developed as a way to "equalize" differing sources to sound similar. By mimicking the frequency characteristic of the location recording you will be able to better blend and mix the two recordings together for a seamless final mix. Room tone will be edited in sync with each take of ADR. If the ADR performance and the lip sync are good, the combination of the correct EQ and room tone will complete the illusion.

The best device to help pinpoint the correct EQ to use is a *frequency analyzer*. A frequency analyzer can examine the ADR recording and display its frequency characteristics. Figure 10.8 is

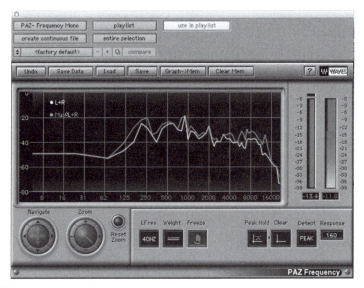

FIGURE 10.8 The material in this example is that of dialogue being analyzed

an example of the results of a frequency analyzer examination of an ADR recording.

The frequency analyzer will examine the tonal characteristics of the location recording. You can then use a graphical EQ to apply frequencies to the ADR to better match the sonics of the location recording. A graphical EQ device can precisely add or remove specific frequencies. Figure 10.9 is an example of a ten-band graphical EQ.

This technique outlined above is the starting point to get the EQ close. It will take some adjustments and critical listening to dial in the exact frequencies and amounts to get recordings to better match one another. It takes time, skill, and a bit of experience to make things sound right. Practice makes perfect.

Reverb

There are a couple of other aspects of the recording that can be manipulated further for better blending with location recordings. *Reverb*, or reverberation, is the result of sound sources hitting objects and walls and returning the sound back to the listener. It is the effect of a sound after the sound is no longer being produced.

Reverberation is something that affects the sounds we hear all day long. A simple example is speaking in a bathroom or talking loudly in an empty parking garage. The voices are moving around these spaces in a different manner. There are digital reverb devices that can simulate the character that various rooms have on sounds.

■■■   AUDIO PRODUCTION AND POSTPRODUCTION

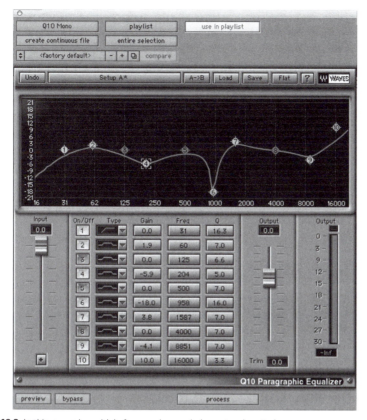

FIGURE 10.9 In this example multiple frequencies are being cut or boosted

Recordings from an ADR booth will not sound quite the same if they are intercut with location audio that was recorded in an empty warehouse. A rerecording mixer will apply a reverb that will simulate the sound of the warehouse on the ADR recordings to blend them with the location recordings.

Reverbs are powerful devices that are used in a number of ways for postproduction audio. They are used extensively in ADR to mimic the sounds of the rooms that characters are speaking in. Reverbs are also used extensively for sound effects, for Foley, and for music. In some instances they are used to mimic the location sounds, and in other instances they are used more for creating special audio effects.

Summary

Dialogue replacement is a highly skilled craft for everyone involved. The main concerns are to mimic the recording quality and capture strong performances while keeping the dialogue in sync with the picture. This is a collaboration of the recordist, the actor, and the filmmaker.

Beep tracks cue the talent for each line of dialogue being replaced. A rhythm gets established for rehearsing the line with the beeps and the guide track and then it is recorded in sync with the picture. The prepared ADR script is notated throughout the ADR session, and the preferred takes are circled. The recordist is also placing the chosen takes on tracks in the recording session for easy referral later. Chosen takes will be cut to sync and mixed. EQ will be used to blend the ADR lines with the location recordings at final mixing. Reverb will be further added during mixing to re-create the specific sound of the locations and spaces that the characters are in. ADR is a technical and exacting process in postproduction audio.

Review Questions

Questions like these are likely to appear on exams to test how well you understood and retained the information in this chapter

1. What is a beep track? How are the beeps edited into the timeline?
2. Why is an accurate script important for the ADR session?
3. What is walla?
4. Why would you use a frequency analyzer?
5. Why would you use reverb for ADR?

Discussion/Essay Questions

Your instructor may assign you one or more of the following questions for discussion in class or as the subject of a paper

1. Describe the ADR process from the preparation to the recording session with the performer.
2. Define and describe the process of cutting ADR takes to sync.

Applying What You've Learned

Research/Lab/Fieldwork Projects

The following lab exercises will give you practice with dialogue replacement.

1. Create a beep track with three evenly spaced one-frame beeps one second apart.

2. Place this new "beep track" prior to the start of each line to be rerecorded.
3. Practice playing and muting the production tracks for the performer.
4. Record several lines of dialogue replacement.
5. Edit these new recordings in sync with the picture edit.

NOTE
Students who have ongoing projects may elect to use their own source material, such as video clips, with the instructor's permission.

Resources

The following resources have more information on the topics covered in this chapter:

Jeremy Hanks, "The Basics of ADR: Secrets of Dialogue Replacement for Video People," *MicroFilmmaker* (http://www.microfilmmaker.com/tipstrick/Issue15/BasicADR.html). This article is a great firsthand account of a filmmaker tackling ADR.

Woody Woodhall, "Dialog Replacement Is Your Friend," StudioDaily Blogs (http://www.studiodaily.com/blog/?p=1703). This is a blog post I wrote regarding ADR. Check out all of StudioDaily's forums and blogs. There is an amazing amount of valuable information located here.

.

CHAPTER 11

SOUND DESIGN

In this chapter, you will:

- Learn about charting a course
- Learn how to create time and space
- Understand how sound affects the timing
- Learn about sound effects libraries
- Learn about building the timeline

Charting the Course

Sound design can be described as the overall scheme for the sonics of every part of the soundtrack. In collaboration with the filmmaker, the sound designer will translate the ideas of what the filmmaker wants to hear into an edit timeline and a mixable soundtrack. They will re-create the sounds of old worlds for period pieces and create new worlds for science fiction. They will interpret the filmmaker's needs and create what the project requires. The ideas discussed in this section are

- Understanding All of the Pieces
- Spotting the Sound Design
- Layers of Sound

Understanding All of the Pieces

Audio post, like all of editing, is a giant puzzle. There are many parts, all of which add up to the whole. The sound designer must be aware of all of the elements to understand how they will be edited and finally mixed together. I need to take a moment and discuss another crucial person in the post audio process. The *supervising sound editor* is typically the person who takes a project through audio post. However, in today's world, where everything is able to be done on a single computer, the lines have blurred between these audio post positions.

Today, the sound designer may well be the supervising sound editor as well. Or that person may be the dialogue editor or the re-recording mixer. Sound design is truly a team effort, and as in many parts of digital filmmaking, the post crew may be wearing more than one hat to get the job done.

Going back to the first chapter of this text, you will recall the elements that comprise a soundtrack. These elements include, dialogue, sound effects, and music. Inside of each of those headings, of course, are many other things. ADR would be included in the dialogue portion, Foley would be included in the effects portion, and popular music and score would be included in the music portion.

Each of these elements will combine to create the final soundtrack of the project. As any designer needs to know all of their elements, the sound designer must understand the various pieces of the project, how they all will work together, and what the final sound should be according to the desires of the filmmakers.

Spotting the Sound Design

Spotting the movie with the filmmakers is central to understanding the sonic universe of the project. During this important meeting, the post audio team will watch the entire project with the filmmakers to determine what each scene requires to achieve the goals of the project. It is highly important to make copious notes during this session.

The sound designer should be at the spotting session along with other members of the post audio team. If there is a dialogue editor and an effects editor on board, it is a good idea for them to attend the spotting as well. If the post audio team has all of the responsibilities entrusted to one individual, namely you, then as long as you are there, everyone required will be in attendance!

The best way to spot the movie is by doing it in the session that you will begin editing in. For instance, if you are creating the sound in a DAW, you will open the OMF and import and sync the video file.

Then spot the project with the filmmakers with that session. That way everything that you will be doing will be in the actual edit session.

Start right from the beginning and ask whatever questions will help you understand the desires of the filmmakers. If they want atmospheres to better define a scene, make a note of it. If there are shots of cars passing and they need those sounds, add that. If they don't like the way a fight scene sounds, ask why. Define "louder," "better," or "more." This is the time for you to understand what they "hear" for each part of the project.

The music tracks may not exist yet at this point. It is important to get an understanding of what the music will be. The filmmakers have probably already begun working with the composer on the music tracks. Find out where the music will be spotted and how it will be used in the scenes. If a fight scene will ultimately be mixed so that it is music only, then you won't need to be spending time editing detailed fight Foley.

This is the time when the core post sound team will be able to ask, interject, opine, and understand exactly what the filmmaker's intentions are. Ask about questionable location recordings, express concern about ADR needs, define and understand the sonic qualities that are being discussed, take notes and try to "hear" the "universe" being created. The spotting session sets the agenda and the game plan for the work to follow.

Layers of Sound

Understanding the layers of sound in the real world will guide your designing and editing skills. For instance, you are editing a scene at a beach. Putting in sounds of the ocean and waves would be logical if you are near the water. Seagull calls are often used in the elements of sound for the beach. Beginning sound editors may often add those and move on. But there is a lot more than that going on at the beach. Is there any wind? Is anyone else there besides you? Traffic? Are there kids playing or people laughing? What other sounds are there other than the ocean? Figure 11.1 is an example of a sound effects session in Pro Tools.

After the spotting session with the filmmaker you will understand what they "hear" for their project. You've spoken in general terms about the overall design of the project. It is good practice to "overdesign" the sound.

It takes time to audition sound effects libraries and your on-set Foley and atmospheres. Some things may work; others you may not be sure. The only way to tell if things are working is to edit them in and

FIGURE 11.1 This is a simple example of stacking effects to create variety

listen to them while viewing the picture. I like to leave the work in the session. Perhaps muted, perhaps not, but this way choices are already built into the project and it's a simple matter of muting and unmuting.

Filmmakers can be very particular about the sound. Maybe there are too many seagulls; maybe there are too many waves crashing on the shore. You won't know until you've played things back for them as they watch the picture. Once you move from the abstract to the concrete, then you will have a real grasp of the sonics that are desired.

Don't get too attached to the work you've done; remember, if you are not the director, the writer, the producer, or involved beyond the sound edit, you cannot be too proprietary about the sound edit. You will offer ideas, opinions, and so on, but at the end of the day the last word will reside with the filmmaker.

Commercial sound effects libraries are a treasure of useful sounds. There you will be able to find all sorts of things like car passes, door slams, animal sounds, and so on. They are very handy to start the process of filling in the gaps left in the sound edit.

Many of these are available royalty free. That means that once you've bought them you own them for life. You won't be able to resell the effects by themselves, but you will be able to use them in your edits on just about any project that you will work on. Be sure to read all of the legal disclaimers to be clear about the proper use of any effects purchased on a royalty-free basis. The terms all tend to be a bit different.

These libraries are quite varied. They can be all encompassing, meaning that they try to cover as many of the more standard sounds that you will need as possible, or they can be highly specific, only covering weapons, or only covering animals, and so on. You'll have to determine what you'll need. Over time, as you buy libraries for each project, you will create a very nice catalog of sounds for your use.

After you've spent a bit of time with these libraries, you will find that these can be used and reused many times over. When you've used these libraries as much as I have, you will begin to hear the effects often, on movie trailers, radio spots, and television. I can hear some of these effects within a complex mix because I've used them so often.

This leads me to the next idea about sound effects editing in general. Imagine a commercial library and its use, every day, all over the world. These sounds get used very often. Now of course a car pass or wind is pretty generic sound, but some of the sounds are highly specific.

Create layers of sound as you design the project. Don't look for one ambience that has birds, traffic, and wind. Find one sound for each and cut them up. Rearrange them into new and interesting sounds. Add little accent sounds, such as an appropriately timed laugh or car horn for greater variety. Listen to the world around you and uncover the layers of sound. Re-create those layers in the timeline. Listen to your favorite sounding movies and discover the layers used there.

Creating Time and Space

Sound can tell us many things about our environment. We take for granted all of the sounds we hear each day. The playback of a dry dialogue track with no atmospheres and no sound effects will be a barren soundscape. The ideas to be explored in this section are

- Ambiences Create the Place and the Time
- Creating Moods—Drones, Beds, and Room Tones
- Real Spaces
- Imagined Spaces

Ambiences Create the Place and the Time

You're sitting outside at a restaurant just about to begin eating breakfast. The birds are chirping, there is a faint sound of plates and silverware, and you can hear the murmurs of the other diners around you. If you heard this scene playing but didn't see the picture, could you get a sense of where, what, and when?

Can you mistake this scene for a boat roaring down the ocean? Would you imagine it was a frosty night in Siberia? Could it be a hard rain in the jungles of Brazil? You could probably quickly decipher that you were outdoors, it was daytime, and that you were eating or possibly even at a restaurant.

The ambiences that surround us on a daily basis tell us volumes about where, what, and when. Sound designers use these aural clues to their advantage and set the scene for the viewers for any given motion picture or television program.

Some filmmakers are quite literal in their approach to sound design. If they don't see a seagull, they don't want to hear a seagull. But as you create more and more soundscapes, you will discover that you must follow your own instincts as to the aural quality of a scene. Filmmakers will make their decisions when they see the edit played against the picture.

Creating Moods—Drones, Beds, and Room Tones

Often when people think of sound design they think about science fiction or otherworldly soundscapes. There is a major use of sound design in such films, but of course as we now know, sound design is a part of all projects.

David Lynch, award-winning director of films such as *Blue Velvet* and *The Elephant Man*, uses sound in very specific and wonderful ways. He has an acute sense of sound and weaves his musical soundtracks seamlessly with his sound-design elements. He is a very hands-on director on each aspect of his motion pictures.

Lynch is a visual artist, a photographer, a musician and composer, and an author with many other talents. He takes a firm hand in all aspects of his projects. Watch and listen to his use of sound to create foreboding. Movies of his like *Lost Highway* employ an amazing sense of aural design.

Drones are powerful sound-design elements used in many types of projects. Drones are typically, low-pitched sounds that play in a continuous manner underneath a scene. *Beds* are a similar sound device, although beds can refer to more musical types of sounds. Drones are more subliminal, monotonous sounds.

Sometimes drones are musical elements. Sometimes drones are the sounds of pipes in a basement, or the rumblings of fans. These deep, dark sound elements when played against picture often give a sense of foreboding and danger. David Lynch, along with his composers, most notably Angelo Badalamenti, uses these sound elements to imply otherworldly times and places. I mention David Lynch because he is a world-class filmmaker with a keen sense of sound but also because he generally makes dramatic works as opposed to science fiction—*Dune* being his rare stray into the realm of science fiction of course! But yet Lynch's movies are filled with many unique sound elements.

Use your critical listening skills while watching thrillers, film noirs, and other films with dark subject matter. You will uncover in your listening extensive use of drones to convey these darker, suspenseful audio elements. There are many room tones and atmospheres that can be used in this manner.

Commercial sound effects libraries have sounds of boiler rooms, machine rooms, and other room tones from industrial spaces that work perfectly as drones for these types of emotional effects. Or go out and record your own! Figure 11.2 is an example of a Final Cut Express timeline with a combination of drones, room tones, and ambiences designed for one scene in a motion picture.

Real Spaces

There's an old saying that "audio follows picture." What that means is that the audio should mimic what is seen on-screen. There will always be exceptions, of course, but typically if you see a car pass, you hear a car pass; if you see waves crashing on a beach, you will hear the ocean.

Here is a great opportunity to crack open the additional audio files folder and see what's been recorded. If you are lucky enough to have

FIGURE 11.2 In this example, effects are stacked to create a layered background of sound

clean ambiences from the location, use them. Be sure to sweeten the scenes with all of the wild sounds that were recorded on set.

If it's a period piece, then use those location recordings of cars, tools, or whatever is pertinent to the scene. All of the recordings done on location should be "real" sounds of real places and real things. Be sure to have a good look over all of the goodies in there to see what you can use.

You can also check for alternate takes of scenes to see if there are snippets of sounds that are clean enough to use to sweeten scenes with. This is great for crowds, fight scenes, or scenes where PFX could be used to sweeten. Alternate takes may have different places where the dialogue was spoken, so they may be pieced together to use as PFX for a particular scene.

Imagined Spaces

Motion pictures and television programs are often set in imaginary and fantastical settings. You could be deep in outer space, deep underwater, or deep underground. You could be zipping across the universe faster than the speed of light. You could be transformed into a beam of light. The options are as boundless as the imaginations of the filmmakers.

Typically, even in fantastical situations, audio will still follow picture. The difference in this case is that the car pass may be a spaceship pass, or rather than the waves of an ocean they are waves of light. Just as the visual effects designers are creating new and unseen worlds with the picture you will be creating new and unheard worlds with the audio.

Ben Burtt, the sound designer of *Wall-E* among many other science fiction classics is the go-to guy for creating new sonic universes. Just take a look and listen to *Wall-E* or any of the Star Wars movies to get a sense of his use of sound. The opening scene of *Wall-E* is a complete creation of audio with no dialogue. Get a copy of the movie and listen to that first scene with critical ears. Uncover the layers of sound used to create that sonic landscape.

Designing sound for these new visuals is an exciting and an exacting skill. The process of the design remains the same. You will add background atmospheres to fill the spaces and define time and space. You will add, create, and sweeten the location recordings with hard effects and Foley elements.

The main difference is that you may be creating all of these sounds from scratch. Sound effects creation is a fantastic and exciting pursuit. You will take the same approach as before. You will spot the movie with the filmmakers, but this time they may act out and vocalize the sounds that they "hear!" Then it is your job to find those sounds or to create them.

There is no "correct" way to create sound effects. Try anything. Layer sounds on top of one another and mix them together for new sounds. Filter them, play them at odd speeds, and manipulate them into something new. You can always start with "real" sounds and in their manipulation transform them into something new.

Sound Design and Timing

The sounds in a movie can heighten and change the feeling of a movie. A judicious use of great sound design, great picture editing, and great sound mixing will create a great final product. Each of those elements contributes to the feeling of motion in and with the scenes. The ideas explored in this section are

- Using the Sound Design to Enrich the Scenes
- Using Dialogue Elements for Sound Design

Using the Sound Design to Enrich the Scenes

There is a wonderful term that is used often in live theatre. That term is *button*. Directors will try to be sure that each scene ends with a button, some nice touch that sums the scene up and leads to the next one. Buttons are wonderful devices to use when designing sound for a project.

For example, you are cutting a scene with two characters arguing in a parking lot. They are standing next to the car, the argument escalates, and then one enters the car and drives off. A simple button could be adding a tire squeal as the car pulls off. Or maybe add a door slam just after a character reaches the end of their speech.

Perhaps there is a scene where one character is getting frustrated. Maybe there was a quick shot of their foot tapping. You could use that visual cue to add more tapping as the scene progresses. The rerecording mixer could take your idea and run with that, perhaps mixing the scene so that by the end of it all that you can hear is the tap, tap, tap of an impatient character.

Sound design also takes the project as a whole into consideration. Rerecording mixers like to create dynamics with the mix. The same way the lighting designer is creating light and dark, the sound designer creates quiet and loud. Help them with your sound design. Give them elements to mix the scenes with dynamics.

Perhaps the movie has a lot of car elements in it. People talking in cars, driving in, driving away, and just plain driving. If one of the characters is increasingly feeling paranoid or suffocating, you can mimic those emotions with the sound design. Slowly add cars and car sounds as you build the scenes in the edit. At a dramatic crisis point in the project the rerecording mixer will then have the elements needed to "suffocate" the sound with an overwhelming presence of cars and car sounds.

The pacing of the actual movie was begun in the picture edit. But the sound design will add to the pacing as you build it. Little elements like those just discussed will go a long way in defining the aural pacing. Know the story, ideas, and emotions that the filmmaker is trying to convey. Use the sound design to heighten and illuminate those ideas.

All of this is project specific. But every project that can be made can use these ideas to define moods, feelings, and emotions. Try to think of those dynamics within the context of the story. Use the real world as a guide and fill things up from there. Many sounds can be enriched and enhanced with the final mixing. Brainstorm sonic ideas, run them past the filmmaker, and if you have access, run them by the rerecording mixer as well. Sometimes the filmmaker will resist but if the rerecording mixer gets what you are trying to do, perhaps you can create a small section to better define your efforts. Filmmakers respect and appreciate their collaborators going the extra mile. You may open a "sonic door" that they may not have thought of. Bring your top game to the process!

Using Dialogue Elements for Sound Design

This discussion so far has centered on sounds, whether recorded on location, copied from sound effects libraries or created from scratch. Although the dialogue track is the domain of the dialogue editor, dialogue elements are fair game for the sound designer.

Sound designers can make extensive use of the dialogue to help tell the story. They don't need to use the sync dialogue for these efforts. There will be crowd sounds and walla sounds that help the design of a project as well. The dialogue elements can be a key aspect of the sound design.

Many sound designers will use voices or human vocal sounds such as screams and yells as sound-design elements. I sound-designed a horror feature where I used the vocalizations of the lead actor as the basis for the movie's demon character. The director had very specific ideas about the soundtrack but was stumped as to what his demon would sound like. I have to say that I was a bit as well.

I began with a lot of the tried-and-true starting points, such as wolf howls, animals in pain, and the like. It wasn't getting me where I wanted to go. He wanted something unique and otherworldly. I tried synthesized sounds as well, but it wasn't quite right. By accident I had dropped some screaming I had recorded from an ADR session from the lead actor into the timeline. It was a pleading woman's yell. I spotted it over the demon, hit play, and I knew I had a direction to go in.

I then spent the next day combing through the ADR recordings finding a variety of vocalizations to alter for the demon. I found mean, pleading, angry, and satisfied vocalizations that I then transformed into other sounds. I was excited by the new sounds but hadn't yet auditioned them for the director. You just never know how they will react.

After discussing other audio matters on the design he asked if I had gotten anywhere with the demon. I said I had a thought or two, nothing written in stone, of course. I then played him what I thought was the best version of a sound for the demon. He sat wordless, emotionless, and said to play it again. And again. And again. Then his face cracked a smile and he told me to run with it. And so I did!

I then realized I had a gold mine of sounds in those earlier ADR sessions. This film took place "in her head," so I used the voices of other characters as elements within the design. After I built up these new tracks I played them against the picture with the "real" dialogue elements and the sound effects elements. The filmmaker made changes and cuts as expected, but he was also excited by new possibilities that were never in the script or in the picture edit. In fact, it was such a successful experiment with this project that we went ahead and recorded new screaming and moaning ADR just for this purpose. Never let a good "mistake" pass!

Sound Effects Libraries

Digital audio has provided the sound designer access to wonderful, clean and clear recordings. Prior to digital audio, analog copies had all sorts of audio issues. Hiss, crackles, hum, and just plain old noise were constant problems in analog transfers. Today's digital sound effects libraries are easily copied, transferred, and edited. The following section will discuss

- Hard Effects and Ambiences
- Processing the Library Sounds with Effects
- Time-Stretching Audio Files

Hard Effects and Ambiences

Hard effects are sounds that are specific to sync action on screen. A door slam, a knife cut, or gunshots are all considered hard effects. Ambiences, also called backgrounds, are more generic and, as noted, help define time and space.

Sound effects libraries excel at both of these types of recordings. With all of the advances with digital recording and capture, the sound quality of these recordings is better than ever. And since they are digital, they can be simply copied, imported, and pasted into timelines.

There are quite a few libraries that are commercially available today. These libraries can be incredibly inclusive, containing thirty, forty, or fifty volumes each. As previously mentioned, they can also be very specific, consisting of only weapons, for instance, or vehicles or period props. There are many varied and amazing recordings available to today's sound designer.

Sound libraries by themselves, with some creativity and excellent editing, will allow you to create realistic sound design. It is preferable to use Foley if possible simply because it is "made to order" but sound effects libraries, edited and mixed well can be quite convincing. Libraries will be needed even if Foley is available. Foley recordings cover the human sounds in a scene. But if there are scenes, for instance with cars, trains, or boats, libraries will need to be utilized. A Foley artist could do the walking on a deck, but a library will provide the boat motor sounds and the ocean splashes.

Sound effects libraries are also now available online "à la carte." That means that if you didn't want to buy a full weapons library, for instance, you could just buy the one machine gun sound that you need. This can be a very expensive way to buy sound effects, however. They may cost several dollars per minute, per sound effect. Although not particularly cost effective, if you are only looking for a single effect, it may be the way to go.

There are also volumes of libraries of ambiences. You could purchase ambiences of exotic locales such as rain forests, the tropics, or even the North Pole. There will also be many useful backgrounds such as a New York City street with traffic and people or a suburban neighborhood on a sunny day. Search for ambiences that are right for your project. They will add a subtle depth to the scenes in final mixing.

These recordings typically vary in length from one minute to three minutes. They serve as a sort of room tone. Edit several layers of similar and complimentary backgrounds for variety. If there were no location recordings made of ambiences, sometimes it is possible to create some in a manner similar to room tone creation.

Processing the Library Sounds with Effects

The sound edit is all in preparation for the sound mix. The rerecording mixer will further manipulate the layers, which you edited to picture. To heighten the experience of the backgrounds or atmospheres, they will apply various EQ and volume levels, creating variety. They may add reverb to affect the audio in various ways. It's important to understand the processes that the rerecording mixer can apply to give them the best edit possible.

Almost all of the sounds that we hear are affected in one way or another with reverberation. Sometimes editors and mixers use the terms *wet* and *dry*. These terms refer to the amount of an effect placed on an individual sound. A sound that is wet contains a lot of an effect, say a reverb, and a sound that is dry has no effect on it. Typically sound effects libraries are recorded dry, or as dry as possible considering the particular situation. This allows the rerecording mixer to add reverb to more than one track of sounds to create the illusion that all of the sound is occurring in the same place.

For instance, a scene is taking place in a parking garage. The voices have a lot of natural reverb due to the location. Let's say that the car door slams were not properly recorded on-set, so they were replaced by library door slams. It is imperative that the mixer finds a reverb similar to the location reverb that is affecting the voices to match the scene. Otherwise the illusion of the door slam will not work and will jar the audience out of the scene. Figure 11.3 is an example of a software reverberation device that uses a type of reverb called *impulse response*.

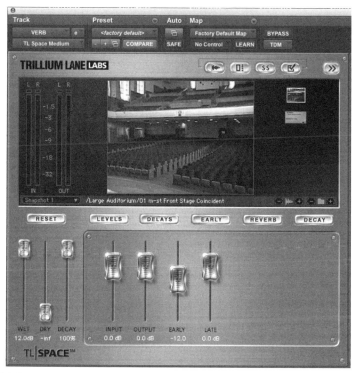

FIGURE 11.3 This is an extremely versatile, very high-quality impulse reverberation unit made by Trillium Lane Labs

Impulse responses are snapshots of the particular characteristics of a given space. This is an example of an impulse response of a specific auditorium. There are many impulse responses available today. You can also create your own impulse responses. Each system does it a bit differently but essentially a device will capture the reverb quality when a short, quick sound is created in the space. The reverb unit will then use the impulse response to create a reverb from that space.

Mixers will also use volume levels in a very skillful manner to achieve affects. They may slowly, almost imperceptibly add level as a scene progresses to achieve a crescendo of sorts. They may use volume to heighten the perspectives of distance. They will use a combination of volume and EQ and reverb to change musical tracks to sound as if they are coming from a radio, boom box, or television set.

Great sound designers will understand how a skillful rerecording mixer will use their layers of sound and create new sonic textures and soundscapes. Give them plenty of sounds to alter, manipulate, and mix; together you will help filmmakers finalize their vision of the project.

Time-Stretching Audio Files

Library sounds may not always match picture in a convincing manner. Manipulating sounds with time stretching can be a powerful way to alter them. Time stretching is a digital process that will transform your audio in length, making it longer or shorter, and in pitch, making it higher or lower. Most NLEs and DAWs offer some sort of time stretching.

There are a number of time-stretching tools that will work with NLEs or DAWs. Figure 11.4 is an example of a sound that has been time-stretched longer than the original file. This can be quite useful since some effects won't edit to sync.

Time stretching and digital audio can produce some very interesting effects as well. You can retain the pitch and quality of a sound source but slow the delivery down, or you can speed the delivery up without affecting the pitch. This can be useful on any number of sound sources including voices.

Time stretching does have its limitations, however. If the transformation is made to a piece of audio that is a blend of a number of different sound sources, then you can stretch things one way or another pretty far. One thing to note, however, is if it is used as a lead or central sound effect with very few other sounds around it, time stretching will need to be used creatively and sparingly. The use of

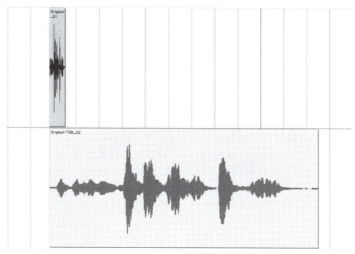

FIGURE 11.4 In this example the file has been stretched to over ten times its original length

time stretching in this sort of instance will limit the stretch to about only 10 or 15 percent one way or the other. The artifacting caused by the time stretching can change the audio in an unpleasant and often unusable way.

An option for using time stretching with minimal artifacts is to time-stretch pieces of something longer and then artfully crossfade the pieces. This can provide a deeper effect with less digital noise, but the quality of the sound itself will determine its ultimate time-stretching capabilities.

Building the Timeline

The edit timeline is the main repository of all of these wonderful sound elements. The sound designer has a task similar to the dialogue editor in that the edit timeline is being prepared for the rerecording mixer. The subjects included in the following section are

- Track Assignments and Preparing for the Final Output
- Preparing for the Mix and the Final Outputs

Track Assignments and Preparing for the Final Output

Rerecording mixers need to have their sessions laid out in an orderly and predictable manner. They all like to see their sessions set up in their own particular way, so it's always a good idea to check with the mixer if possible.

A good rule of thumb is to always have similar tracks organized together. For instance, keep the mono effects tracks grouped together, keep the stereo effects tracks grouped near them. Keep all of the Foley tracks together, and all of the backgrounds or all of the ambience tracks together.

It is very frustrating trying to find tracks that are scattered all over the timeline. By working in this manner, the rerecording mixer will be able to easily route these tracks to all of the output locations that are necessary. Also, while mixing, if all of the like tracks are in proximity to one another, then it will be easier for the mixer to mute and unmute the tracks that he or she may need.

Rerecording mixers will be in charge of every single recording that is on the timeline. If the mixer is not the person who built the edit, then it will take some time to learn all of the pieces that are available. It is important that the track layout and assignments facilitate an easy find for all of the elements at any given point in the mix to be able to clearly focus on the complete mix.

When the final edit is complete, the track count will fill up quickly with sound effects tracks, Foley tracks, ADR tracks, and all of the dialogue tracks, so it is an excellent practice to make the session easy to understand and well grouped.

Preparing for the Mix and the Final Outputs

We will be discussing the mix and the final outputs at length in a later chapter but I want to touch on it here as well, since all of these pieces fit into one whole, the final mix. The rerecording mixer will be splitting out all of these different elements into separate tracks. There will be the mix tracks that could be stereo mixes or surround mixes. These mix tracks will also be split up into their individual parts. This is important since the mixes may need to be repurposed later by the distributor. Figure 11.5 is an example of the output mix from a Pro Tools session. You can see the stereo tracks and also the individual components of the stereo mix.

The mixer will need to take the outputs of the edit tracks and send them to all of the various places to properly create the final mix files. For instance, the sound effects will need to be sent to the final mix output and also to an effects mix output as well as to a music and effects (M&E) mix output.

Depending on the delivery requirements, these outputs can get very complicated quickly. If everything has been properly arranged by the dialogue editor and the sound designer, then the job becomes a bit easier on the rerecording mixer, who will be responsible not only

FIGURE 11.5 In this example, the stereo mix is the top tracks and the stems are located beneath them

for the fantastic-sounding mix but also the mix outputs to be split as described.

All of this hard work has been leading up to the mixing of the project. The dialogue tracks have been cut at this point and the effects tracks have been built and have filled the gaps left from the original sound edit by the picture editor. In the following chapters we will discuss Foley and music and finally the mixing and outputs. Each step of this process is leading to those final sessions. The sound designer and the supervising sound editor are the ones who pull all of these elements together to assist the filmmaker in getting the exact aural universe that their project requires.

Summary

The sound design is the overall template for the final sonics of a project. The sound design process begins with the spotting session. Once the sound designer and the post audio team have a clear understanding of the project from the filmmaker they can begin to create that "vision." By using the location recordings and sound effects libraries to sweeten the scenes, the sound designer fills the timeline with all of the appropriate sounds necessary to create the desired soundtrack.

Sound designers use ambiences to define time and space. They will also create sounds if there is no real-life corollary to the needed sounds. They will use sound libraries in a creative and layered manner.

They will use drones and beds and room tones to create suspense. Sound design will help punctuate moments in scenes as well as help pace the scenes. Finally, the sound designer will assign all of the tracks in a simple manner so that the rerecording mixer can take all of those sounds and create a stunning, final mix.

Review Questions

Questions like these are likely to appear on exams to test how well you understood and retained the information in this chapter.

1. What is a spotting session and why is it important?
2. Why are ambiences useful in sound design and what illusion do they create?
3. What is the purpose of drones and beds?
4. When editing ambiences what special things should you check for? Are there special editing concerns as well?
5. Why should a sound designer understand the rerecording mixing process?

Discussion/Essay Questions

Your instructor may assign you one or more of the following questions for discussion in class or as the subject of a paper.

1. Describe a spotting session. How will you communicate ideas with the filmmaker to best design the project?
2. Describe how you would approach designing the sound for a movie. What steps would you take, what materials will you use, and how would you create the edit?

Applying What You've Learned

Research/Lab/Fieldwork Projects

NOTE
Students who have ongoing projects may elect to use their own source material, such as video clips, with the instructor's permission.

The following lab exercises will give you practice working with sound design.

1. Add ambiences from your location recordings under an edited scene.
2. Add "hard effects" to an edited scene.
3. Add library effects to sweeten an edited scene.

Resources

The following resources have more information on the topics covered in this chapter.

Dave Whittaker, "How to Do Some Quick and Dirty Sound Design Without Getting Any Dirt Under Your Fingernails," *Motion Picture Editors Guild Newsletter* 6, no. 6 (Nov/Dec 1995) (http://www .editorsguild. com/v2/magazine/Newsletter/pt-quicksd. html). This is a terrific article written by a professional picture editor about some Pro Tools tricks and tips.

Sven Carlsson, "The Sound Design of Star Wars," FilmSound. org (http://filmsound. org/starwars/). This is a fascinating and comprehensive account of the some of the iconic sonics of the Star Wars movies.

CHAPTER 12

THE FOLEY PROCESS

OVERVIEW AND LEARNING OBJECTIVES

In this chapter, you will:
- Understand the Foley process
- Learn about the history of Foley
- Learn to record Foley

Understanding the Foley Process

Foley is the re-creation and rerecording of all of the human sounds in a motion picture or television program. The Foley art came into being just at the time that "talkies" became the new paradigm for the motion picture industry. A *Foley artist* is a highly skilled performer who mimics the action on-screen and recreates the sounds produced by that action.

Over the years Foley has been refined to not only mimic the actions of characters on-screen, it is now a key part of the storytelling process in sound. The Foley process consists of several important steps and several key individuals. There is the Foley recordist, who is responsible for running the recording session. There is the Foley artist, who will perform all of the activities required to match the on-screen movements. There is the Foley editor, who will take the recordings and cut the actions to better match sync with the picture edit and prepare them for final mixing. Finally, there is the rerecording mixer, who will take the edited tracks and blend them seamlessly with all of the other edited audio tracks into the final mixed soundtrack.

As with so many of the audio duties that are detailed in this text, in the DIY filmmaking world, all of these duties may be tasked to just one individual. Foley in particular, however, is a tough one to do alone. No matter the size of the team completing the work, Foley is a challenging, dynamic, creative, and labor-intensive part of the audio post process. The topics discussed in the following section are

- Jack Foley
- Location Recordings and Foley
- A Performer Acting in Sync with the Picture Edit
- A Recording Session That Mimics the Production Quality

Jack Foley

The term *Foley* comes from the man who created and developed the process for Universal Studios, Jack Foley. Jack Foley was an athlete, a writer, a Hollywood stuntman, and a silent film director, among many other exploits. One of the first documented sessions of "Foley" recording came during a sound recording session for a Universal motion picture called *Showboat*. *Showboat* was originally released as a silent film. It was competing with *The Jazz Singer*, one of the first "talkie" motion pictures.

Universal understood that they had to compete in the marketplace with their own "talking films." For the film *Showboat* Jack Foley was tasked with re-creating the sounds of the actors while a full orchestra was also being recorded for the score. During his tenure at Universal Studios, Foley came to perfect this process of recording human sounds after the picture edit.

People at the time were amazed at his ability to use a cane to mimic the sounds of several people walking. He also developed a technique of rubbing cloths together to better mimic character's movements. He loved to do the walking aspect of the work but found walking for women to be particularly difficult. It wasn't the fact that he was two hundred and fifty pounds; he could mimic their gait, it was just that they walked so fast it got him winded!

Jack Foley was a pioneer of film sound. Eventually the techniques he developed were adopted, adapted, and refined by others. His real gift was that he performed as if he were the actor on-screen, and he imbued his actions with purpose and meaning. His last name has become the term for the work of legions of film professionals. He was eventually awarded a Golden Reel Career Achievement Award from the Motion Picture Sound Editors Guild for his contributions to film art.

Location Recordings and Foley

Since the recordings of character's movements are so important why not just use what is captured on-set? As you now know, the key to excellent location recording is to get the microphone pointed at the actor's mouths to capture clean dialogue. This being the case, microphones are rarely, if ever, pointed at an actor's feet.

Many of the types of sounds that occur during location recording are either not properly miked or are obscured by the dialogue itself. The dialogue editor will painstakingly create a production effects track (PFX), but since most of the location action will be masked by the dialogue, the PFX will be incomplete.

Foley will be created and used for several reasons. First, it can be used to sweeten the location audio tracks to heighten moments in scenes or focus the storytelling. Foley is also used extensively for the augmentation of a music and effects track (M&E) that will allow the project to be dubbed into other languages for international distribution.

Foley is also a major component in animation. Imagine *SpongeBob SquarePants* or *Ratatouille* with only dialogue and music. Those cartoons are far richer with all of the mimicked human sounds and actions created and recorded by a Foley team. Obviously the "location audio" for cartoons will not provide a suitable PFX!

A Performer Acting in Sync with the Picture Edit

Foley artists are a special breed of performers. They are usually not actors but they are typically very athletic and physically agile. They will cover all of the action occurring in any given project. Foley can be not only a physically demanding job, but also one of deep concentration. Foley artists are glued to the screen to properly understand the dynamics of a given scene and re-create its emotional qualities and perform it in sync.

Prior to the Foley recording session, the Foley artist may watch the project or at least at a minimum understand the basic actions to be performed for the session. They will need to know exactly what action is to be covered for the scenes and will, typically, bring all of their own specialized "tools" to the session. A Foley artist's bag of tools is different from most. It is generally filled with the types of things you might find at a thrift store or a garage sale. They will bring along shoes, clothing, papers, and hinges. They will bring bags of leaves or twigs, creaky

FIGURE 12.1 Just about any prop can and will be used for the numerous productions that go through a busy Foley stage

chairs, balls, bags, or whatever is required to fulfill the action in a scene to be recorded. Figure 12.1 is an example of a Foley props room.

A Recording Session That Mimics the Production Quality

This concept is one we've explored while recording ADR. It is very important that the sound elements that are used or created after the location shooting is complete match the quality of the production tracks. Today's audiences are very sophisticated. They have gotten very used to high-quality audio and images. When things don't match they will spot it and their minds will wander away from the story being told. Our goal is to fool them into believing that the story is unfolding right before their eyes. Technical matters will adversely affect their enjoyment of the story.

Many of the same rules and strategies apply as in recording ADR. It is a great idea to use the same or similar equipment to record the Foley that was used on-set. Many times Foley is recorded with shotgun microphones placed at similar distances and perspectives as the images on-screen.

Foley recording is a highly skilled craft. There is also a deep collaboration between the recordist and the Foley artist. The recordist and the Foley artist must determine a way of working that captures the essence of the movements as well as the quality of the location recordings and work in a coordinated and relatively quick manner. Unless the production is an expensive Hollywood feature, most shows don't have the time or the budget to do weeks of Foley recording and editing.

The Foley Session

Foley sessions are fun, creative, and labor-intensive work. The qualities of the recordings have to be similar to the production tracks, the action being recorded must be in sync with the cut picture track, and the tracks must be recorded and arranged and assigned in an orderly and predictable way for the rerecording mixer. The ideas explored in this section are

- How to Record a Foley Session
- What Do You Record
- Acting "Human Sounds" in Sync to Picture
- Additional Foley Considerations
- Microphone Placement
- The Cloth Pass
- Editing Foley Recordings
- Mixing

How to Record a Foley Session

There are a number of things that must be available and prepared for a proper Foley recording session. There has to be a final version of the cut picture for the Foley artist to watch to re-create the action. The recording space, ideally, will have a separate control room and recording booth for the recordist and for the Foley artist to do the work. The Foley artist should be prepared with all of the props that will be necessary to match the on-screen action. The recordist should be using the same or similar equipment to create the recordings. The recording room should be a quiet, controlled space so that the only thing being recorded is the action on-screen. No birds, traffic, or air-conditioning please!

> **TIP**
>
> Meet with and discuss the scenes with the Foley artist prior to the session. Foley artists are creative, sound-obsessed individuals. Typically they will supply a great deal of the props that will be needed for the session. Describe the scenes and determine what props they don't have that will be needed for the session. These creative professionals can make the unlikeliest of items into sound sources. For one session I needed a skateboard. The Foley artist did not have one and neither did I. I was almost out the door to buy one when he called to ask if I had a paint roller. With a thin piece of plywood and a paint roller we had all the skateboard sounds that were required. Always check with them first. You will be surprised with the creative solutions they will devise to create sounds.

The booth where Foley is performed is sometimes called a *Foley stage*. Foley stages are usually large rooms that can hold many different

FIGURE 12.2 Notice the various surfaces that include wood, sand, gravel, and concrete

types of props and can provide distance and recording perspective. Foley stages are unique in that they are built with various surfaces covering the floor. These surfaces are typically concrete, wood, carpet, tile, linoleum and dirt. They often also have pits that may be filled with sand or gravel or water. Pits can also be used as a safe place to record breaking glass or breaking bottles. Figure 12.2 shows the surfaces on the Foley stage of Chace Audio by Deluxe in Burbank, California.

Typically, during most Foley recording sessions, the Foley artist is in charge of placing the microphone. When recording Foley, it is not practical for the recordist to keep moving from the control room to the stage to reset the microphone. They would have to set the mic, get back and listen to its placement in the control room, and then rearrange until it's correct. From the point of view of logistics, it would be prohibitively time-consuming to work in this manner.

In consultation with the Foley recordist, the Foley artist will move the microphone for each recording. This way the recordist can critically listen to the microphone placement and make suggestions until things are set just right. They can also change microphone positions for various recordings quickly. Figure 12.3 shows the microphone near the action being performed by the Foley artist.

The Foley artist, in collaboration with the recordist, will determine the flow and movement of the session. Each artist has his or her own way of working and will cover things in a particular order. Also, if a particular prop is used throughout the project, it may be better to do all of those elements together. For instance, if there is a particular prop whose sound is important through different scenes, perhaps a specific footfall of a character with a broken shoe, it may be better to do all of those scenes together and then go back to get the other sounds required later.

NOTE

The same rules apply for microphone placement for Foley as for all of the other recordings we've discussed. Ideally you want to get the microphone in close for a nice clean recording. There is no hard-and-fast rule, of course. If the recording needs perspective, then the microphone will need to be adjusted accordingly.

FIGURE 12.3 Foley artist Monique Reymond pours liquid in a glass after adjusting the microphone in consultation with the Foley recordist

One Foley artist may like to start with a *cloth pass*. A cloth pass is a mimic of the sounds of the characters' clothing as they perform action in a given scene. Clothing movement can create a substantial amount of sound. There is a resulting sound as pant legs rub together, there are sounds as characters touch or rub or scratch, and there is the sound of clothing as individuals move around within a scene. Some Foley artists like to record a cloth pass first because it allows them to get a feel for all of the various movements and actions in the scene.

Some artists prefer to walk the characters first. Foley walking is a very important part of the Foley process. Foley artists tend to bring many pairs of shoes to these recording sessions. They will have a wide assortment of men's and women's shoes. The artist and the recordist will plan out the surfaces and the microphone placement for each of the walking sequences. Many scenes are simply one or two people walking. But there can be scenes that require many different individuals walking and will require a strategy to complete the recordings. Figure 12.4 is an example of a Foley artist walking a character.

Bear in mind that these recordings need to be "clean." The process is about recording the actions and not the sounds of the Foley artist. This is more difficult than you might think. No stomach gurgles, coughs, sneezes, or exertions are to be contained in these recordings. Unless that is what you are recording!

Critical listening skills are required of the recordist to be on the lookout for any of these intrusive noises. Sometimes simply the performance of a particular action will invoke unwanted noises. Listen carefully for a swinging headphone cable hitting a microphone stand or the inadvertent tapping of a microphone stand while running and recording big body

FIGURE 12.4 In this example the character on-screen is running down a gravel road

movements. Make an effort to get only the actual recordings needed to minimize the editing time once everything has been properly recorded.

What Do You Record

Sometimes when discussing a project with someone I am told that they need a "little bit of Foley and a little bit of ADR." As should be clear by now, there is no such thing as a "little bit" of either of these highly skilled tasks. Even if only one scene of two characters is to be completely rerecorded with ADR and Foley, it will still consume a lot of time, energy, and effort.

When budgets are tight, often only very limited Foley sessions occur. When complete scenes have been rerecorded with ADR, then at a bare minimum, all of the human sounds in those scenes will need to be recorded. Other than that, with limited Foley recording time, projects will only Foley the scenes that can be enriched or heightened with additional Foley sweetening. Typically, however, when producing an M&E soundtrack, all of the human sounds get recorded for every scene in a motion picture or television program.

The purpose of an M&E track is to provide all of the sounds on-screen without the dialogue tracks. This will allow the distributor to rerecord the dialogue in other languages for international markets. International sales can make up a large chunk of the profits of these programs, so a proper M&E track is essential to be released into these other markets.

Let's have a look at what a typical session may be like. For instance, the scene to be Foleyed is a scene taking place between a husband and wife in their home at dinnertime. The husband arrives home, walks in, and hangs his jacket in the hall closet, and walks into the dining room.

The wife has just finished setting the table and walks back into the kitchen to grab a large salad bowl and bring it to the dining table. The husband in the meantime puts his keys on a console in the room and starts rifling through the day's mail found there. He grabs a couple of letters and then walks over to the dining table and pours himself a glass of wine and sits. He takes a gulp of wine and opens one of the letters. The wife comes back in from the kitchen with two plates of steaming food.

This short scene is a typical domestic scene in a motion picture or television program. It is a simple enough scene, with maybe twelve or fifteen picture cuts to tell the scene. Perhaps there is a lot of dialogue between the characters as well. If you were thinking about the Foley process as I described the scene, you probably had a pretty good sense of the complexity of the sounds to be recorded. How would we approach this recording session and what do we need?

If the Foley artist wanted to start with the cloth pass, perhaps it could be the male character. Watching the following action they will rub cloth in sync with the scene, mimicking the actions of the character's clothing movements. For instance, the man is wearing a suit and his pants will rub together as he walks. Then he removes his coat and hangs it up on a hanger. Since we are only doing the cloth on this pass the closet and the hanger and any other prop incidentals will be recorded separately later. He then walks over to the console and is looking through the mail. All of these actions make noise as he moves through the scene. He pours the wine, sits, and so on, each of these will make specific movement sounds, starting and stopping with each movement of the arms or legs.

The wife is also moving around. Let's say that she is wearing a dress of thin cotton. Each one of her actions will also produce sound as well. Moving in and out of the room, placing props and so on. So a full cloth pass will be required for her actions as well.

Perhaps next you will cover the footsteps. Starting with the man, you will follow the action of his walking in, stopping to put away his coat, then walking again to the console and finally to the dining table. Move on to the woman's footfalls next. Hers may be a bit trickier. Let's say the dining room has carpeting and the kitchen is linoleum. Her footstep sounds must move from the clack of the linoleum back to carpet back to linoleum and back to carpet again.

Now move on to each of the individual sounds within the scene. These recordings can sometimes be called *specifics*. They are the specific props that are being handled for the scene. The Foley artist will mimic and record each property's sounds. In this case, the woman is placing the food on the table. The man enters and opens a closet door, perhaps makes a bit of noise with the hangers. He then moves over to the console, leaves a jangle of keys and shuffles through mail.

CASE STUDY: MONIQUE REYMOND— FOLEY ARTIST

Monique Reymond is an award-winning Hollywood Foley artist. She offers a few thoughts about her work.

On Collaborating with a Recordist

"Whoever is recording the Foley has a very heavy influence on the creative process. I don't really know how to articulate how important the recordist is in the entire process. Usually we will have a discussion as to what we are going to cover first or what we think is the most important thing and we will do that first. If there is something that is a really key prop that's used over and over and over again, then that's something that we really want to establish. Sometimes we will record that in its entirety throughout the film all at once for consistency's sake.

"I can't always tell how the microphone is picking up what I'm doing and I heavily rely on the recordist's judgment. I work with a bunch of different types of engineers. Some are mixers who have truly taken it to an art form, they EQ and modulate and do all sorts of things. Others that I work with just do straight recording, but are very picky about my interpretation of what I am doing. The people that I work with are really quite incredible."

On Tools of the Trade

"I've got a small portable kit that I bring with me. Things are basically categorized into like materials. I have a backpack with various papers in it such as photos, newspaper, cellophane, wax paper, etc. I've got different clothes that I carry with me such as a leather jacket, a nylon windbreaker, denim, etc. I've got about forty pairs of shoes. I have a Foley purse with some stuff in it that rattles in a kind of cool way. I've got a lot of metal things, some hinges and wood, glass, plastic and rubber items. It's really great when you can find something that squeaks or creaks. It's invaluable stuff to me.

"Lately, my favorite props are a couple of pillowcases filled with cornstarch, which I use for snow. Cornstarch has a nice screech and creak to it. The crunch sounds like snow. It also works really well for body falls in animation. If somebody falls in sand, it's got a nice feel of "loft" to it, and it's more of an interesting sound than just using sand, for example.

"A chamois has been a versatile and useful tool for me. When you get them wet, they make lots of cool, dimensional, gushing sounds. I also get a lot of mileage out of a pinecone. I can step on a pinecone and the cracking of it can sound like ice breaking. If the pinecone is worn down a bit and I manipulate my fingers on it, it can sound like little bug legs. It can sound like all sorts of things. It's a secret favorite of mine. I remember telling a recordist I worked with, 'don't tell anybody about the pinecone.'"

Each and every one of his actions described gets covered in detail. Then all of the woman's actions get covered in detail. There is not a moment of movement that won't get covered in this scene. And this is just one "simple" scene. Now magnify that with every scene in a motion picture and you can see the scope of the work the Foley process entails. For an interview with a working Hollywood Foley artist see the accompanying sidebar, Case Study: Monique Reymond.

Acting "Human Sounds" in Sync to Picture

Foley artistry is an extremely creative and demanding skill. They are expert mimics, but they also excel at hearing the layers of sound in the real world. When a Foley artist walks a character, they are re-creating a performance, and it isn't merely stepping one foot after another. The feet may start and stop with a scuff here and a clomp there. The Foley has to match the performance. Figure 12.5 is Monique Reymond at work on a Foley stage.

Foley is to the sound effects track what ADR is to the dialogue track. Hence, the same issues face the Foley team. The Foley has to be performed with the same emotions and intention as the location recording but also, of course matching sync. It doesn't matter if the Foley artist is a five-foot-tall woman and the character she is walking is a six-foot-ten-inch man in cowboy boots. That walking performance must match the scene.

This is where the real gift of Foley artistry lies. A single Foley artist must portray a small child playing or a large man, drunkenly walking, and even a dog or a bug scampering along a wooden floor. These and countless other sorts of characters and situations must be believably performed by the Foley artist.

FIGURE 12.5 Car doors are useful Foley props

FIGURE 12.6 Many types of shoes and boots are required to walk a range of characters

All of the props in a scene are moved with emotion and feeling. It is not a rote mimicking of actions. All of these movements and events are imbued with the feelings of the actor's performance and must be re-created appropriately. Foley artists' gear usually consists of men's boots and shoes, women's shoes and heels, and all sorts of doodads that make funny little noises. Ask any professional Foley artist about the props they've acquired and they will focus on one quality, the emotions that can be wrung out of them. Figure 12.6 is an example of different footwear used for Foley walking.

Additional Foley Considerations

Recording Foley is a methodical undertaking. Capturing the re-creation of the sounds of human action performed in sync with a motion picture or a television program can be a challenge. There are some practical ideas that can assist the Foley session's success. The following section will examine

- Microphone Placement
- The Cloth Pass
- Editing Foley Recordings
- Mixing

Microphone Placement

The quality of the Foley recording depends on the performance of the action by the Foley artist and the proper microphone placement.

FIGURE 12.7 In this example, characters on-screen are fighting with swords

Foley recording is a highly creative collaboration. The types of the actions and recordings can run the gamut from tiptoeing up the stairs to running through a forest, to pulling up the covers to fighting a fearsome dragon. Since the Foley process records several passes for key props, the Foley artist doesn't need to be an expert swordsman Figure 12.7 shows a foley sword session to achieve the effect.

Microphone placement is key when mimicking the perspective of the on-screen action. Feet are generally walking to and from places. Experiment and find the ideal location to mimic not only the perspective of the walking, for instance, but also the appropriate sound of the flooring. It's more than just walking on a wood surface; it's the type of shoe, the weight and gait of the character, and the sound of the room they are walking in, which sometimes is not quite the sound of the room the Foley is being recorded in. In Figure 12.8 the large Foley room diffuses the sound to better create the illusion of being outdoors.

Moving the microphone just slightly in one direction or the other can completely change the character of the sound. Experiment with the placements for optimal recordings.

Proper microphone placement can also reduce and minimize the effects of an acoustically inferior recording space. Perhaps there is a reverberation that is adversely affecting the recordings. By close miking the action you can reduce the amount of "room" captured. Close miking also gives the advantage of proximity effect that can give a sound a feeling of "depth" or "weight" and "intimacy" to the recording.

FIGURE 12.8 In this example characters are jumping over cars and fences fleeing the police

Sometimes Foley sounds are used to heighten the mood of a suspenseful scene. Imagine a scene in a thriller feature film; there is a woman, barely breathing, balancing quietly on a floor filled with broken glass, while a killer is approaching. Each time her weight shifts, the glass makes a sound.

The way that the glass is recorded in Foley will be a key factor in the final mixing of the scene. If there is a tight close-up shot of her heels as she totters on the glass shards, then a hot, clean recording of that glass could be ideal. Get the microphone right next to the glass in the Foley pit to induce a fingernail-biting recording of a glass crunch. The Foley artist and the recordist have many opportunities to be original and unique in their recordings.

Foley is also, often, recorded with two microphones, one is used for close up and the other, typically a shotgun, is used for perspective. As with all things having to do with production and postproduction, every situation is unique. The Foley team will use the tools at hand to create excellent recordings within the context of their particular situation.

The Cloth Pass

Digital filmmaking, whether it's reality television, motion pictures, documentaries, or any type of project in between is made of many different parts. Some parts are recorded on location; some parts are recorded, created, or re-created later. There are not many contiguous audio moments in an edited project other than the room tone and the musical score.

The cloth pass is an audio element that is typically recorded through an entire scene. The cloth pass, if recorded properly, can act as an additional room tone track. It provides a constant sound, throughout any given scene. The cloth pass can be a very valuable track in the mixing process. It is one more element that provides continuity between cuts.

Some filmmakers will forgo a cloth pass in Foley. I recommend always recording a cloth pass, even if there will be no other Foley recording for any particular scene. There is a wonderful intimacy in a cloth pass. For a rerecording mixer, to have that track available can often be invaluable. It can capture intimate moments in life. Imagine a heart-wrenching scene of a breakup. At the end of an emotional scene all you can hear is the slight swishing of pants walking away. These sorts of subliminal sounds exist in our everyday life. By having this track, those sounds can be heightened to increase the emotional impact of the scene.

Editing Foley Recordings

Foley artists are very skilled at getting the proper sync for the actions on-screen that they are re-creating. However, just by nature of the process, there is an inevitable lag from time to time. Foley recordings can be a couple of frames behind the action. This is due to the fact that the Foley artist is reacting to the action.

Cutting sync in Foley is no different than cutting sync with any sound effects. A knife hit, a body fall, or high heels on tile should all match the sync of the on-screen performance. When Foley recordings do not match, they need to be nudged to properly align the sync.

Foley recordings will often contain additional items that will need to be edited out. The Foley artist may laugh or gasp at the end of an extreme action or may be talking as the recording is just starting. Obviously, Foley tracks need to be clean of any such intrusions and contain only the recording of the action itself.

Many NLE and DAW programs allow for *locking*. Locking tracks puts them in a state that can keep them safe from additional changes. Once you have cleaned, edited, and synced all of the Foley recordings, it is a good idea to lock those recordings. This way, as you continue working on other elements or prepare for final mixing, you are not inadvertently knocking sync on edited tracks.

Foley professionals do an excellent job of performing and maintaining sync. They will often request an additional recording when they feel that they can offer better sync as well as a better performance. Completed Foley tracks can be high in number and contain a great deal of minute recordings. Be sure to watch and listen to all of them and take the time that is needed to properly sync the Foley recordings. A rerecording mixer will use those tracks for the final mixing. Properly recorded and synced Foley tracks are expected when they reach final mixing.

Mixing

Foley mixing entails many of the same strategies as were applied for ADR mixing. The main tools utilized are the EQ, compressor/limiters, and reverb devices. This makes sense because the recordings are created the same way as ADR is, in a booth, performing with a screen.

The Foley tracks, after they've been neatly edited and placed in perfect sync, will be ready to be mixed into the scenes. You will need to spot the Foley with the filmmaker to determine the extent required of the Foley. Often much of the Foley that is recorded is not used in the final soundtrack. Now is the time to get clarity on the extent of its use. You don't want to carefully mix footsteps only to discover the scene will played with music only.

The strategy is to make the Foley tracks sound as if they were recorded in the same room as the all of the location audio. You will use a frequency analyzer to determine the inherent EQ qualities of both the Foley recording and the location tracks. Then use an EQ device to better match their qualities.

One of the key processes required for believable Foley mixing is a sparse but judicious use of reverberation. If there are characters walking briskly through a large reverberant space, then the Foley walking should sound very wet with reverb. Dry walking will not match, and even if it is in perfect sync the audience will not accept it. They may not have ever heard of reverberation, but they will know that the recordings don't match. The key to the proper use of reverb is to find a close match to production. Be sure to use it very lightly. Unless you are going for an effect on the Foley, other worlds or dreamlike, stay as realistic as possible so the tracks blend rather than stand out.

Summary

Foley is a fascinating, labor-intensive, highly creative skill. Typically, there is a minimum crew of two, the Foley artist and the Foley recordist. The Foley process can be broken into a couple of major categories. They can be described as the cloth pass, the walking, and the specific properties actions. These elements will be broken into as many different tracks and performances as are necessary for the sounds required to be captured for each character in each scene in a motion picture or television program.

The Foley team will cover all of the human sounds in any given scene in a project. The Foley artist is typically in charge of placing the microphone on the Foley stage at the direction of the recordist. The Foley artist will provide props that are necessary for the project such as shoes, handbags, and other small items. The Foley stage will have surfaces for walking and larger items such as car doors, tables. and chairs.

Once all of the scenes have been fully recorded a Foley editor will trim and sync all of the performances to picture. Then a Foley mixer will mix the Foley tracks to blend them seamlessly with the location audio.

Review Questions

Questions like these are likely to appear on exams to test how well you understood and retained the information in this chapter.

1. What gets recorded at a typical Foley session?
2. What is a cloth pass and what are specifics?
3. Who is in charge of microphone placement and why?
4. What is Walter Murch's "Law of Two and a Half?"
5. What is a Foley stage and what sorts of things will you find there?

Discussion/Essay Questions

Your instructor may assign you one or more of the following questions for discussion in class or as the subject of a paper.

1. What types of on-screen actions are typically performed by a Foley artist?

   Discuss a typical Foley session describing the functions of the recordist as well as the functions of the Foley artist.
2. What are the differences between Foley tracks and the sound effects tracks?

Applying What You've Learned

Research/Lab/Fieldwork Projects

The following lab exercises will give you practice working with Foley recording.

1. Determine the props, shoes and specific requirements to Foley an edited scene.
2. Record the various elements of the scene with your Foley artist.
3. Edit these new recordings into the scene.

> **NOTE**
> Students who have ongoing projects may elect to use their own source material, such as video clips, with the instructor's permission.

Resources

The following resources have more information on the topics covered in this chapter.

Philip Rodrigues Singer, MPSE, "The Art of Foley." (http://www.marblehead.net/foley). This site is filled with excellent articles and links.

Woody's Sound Advice (http://woodyssoundadvice.com/category/interviews/). This is the interviews page of my sound blog. Here you can find an in-depth interview with Monique Reymond. There are also interviews with a dialogue editor, a music editor, a feature film director, a location recordist, and more.

CHAPTER 13

THE MUSIC SCORE

OVERVIEW AND LEARNING OBJECTIVES

In this chapter, you will:
- Learn to create a temporary music score
- Learn how to work with composers
- Learn how to work with library music
- Learn about scoring software

Creating a Temporary Music Score

Music is a major part of just about any motion picture or television soundtrack. In many cases it is a major component in the final mix. Great cinema composers are renowned artists in their own right. The power of marrying music with moving images is profound. Music has such a pull on our emotions and feelings that it is often used to mask deficiencies in either the storytelling or the performances. In fact, most producers will go so far as to not show any edit of a project until there is some sort of music included to at least indicate the emotional feeling of scenes.

During the editing phase of a project the first step for adding music is called the *temporary score*. A temp score is a score created from bits and pieces of already produced music tracks that serve as the score until it is replaced by the final tracks. The ideas explored in the following section are

- A Template for the Final Musical Soundtrack
- Pacing the Picture Edit

A Template for the Final Musical Soundtrack

Big budget Hollywood features employ an editor who is known as the *music editor*. A music editor is the liaison between the director, the composer, and the sound-editing team. The first task before the music editor is to create a temp score for the project. Often, music editors are working on a project prior to a composer.

Music editors can be brought on early by picture editors who don't have the time or inclination to deal with the music or by the supervising sound editor. They will watch the program, and in collaboration with the editor or the director they will decide what the emotional qualities of the scenes are and match them with musical scores for the project.

Because the temp score is only used as a reference for the final soundtrack, it is all right to use commercially available scores, and this has become standard procedure. The advantage for major motion pictures is that they can temp a James Horner score using James Horner's previous scores, and then have James Horner write a new score for this one!

If you are tasked with being the music editor for the project and have never done it before, there are a few things to consider. To begin with, it is important to understand the type of score that will eventually be conceived and written for the program. If the eventual score will be a string quartet, it wouldn't be wise to temp the score with rock and roll music.

Discuss with the filmmakers the various types of music that they desire for the soundtrack. Once the style and genre of music has been decided, then it is time to explore composers whose *oeuvre* matches the desired style. *Oeuvre* is a term that means the body of work of a composer. Explore the music and moods of various composers' scores to determine suitable music pieces to temp into the sound edit.

Most feature-length projects will require a substantial amount of music in varying moods. Spot the project with the filmmakers to determine where they think music tracks and score elements are needed. Try to elicit emotional descriptions for the music requirements. Ask the filmmakers if the moments should feel "sad," "foreboding," "mysterious," or "joyous." These words mean different things to different people. Be sure to define the moods and feelings to create a temp score appropriately. Figure 13.1 is an example of a temporary music score edited into Pro Tools.

A good way of working is to make a map of the requirements for the temp score. For instance, one scene may require a "mysterious" bed of music for two minutes, then it is followed by thirty seconds of music that has a "sense of motion" and finally ending with a fifteen-second bit of music that has a "sense of resolution."

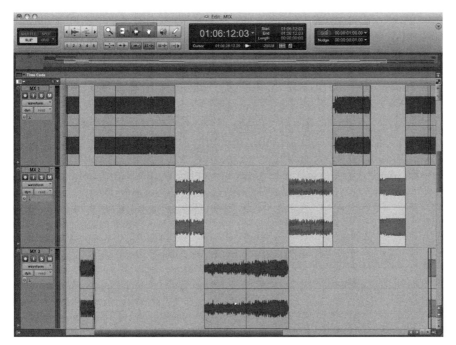

FIGURE 13.1 In this example three sets of alternating music tracks are used for the temp score

Those are all very vague and hard-to-quantify qualities. Although you may have diligently noted and sought these emotional qualities, they may actually differ from those of the filmmaker.

What I try to do is find many types of music in the style desired, with the emotional qualities desired. I will then cut the various pieces of music into the sound edit and play them with the sound elements as well as the picture. You just will never know how it will work out until the music and picture are playing together. The marriage of music and images is a miraculous thing. Suddenly, slow camera moves gain importance and scenes that didn't seem to play well are imbued with majesty, horror, or joy, depending on the scene and the music.

I cannot express strongly enough the need to play the music tracks against the picture. It is a good idea to audition a whole range of tracks. It can be a surprising thing when one piece of music that should be perfect doesn't play properly and another that seems too "light," too "strong," or too "happy" actually fits the moment just right. You won't know until the two are married together for a look and listen.

Once the moments that require music have been spotted to the picture, you will begin to add temp music cues into the edit timeline. It is a good idea to meet with the filmmakers once you've started choosing music tracks. Play a couple of scenes to verify that you are indeed on the right track.

As a beginning sound editor I once created a temp score for a "road movie." The director was not available, and the postproduction supervisor wanted me to begin regardless. The film was about two characters running from the law, and I created a gritty rock score to play throughout the project. When the director came back into the country to have a listen, he informed the team that he actually would prefer classical music to act as a counterpoint to the action.

Be sure to understand the requirements of your individual project and listen to a lot of music. Even though the temp is temporary, the filmmakers will still want it to be an accurate representation of what they "hear" for the score.

Pacing the Picture Edit

Just as an example, take any narrative scene that is playing on the television. Turn on some music. Turn off the sound on the television. In a short amount of time you will find that the music, whatever it is, will "match" the scene on the TV. It may be a fleeting match—maybe a cut will line up to a beat or a slow zoom-in will match a build in the music. Try it again with another scene and choose a different music track. It probably isn't perfect, but you can immediately see that the addition of music to an edited picture sequence can be magical.

An excellent music score will not only create moods and feelings but will also change the feel of the edit. Scenes that played "too long" without music may now feel just right. Perhaps the scenes were missing some feeling of forward motion; music can help create a feeling of movement.

Music makes extensive use of *hit points*. Hit points are moments in scenes where the music is used as an accent in the scene. For instance, perhaps there is a fighting scene and drums are used to accent each hit. Hit points are very common and will pace a scene to its ultimate conclusion.

Directors will try to describe the feel of the music required for any given scene. Often, the terms they use will relate to the pacing of the action. One scene may require a "feeling of motion" and another scene may need to feel very "still and mysterious." These descriptions indicate how the scene should pace for the audience.

Watch a scene from an action movie. Listen to the musical score. Is the music pushing the scene forward? Is the music driving the scene and creating a feeling of "motion"? Watch a scene from a horror movie. What is the music doing there? Is it creating a feeling of pacing as well as a feeling of "foreboding"? Watch a series of scenes, from a number of different genres. Watch romantic comedies, science fiction, and thrillers, and listen to how the music score is used to move the story.

Critically listen to award-winning motion pictures. You will discover that the music score is pulling the audience in one direction or another. Seek out the world's premiere film composers and listen to their works. You will find artists such as Bernard Herrmann, who composed the music for Alfred Hitchcock's *Psycho* as well as five other Hitchcock films. You will find John Williams, who has worked extensively with Steven Spielberg, creating scores for films like *ET* and the iconic theme for *Jaws*. You'll find Ennio Morricone, who created a type of music for a whole subgenre of films called "Spaghetti Westerns." His classic score for *The Good, the Bad and the Ugly* has inspired scores and themes for many other films.

Working with Composers

Composers write the musical scores for motion picture and television projects. Typically, composers are brought on near the end of the editing process. Often they will use the temp score as a starting point for their musical compositions. Like all artists, each composer brings his or her own strengths to the effort. Some will be skilled at orchestral music, others at hip hop. Although they will be writing the actual music, you, as the music editor, will direct their efforts to match the ideas that fit the concept for the show. The following topics in the this section are

- The Temporary Score
- Choosing Instrumentation
- Tempos and Key Signatures
- Composer's Agreements

The Temporary Score

As described earlier, the picture editor or a music editor will take the first pass at the musical score. This is just a starting point for the composer, of course. It becomes an excellent way to pre-spot the project for a composer. The temporary score will note the desired spotting of the musical cues and the general feeling and moods needed for particular moments in the project.

The composer will use the temp score to create a kind of language with which to communicate with the filmmaker. Most filmmakers are not composers or musicians, so descriptive words are often used in place of compositional terms. For instance, a filmmaker might not know what a diminished chord is, but if this chord appears in a cue on the temp score, the filmmaker may explain to the composer "this section right here has the correct feel for this scene." Then the composer can translate the "correct feel" generated by the diminished chord into a musical composition.

The temporary score is invaluable for understanding the pacing, the mood, and the overall feeling that the music will add to the final project. The one problem with temporary scores is that they can become more than a template for the final musical score. Often, filmmakers become so enamored of the cues in the temp that it can be a frustrating experience for a composer who wants and needs to put his or her own stamp on things.

It is important for every person involved to understand that the temp is merely that, a placeholder for music to come. A composer will not want to hear that they should be writing music that matches the temp. They will use the temp to understand the needs of the project, but most composers will not use its cues for "inspiration."

It is important to not only use the temp score for discussion but as a jumping-off point for further ideas. The filmmakers should also have other musical cues at the ready that may not have made it into the temp and yet still contain the feeling or style that is desired. Not all of the temporary cues will fit the editing, but the music can be used for further discussion and enlightenment for the composer.

Choosing Instrumentation

Every aspect of the musical score will have an impact on the energy and feeling of the final mix. The tempo, be it fast or slow, will contribute one feeling. The key signature, be it major or minor, will contribute one type of feeling. The type and genre of music, be it classical or rock and roll, will contribute another feeling. The choice of instruments, whether it is a bamboo flute or an electric slide guitar, will contribute different feelings.

Instrumentation is a key component in defining a genre or style of music. If a piece of music is played on an acoustic guitar, it will evoke a different feeling than a slide trombone playing the same piece. Filmmakers may not know about instrumentation or the different effects that certain instruments have over others, but they will know whether the score should be a piano and violin score versus a drum and bass score.

The temp score will again be a very useful device for discussing the various parameters of the musical score. A filmmaker may like one piece of music but "without the strings" or if it were played faster with a distorted electric guitar. As previously stated, since many filmmakers are not musicians or composers, it is imperative that they listen to and share various types of music that they think is "in the right direction," "has the right feel," or evokes "the emotional quality" of a particular scene.

Many of these considerations won't materialize until a particular piece of music is written and played against the picture. There is something to be said for the intangible quality of marrying music and moving images. Sometimes the oddest elements will work together that "on paper" don't seem to fit. A melody may seem correct, but when played against picture it just doesn't work. Then, experimenting, the composer may try an instrument that seems unlikely, but it just works.

A way of working that is successful for some composers is to write the grand themes and melodies first and get those ideas approved. Then they can try out different arrangements and instrumentations to flesh the composition out. With digital audio and *midi*, modern composers have substantial means at their disposal. Midi, an acronym for *musical instrument digital interface*, is a protocol that sends information to electronic instruments from computers.

Midi revolutionized music when it was developed in the 1980s. It has grown over the years into a very sophisticated musical system. What it allows composers to do is to write a score in midi information. The computer will then play this midi file back into the electronic instrument device that can change from piano to guitar at the flick of a switch.

For instance, a composer can write a melodic theme for a scene. Let's say that it was written with a piano sound. Once the program has recorded the midi file, it will play it back note for note. During each pass of playback, the composer can switch from piano sounds to flute sounds to xylophone sounds to trumpet sounds. Any sound that the electronic instrument offers can be triggered and will play back from the midi file.

Tempos and Key Signatures

Tempo is the speed at which a musical composition is performed. Tempos are denoted by beats per minute (BPM). For instance, a tempo of 80 BPM is a slower tempo than 120 BPM. Composers use tempo for various effects. Slow tempos can be ominous or they can be elegant, and fast tempos can be exciting or frenetic.

Tempos are used to pace music and music is used to pace scenes, so the tempo of music is a key determinant of how the music affects the pacing of any particular scene. Tempos are not necessarily uniform throughout the music. Tempos can change from piece to piece and within any given piece as well. A tempo can start slow and continue to increase in speed to help heighten the emotional intensity of the scene as well as pace the editing.

Key signatures denote the key in which a piece of music is written in. There are major keys and minor keys and other types of key signatures as well. Typically, major keys evoke a feeling of "confidence," "joy," and "resolve," whereas minor keys can invoke a feeling of "sadness," "despair," or perhaps "desperation." Of course, these terms are somewhat arbitrary and also a bit misleading, since a composer can write "happy" music in a minor key and "sad" music in a major key. But in a general sense, these terms are a good approximation of the "feelings" that certain key signatures can evoke.

Key signatures, just like tempos, can change any number of times during a piece of music. The changing of keys within a piece of music is called *modulation*. Modulating a musical cue from major to minor back to major, for instance, can be an excellent mimic of an emotional quality within a scene. Couple the modulations with increasing and decreasing tempos and you have the ingredients for a powerful musical score.

The true power in a film score comes from the skillful combination of tempos, key signatures, and instrumentation. These limitless possibilities give composers the power to vary the qualities and evocations of their musical themes and compositions.

Composer's Agreements

The contribution that the composer makes to the project is different from other departments in that the music can be enjoyed on its own merits without the picture and the other sounds. Soundtrack albums, as they are called, are typically the main themes of a score for a film and are sold at music retailers. Many musical films have spun off major hits, such as *Grease*, *The Sound of Music*, or *Rock 'n' Roll High School*.

The main right that will need to be agreed upon will be who retains the ownership of the music. In *work-for-hire* agreements, every musical idea, song, or score that the composer creates in regard to the project is owned by the producer or production entity. However, if a composer is well established, he or she may be able to retain all of the rights to the music and license its use to the producer or production entity.

Composers can also maintain separate contracts with *music publishers*. Music publishers split the rights with composers and in turn administer the music's royalty collections, usage agreements, and infringement issues and may seek new opportunities for the music to be heard.

It is important to be clear at the beginning of working with a composer about the needs and expectations with regard to the music rights. Do a search online for "composer agreements" and you can find many examples. They can help you understand the various distinctions in music rights discussed here. Negotiate the terms with your composer and then have a new agreement drafted and make it binding. You should have a lawyer write it or at the very least look it over.

Working with Library and Contemporary Music

Motion pictures and television shows make use of library music as well as scored music tracks. Today there are many commercially available music libraries that can be found online. These libraries can be purchased whole by the CD or bought à la carte, track by track.

Since the mid-1960s contemporary music has often been used as an additional musical element in a soundtrack. Typically, these songs are popular songs with lyrics and contemporary instrumentation. The key to using this type of music is in securing the proper rights to use and edit these tracks. The concepts described in this section are

- Music Libraries—Understanding Your Rights
- Contemporary Music
- Music Supervisors and Licenses

Music Libraries—Understanding Your Rights

Today there are countless music libraries that are available as simple downloads. You can audition track after track, search for style, instrumentation, tempo, and many other variables. It used to be that you had to license a complete library or that the tracks that were available were electronic compositions using electronic instruments. Today you can find orchestral cues or exotic instrument cues played by world-class musicians and conductors.

Each library has its own legal requirements for usage. There are numerous libraries that bill themselves as *royalty free*. Royalty-free libraries assign the rights to the purchaser of the tracks or libraries for life. But beware; although they are listed as "royalty free," they are not free in all cases. Be sure to check the fine print for all of the various exceptions to the "free" status of any given library.

Sometimes "free" means that it is free for podcasts or webcasts, but if it is used in a commercially available DVD, for instance, you may have a limited number of copies before a different license kicks into play. Always check what your specific use is and follow that to the letter. You can be held liable for copyright infringement.

Other license schemes are called *blanket licenses*. In general, a blanket license will cover a specific type of programming, television for instance; a territory, the United States, for instance; and a time period, three years for instance. There are many blanket licenses available in limitless configurations, and licenses can also be drafted specific to your needs. Do a simple Internet search on music library rights and you will see the countless variations that are available.

One item is a given, whether the license is royalty free or a blanket license, and that is a *music cue sheet*. A music cue sheet is a listing of the composer, the track title, the usage of the track, the duration, the publisher, and the performing rights organization that the composer has enlisted to enforce the royalty payments. The major performance rights organizations for composers are BMI, ASCAP, and SESAC. Figure 13.2 is an example of a music cue sheet.

Every library is a bit different, but the fact remains that you must be clear about the usage of any particular piece of music prior to using it. There are other rights that are included in these licenses that you should also be aware of. *Synchronization rights*, also known as sync rights, refers to your right to use, edit, and mix a particular piece of music in sync with a moving image. *Performance rights* refers to the right to perform a composition that was written by someone else. There are also other legal terms and rights that may be applicable to your situation.

Do not attempt to navigate the minefield of rights without the assistance of a professional. These are legal matters, and in some cases they can be quite serious. Professionals involved in music clearance know about all of the various terms, rights, and requirements regarding music usage in film or television. There are many things

MUSIC CUE SHEET

| PAGE | OF |
| DATE | |

SERIES/FILM TITLE:

EPISODE TITLE:
EPISODE NUMBER:

AIR DATE:
PROGRAM LENGTH:

PROGRAM TYPE:

PRODUCTION CO. NAME:

ADDRESS:

PHONE:
CONTACT PERSON:

TRACK NUMBER	TRACK TITLE	USAGE	DURATION	COMPOSER	PUBLISHER

USAGE ABBREVIATIONS	
MT	MAIN TITLE
ET	END TITLE
BV	BACKGROUND VOCAL
BI	BACKGROUND INSTRUMENTAL

FIGURE 13.2 Typical music cue sheets contain spaces to include the composer's name, the track title, and the usage

in DIY filmmaking that are truly "do-it-yourself." Legal matters are not one of them. Copyright infringement is a serious legal matter. I recommend seeking out the pros.

Contemporary Music

There are a lot of songs out there. Many of them may exactly express the mood, feeling, and situation of a particular scene in your movie. These songs are easy to find and download, and you probably have a personal library of music that you enjoy. Unfortunately, the same sorts of rights, contracts, and usage fees that were discussed with library music also bind these songs.

The record companies that release these types of songs into the marketplace are very protective of their music. I would not recommend that someone "chance" it. There are countless stories about small filmmakers being sued for illegally using songs. There are some rights that are less stringent than others, such as "film festival" rights or "student film" rights. But using a song from a popular band is generally not a good idea.

One advantage of the Internet today is that there are scores of unsigned and unpublished bands offering their music online. All of the same rules apply regarding rights and usage, with one major difference; it is completely possible to have a new and upcoming band offer you those rights for free. Popular websites such as MySpace, Vimeo, and YouTube have a large and ever-growing selection of music from across the spectrum. You will literally be able to find just about any type of music online.

It is a time-consuming endeavor to listen to endless songs by amateur songwriters and musicians. Much of the music is unsigned and unknown for a reason—the music is just not very good. However, you may be looking for just one small section of a song, and there is a lot out there to choose from.

Don't discount the local music scene either. Perhaps you know of someone in a band whose music you enjoy. Or perhaps you were at a club and heard a new band whose music you liked. These musicians are hungry to get their music out in the world. They would be flattered and maybe even honored that you would want to showcase their music in a movie or television program. Do not, however, simply ask for a recording and use it.

You will still need to clarify, in writing, the exact terms that grant you the right to use this material. You never know; you may just get lucky and happen upon a band that is just about to break big. Spend the time seeking out this new music; there are some very talented newcomers who would embrace a chance at being in a movie.

Music Supervisors and Licenses

Music supervisors are professionals whose main task is selecting and licensing music for motion pictures and television. Music supervisors help select music and will negotiate usage licenses, clearance, contracts, and all of the terms relating to music content.

Music supervisors fulfill a producing function. They are music experts and know about new bands, established bands, and many genres and styles of music. They provide a key role in *music placements.* A music placement is the use of a particular song or composition in a television program or a motion picture. Many bands seek out placements for the exposure the project will bring to the band and its music, as well as the possibly lucrative contracts that are offered.

Music supervisors are experts in the minutiae of contracts, rights, and usage as it pertains to music. They have developed relationships with record companies, record labels, and bands. They are the key individuals who make the deals for each song placement.

Every placement, every contract, and every deal is specific to the music and to the project. A producer or other member of the filmmaking team could act as the music supervisor. However, it is more than just assembling legal papers and bringing music to the table.

Music supervisors have deep relationships and can make difficult deals that others may not be able to. Some bands will not readily license their music. Some bands may ask exorbitant rates for a short section of a song. An experienced music supervisor can call on their contacts and help get better deals for the filmmakers and in some cases make deals that may have not been possible otherwise. They are also excellent dealmakers, so they will work within the budget allotted for music and seek the appropriate music for the budget.

Scoring Software

The advent of personal computers has revolutionized music as much as digital filmmaking. Midi, computers, and electronic instruments have put music creation at the fingertips of anyone with a keypad or a keyboard. The development of these music creation tools has led to quite a few interesting approaches to music scoring for sync picture. The music creation programs discussed in this section are

- Garageband
- Loop Disks and Software Instruments
- Sonicfire Pro

Garageband

Apple's Garageband is a program that makes extensive use of musical *loops* for music creation. Loops are short recordings of music that when placed back to back in a timeline can play back in a rhythmic way. Loops can come in many different types. There are loops of just a bass guitar or just a jazz piano or maybe a harp or an oboe. A loop can also be a full orchestra, a rock band, or just about anything you can imagine. With the advances today in digital audio, loops from all sorts of loop libraries and sources can be combined for unique compositions.

Garageband comes preloaded with a full assortment of loops. It provides a simple and ingenious method for browsing the loops included with the program. Its loop browser breaks into a hierarchy of categories. For example, you could choose, "orchestral" as a genre, then navigate to "strings" and then further refine your search by adding "melodic" and even further by "intense." You would then be brought to a folder of these specific loops for immediate use. Figure 13.3 is an image of the browser in Garageband.

Main categories include: cinematic, jazz, country, world, urban, and rock. There are many others available as well that have different distinctions, for instance, "textures" or "effects." You may also buy additional libraries for Garageband that have many more styles, genres, instrumentations, and moods.

Garageband then provides a timeline that has a key signature and a tempo. You drag the desired loops from the browser onto the timeline to build your composition. It is a multitrack timeline, so you can place drums on one track, bass on another, and piano on another, for instance. You can change the key and the tempo at any point to better suit the composition. Drag and drop and make music!

Garageband also allows you to record midi information to trigger and play back software instruments such as pianos, basses, and guitars. You could "play" one of their software instruments with a midi input device such as an electronic keyboard. You could then record the midi notes into Garageband and move and edit them. That same midi information can be copied and pasted to trigger other instruments. You can also create loop-based sequences that you play along with using a software-based instrument.

Garageband also has a "Movie" project type that allows you to import a video file to play within the Garageband timeline. You could add markers to various important moments in the video and use Garageband to add a musical score and sound effects. Garageband is not designed or optimized for video, and its functions are rudimentary compared to programs that we've discussed such as Final Cut Express

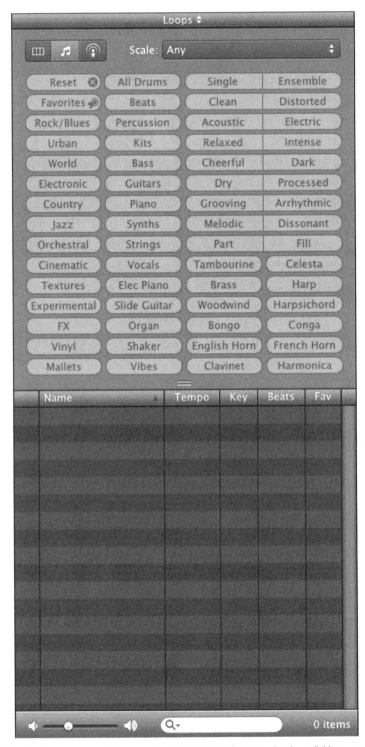

FIGURE 13.3 This image from the Garageband browser shows the range that is available to a composer

■■■ AUDIO PRODUCTION AND POSTPRODUCTION

FIGURE 13.4 In this example of Garageband there are several instrument tracks playing along with a video that plays in the top track

or Pro Tools. However, it is a very clever, intuitive program that can get you creating music even if you've never taken a lesson in music and can't hum a tune. Figure 13.4 is an image of the movie project window in Garageband.

Loop Disks and Software Instruments

Major music creation programs are often referred to as *sequencers*. Sequencers are sophisticated software programs that can playback and record both midi and audio. Sequencers work in the same manner as described with Garageband. It is a timeline that loops and instruments are added to and triggered from. You can drag and drop, rearrange, and reedit all the loops as you see fit. Dedicated software musical sequencers are much more sophisticated than Garageband. Most of these programs usually include advanced video capabilities as well.

One of the main sequencers on the market today you have already been introduced to, Pro Tools. As we've learned, Pro Tools is a very sophisticated audio recording and editing program, but it also can record and playback midi files, has world-class software instruments, and can use loops in a manner similar to Garageband. Figure 13.5 is an image of the piano software instrument that is included in Pro Tools.

FIGURE 13.5 This is a great-sounding software instrument that can be triggered by a full-sized midi keyboard

Other major sequencers include Logic, Cubase, Cakewalk, and Nuendo, among many others. They each offer a feature set that has a particular area of excellence similar to all of the different NLEs that are available today. They all offer video playback as well as multitrack audio capabilities. Some of them have the time-stretching audio capabilities with loops similar in operation to Garageband.

Just like the music libraries market, the loop market is enormous. You can find just about any type of musical loop, bed, or drone imaginable. From otherworldly textures to bluegrass to sweeping orchestral loops, these disks have limitless possibilities for editing and mixing. None of these sequencers will offer the same sort of browser simplicity as Garageband, but with these disks you are not limited to the proprietary Apple file type used in Garageband called "Apple Loops."

There are other advantages to creating music this way besides the incredible variety of material that is currently available. Since it is being used as a musical element within your musical composition you can use any loop as you see fit, with no additional royalty payments. Not every single loop disk on the market has this broad a usage policy, but the vast majority do. You retain all of the rights as a composer to whatever original music you create with these loops.

Inside of these sequencers you can build complicated patterns and textures with these loop disks. You can also input midi into their

■ ■ ■ AUDIO PRODUCTION AND POSTPRODUCTION

respective software instruments and play with those loops in real time with the video, similar to the movie project function in Garageband.

Sonicfire Pro

SmartSound's Sonicfire Pro is a unique program that is sort of a music library with an intuitive interface that is in some ways similar to Garageband. Garageband however, is a music creation program and Sonicfire Pro is a music library. The tracks available in Sonicfire Pro are completely composed pieces in just about any style or genre that you could possibly need.

Sonicfire Pro has a unique interface that allows you to sample and browse music tracks in a manner similar to how you would browse for loops in Garageband. You can use key words such as "orchestral" or "rock" and also define moods and tempos. But what makes this even more unique are several other features. You can easily define a duration for a track. For instance, a track is one minute long, but you only require ten and a half seconds. You can type your desired duration into the program and it will reedit and rescore the music to that length with a new beginning, middle, and end point! You can then just drag and drop this new version of the song into your edit.

The duration feature is impeccably implemented in Sonicfire Pro but they offer an even greater degree of control for their library. They also offer quite a few of their titles as multitrack files. You could then completely remix the track to your liking. You could remove the drums for a section or only use the strings for a section. The possibilities are limitless; they even provide a virtual mixer so you can change the relative levels of any given track within a composition. This is a truly useful and remarkable feature.

The magic of this interface does not stop there. You can "mood map" the tracks as well. Mood Mapping is a proprietary function of the Sonicfire Pro software that allows you to mark certain sections of a track, to better match your video. For instance, you can define the track as "full" followed by "dialog" followed by "bass only." You can define each of these points with key frames in sync with your video file. Sonicfire Pro will rewrite the track magically to match all of the parameters you've added. Figure 13.6 is an image of Sonicfire Pro's timeline with video.

Sonicfire Pro's music tracks, like most music libraries, are available instantly online. Through their browser window your search can include not only the tracks that you've already purchased but also any tracks that meet your specific search criteria online. You can audition the track from your Sonicfire Pro timeline and download the volume of just a specific track. Search for Sonicfire Pro from SmartSound

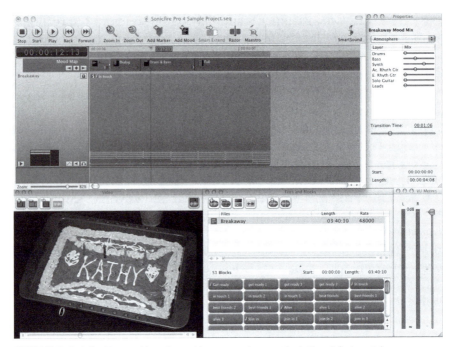

FIGURE 13.6 Sonicfire Pro provides a large video screen, here on the bottom left, to watch as you compose the score

online and have a look at all of their various tutorials. If you need to create a score quickly and with specific elements, hit points, and moods, Sonicfire Pro might be the solution you require.

Fast computers and software technology have revolutionized music creation as much as they have for video and film creation. These tools are powerful for professionals, but they also make it relatively easy for a nonmusician to create original music as well. Today you can literally have an orchestra playback from your computer, playing parts and sequences of your own design. If you've always wanted to make music, loops and software instruments can get you started. The only limit, truly, is your imagination.

Summary

Music in motion pictures and television programs typically starts with a temp score. This score can be comprised of many different sources of music; it will never be used beyond the early part of the composing process. The temp score will map out the desired spotting of the music cues as well as indicate the mood, the style, and the type of music needed. Music serves several main purposes for the project. It can set a tone and mood for a story, it can pace and heighten key moments, and it can move audiences on an emotional level.

Research great composers and see how their music affects the overall experience of a motion picture and television program. Their contribution is immeasurable. When working with composers on creating a score for your own projects, the main concerns are the key emotional qualities that are needed. Then the genre of music, the instrumentation, and the general feel and tempo of the cues are determined.

Music libraries are very useful tools for digital filmmakers who want a world-class score but can't afford the composer and musicians. There are many different types of music libraries available online for immediate auditioning and use. Be sure to fully understand the rights and terms in the music you plan on using.

You might also choose to use popular or contemporary songs as a part of your overall soundtrack. Here again, rights, terms, and usage must be determined and signed into a contract. Music supervisors are excellent sources for finding the right music as well as experts regarding legalities involved with licensing music tracks.

If you are a composer yourself, you can create a score. Today, even if you are not a composer, there is music creation software that is available to make music with. Garageband, loop-based options for sequencers, and music libraries with a software component like Sonicfire Pro make musical soundtrack creation, even for a nonmusician possible.

Review Questions

Questions like these are likely to appear on exams to test how well you understood and retained the information in this chapter.

1. What is a temp score and what is it used for?
2. What sorts of ideas need to be conveyed to a composer regarding composing music for a project?
3. In what ways does music affect a motion picture or television program?
4. What is the role and function of a music supervisor?
5. What is a sequencer and how is it different than an NLE?

Discussion/Essay Questions

Your instructor may assign you one or more of the following questions for discussion in class or as the subject of a paper.

1. How do you discuss musical ideas and strategies with a composer?
2. Why is it important to understand and secure the various rights that are required to use contemporary music in a motion picture or television program?

Applying What You've Learned

Research/Lab/Fieldwork Projects

The following lab exercises will give you practice creating musical soundtracks.

NOTE

Students who have ongoing projects may elect to use their own source material, such as video clips, with the instructor's permission.

1. Create a temporary music score with tracks of your choice.
2. Experiment with different types of music. Try a scene with classical music, and then try the same scene with rock and roll music.
3. Add contemporary songs to your timeline to gauge the effect of how these types of music affect your picture edit.
4. Download music loops from the Internet and create a short piece of music in your NLE or in Garageband if available.

Resources

The following resources have more information on the topics covered in this chapter:

Artist House Music (http://www.artistshousemusic.org/Home). This website is filled with articles and video clip interviews with many top industry professionals specifically working in music today. There are music publishers, music supervisors and composers, and other music professionals speaking at length about their process, their projects, and the music world at large.

Mark Litwak (http://www.marklitwak.com/articles/). Top Hollywood entertainment lawyer Mark Litwak hosts this informative and fascinating website filled with articles about contracts, licensing, and deals specific to the motion picture and television industries. This website is a must read for those who would like to know more about the many legalities involved in the world of entertainment.

CHAPTER 14

MIXING, FILTERS, AND EFFECTS

In this chapter, you will:
- Learn about putting it all together
- Understand effective track layouts
- Discover how to use filters
- Learn the basic concepts of mixing

Putting It All Together

It's been a while since you had microphones attached to actor's bodies and worried about the sound qualities on-set. It's been some time since the dialogue edit, the ADR and Foley recording, and all of the editing and sound designing. The composer has delivered the music tracks and their deal has been made. All of the rights have been assigned and contracted for the popular music. Now, the complete sound edit with all of these elements goes to the rerecording mixer to put it together for the final mix. The following concepts explored in this section are

- Overview of Mixing
- So Many Tracks—What Now?
- Understanding the Delivery Requirements

Overview of Mixing

Final mixing of a project is the balancing of all of the elements that were created and manipulated in post audio to a final set of outputs that will be married to the final picture version of the project. The job of a rerecording mixer requires extensive audio knowledge as well as a wide skill set. Final mixing is where all of the hard work and dedication of the location and post audio teams comes together. This is where room tone, re-creating the quality of the location audio for ADR and Foley, and great sound design and music magically gel into one final, complete form.

The rerecording mixer will use filters such as EQ, add effects such as reverberation, and raise and lower gain levels to focus the correct elements of the mix to the appropriate moments in the project. The ultimate goal of a superior mix is that it is "never noticed, never considered." What does that mean? That means that the mix of the program should be so engrossing, so moving and emotional, so seamless that it would never occur to the audience that the sound was created over days, weeks, and months but instead is a reflection of real time.

This is when the room tones are put to the test. This is the time to see if the ADR is in sync, has believable performances, and blends perfectly with the location recordings. This is when the final music is played with all of the sound elements to see its emotional impact on the scenes. Final mixing is a joyous, frustrating, delicate, time-consuming, and supremely satisfying part of the post audio process. This is it, the end of the line, where the rubber hits the road. You are almost there!

So Many Tracks—What Now?

A final timeline of a sound mix can contain many tracks. Hollywood features will often have hundreds of tracks prepared for the final mix. In fact, most Hollywood feature films won't have one rerecording mixer, they will have three. One mixer will focus on the dialogue and ADR, one mixer will focus on the effects and the Foley, and one mixer will be in charge of the music.

The world of DIY filmmaking is a bit different of course. Just like many aspects of the project, all of these duties may be tasked to one individual. It is quite conceivable that the post sound department consists of a team of one. As this book has illustrated, one person will have to have a very broad skill set to achieve a successful sound edit and sound mix.

One way, particularly if you are understaffed, to achieve a high-quality mix with many tracks and elements is to *predub* the tracks. Predubbing is the process of premixing tracks together to make the mix more manageable. For instance, it may make sense to predub sound effects to fewer tracks if there are many sounds and they have all been approved.

Predubbing is very common. The beauty of digital audio is that you can predub elements and if everything is working properly, you've just reduced the track count. However, if you need to "get inside" of the predub to make changes, you can simply reload the session that the predub was created from and make the fixes there and output the predub again.

In the "old days" of analog audio, each dub was a generation loss. A generation loss means that it is not an exact duplicate but a copy that loses signal in the process. Each dub is another generation, and with it more signal is lost. Today, with digital audio, mixing does not incur additional noise and loss. With the excellent audio practices discussed in this book, most notably proper signal gain, these predubs will be of extremely high quality.

Understand the Delivery Requirements

The final mixes are married to the final picture file when the mix is complete. For television, the mixes are typically laid onto the master. For theatrically released motion pictures the final output is called a *printmaster*.

It is imperative that you understand what the final outputs need to be for the audio for distribution. For instance, one of the delivery requirements could be a stereo mix of the program. Then the elements of that stereo mix can be split out into something called *stems*. Stems, also called *split tracks* or *splits*, are the various elements of a mix that comprise the final mix, for instance, a dialogue-only stem, an effects-only stem, a music-only stem, an M&E stem, and just about any breakdown of the mix that can be thought of. There is no such thing as a "standard" for stems. Every motion picture and every television program will have different requirements.

When the stems are all played together at *unity gain*, the result is a re-creation of the exact stereo mix of the program. At unity gain you are not adding or in any way changing the gain of the actual signal that is passing through a mixing board or a tape recorder; in this case the signal is a recording playing back.

Look at the fader strip of any console. When the faders are pulled down they have turned off the flow of signal. If you bring them up to the "0" on the mixing board, you have set the board to unity gain. If you play a recording through that channel you are not affecting the gain in any way. Stems should be played back together at unity gain to re-create the mix.

What is the purpose of stems and why would you need them? Stems are an important sound delivery for a finished program because they allow the filmmakers to repurpose the program in various ways. Figure 14.1 is an image of a stem mix from a Pro Tools mixing session.

Let's have a look at one purpose for the dialogue-only stem. Perhaps a picture editor needs to edit a trailer for a feature film and only has the fully mixed program to take the edits from. None of the audio will match up for a proper final sound track. If each of the edits had different music tracks from various scenes within the film, there would be no way to fix the audio. The best approach would be to have the separate elements of the final sound mix to edit the new trailer with.

What will happen instead is that the editor will lay the dialogue-only stem to the final edited picture file. He or she will then cut the trailer using that audio track. Once the trailer has been to cut, the editor will lay, perhaps a single music track under the entire trailer to fit the edit. The effects stem may also be used if it is a sound effects–heavy film.

As noted numerous times through this book, the M&E is a key stem for the final mix. When a film is repurposed for foreign delivery, the dialogue stem will be muted, but all of the other stems will be used to create a new mix. Actors of whatever language is required are cast

FIGURE 14.1 In this example of a stereo stem mix, the dialogue, music, and effects are all split from the main mix

to rerecord the voices. Since the muting of the dialogue track can also mute important PFX from the dialog tracks, Foley is recorded to fill those moments.

There can be many different types of stems required. There could be a surround 5.1 final mix file that then could be broken into various 5.1 stems, and further broken into stereo and mono stems from the final mix. The track count of the outputs can get overwhelming. If you think of each 5.1 track as being six mono tracks, *left, right, center, left surround, right surround, low frequency channel,* and each stereo track as being two mono tracks, *left and right,* you can very quickly have a very high track count in the final delivery requirement.

By understanding the delivery requirements, you will be able to determine how to split out the final mix into the stems that are required. The stems suggested above are just a starting point. Sometimes there are foreign languages in a project. They may want you to split out just those dialogue segments onto a separate stem. Sometimes they may require that you send out the ADR separate from the dialogue stem. When I split out a Foley stem, I will typically separate the walking from the other Foley elements. This gives additional flexibility in remixing the stems if needed. You will need to understand the stem requirement to properly edit and route the audio.

Effective Track Layouts

Since there are so many tracks from a final edit, and so many discrete places they must be sent to for proper stem outputs, organization is imperative. You need to be sure that effects are not being sent to a music-only stem and dialogue is not being sent to an effects-only stem. You must be sure to properly lay out the tracks and route them to their outputs or you will not send the correct elements of the mix to the proper stems. The ideas explored in the following section are

- The Organization of Tracks and Audio Files
- Auxiliary Sends and Bus Sends

The Organization of Tracks and Audio Files

It is a pretty straightforward exercise to group and route tracks to the proper places. In a timeline, keep the dialogue tracks together, keep the effects tracks together, and keep the music tracks together. When mixing, you will spend a good amount of time muting and unmuting tracks to seek specific sound files or to check filtering and effects. By keeping a clear organization of the track layout, you will be able to better find what you need.

In the example stated above, where it is requested to separate out a portion of the dialogue stem, in this case the foreign language elements, it is necessary to put that dialogue onto a separate track. You can then send the output from that track to the special stem and not send it to the dialogue stem.

This sort of specialized split is very common in sound mixing stems today. There are so many ways to repurpose programming for so many places that producers want to be sure that they have their audio outputs covered. A foreign language stem mix was needed on a program I mixed for television. In this episode there were people speaking languages on-screen other than English. The producers required a mix of the non-English voices lower so they could overdub an English translation for English-speaking audiences. They required another version where the dialogue level was not lowered to in play Europe with the foreign language mixed at the standard volume.

To be able to do this sort of precise mixing, the audio files need to be placed onto the properly assigned tracks. The tracks then need to be routed to the proper stems and the stems to be outputted according to the particular needs of the program.

Auxiliary Sends and Bus Sends

Auxiliary sends and *bus sends* are the sorts of concepts that can make people's heads spin. Auxiliary sends, also known as auxes, are tracks where signal is sent to be processed and is also then sent to other places. A bus send, also known as a bus, is simply the path or signal flow of a particular signal. Another way to think of it is this: the bus is the place where the signal travels, the aux is one of the places where the signal arrives.

Buses and auxes are one way to split out the signal that you need to create stems. Let's create a stereo mix and some splits to better explain the process. Typically, output channels are referred to by number. Also typically, channel 1 is designated as being left, and channel 2 as being right. If you look at the rear of mix consoles and recording decks, you will see that channel 1 is left and channel 2 is right.

Let's create an eight-track session that needs to be broken into stems. The session is made of these tracks: dialogue 1, dialogue 2, mono effects 1, mono effects 2, PFX, and stereo music. If you send the output of each track to 1 and 2 you will create a stereo mix of all of those tracks. Figure 14.2 is an image from Pro Tools of this example session.

Besides the stereo mix of the program there is a requirement of the following stems: dialogue only, music only, and effects only. You will then send out from buses to auxes the following signal routing: dialogue 1 and 2 and voice-over on one bus to a dialogue-only aux track, mono effects 1 and 2 and PFX to an effects-only aux track, and the music track to a music-only aux track. Figure 14.3 is an image from Pro Tools of this busing scheme.

The tracks in Figure 14.3 are laid out in this manner: the blue tracks are the audio tracks from the sound edit, the yellow tracks are aux tracks, and the red tracks are the record tracks. A concept often discussed in audio is *sends and returns*. The idea is that you will send audio somewhere and then it will return to somewhere else. In this example we are sending audio to auxes, and the auxes are sending audio to the record tracks, or returning the audio to the record tracks.

If you look at the sends for the blue tracks, you can see that each track is being sent to the stereo bus; the dialogue tracks are being sent to a dialogue bus, the effects tracks are being sent to an effects bus, and the music is being sent to a music bus. This is one way to create stems from the original mix. Each track is sending the audio to the stereo bus and then each track sends out the audio to its particular stem.

FIGURE 14.2 In this example buses feed the aux tracks, which then feed the record track

FIGURE 14.3 A closer view of an example of aux and bus routing in a Pro Tools mixer

The outputs of the aux tracks then are sent to the inputs of record tracks. The power of DAWs like Pro Tools is that they can send and record all at the same time. When you hit record on this session, the audio will play back through the auxes, get sent to the record tracks, and then be recorded back into Pro Tools as the mix and the stems, all at once.

This is standard procedure to create stems for those with DAWs. If you only had an NLE but had a stem output requirement, it could still be done. Instead of using auxes and busing to break the mix out into its separate elements, you would simply mute irrelevant tracks for the output. For example, you would play all of your tracks for the stereo mix. You would then mute all of the tracks except the dialogue tracks and output the show again. This would be the dialogue-only stem. Then you would mute all of the tracks except for the music tracks and output the show again. This would be the music-only stem. Outputting in most NLEs is faster than real time so you can create these stems by muting in short order.

Using Filters

During the mixing process filters are used extensively to add, remove, and limit certain noises and frequencies. There are many types of filters available to process audio with. A few, however, are the most common as well as the most useful. The filters discussed in the following section are

- Equalization
- Noise Reduction
- Special Effects

Equalization

EQ has been discussed before in relation to matching new recordings such as ADR and Foley to the original production audio. EQ is a common and useful filter that can be used for many other purposes as well.

EQ alters the frequency characteristics of a recorded sound. It can enhance recordings by boosting, reducing, and removing certain frequencies. But caution must be used in the application of EQ. Digital audio is no different from anything else in life; you may be able to change it, but that doesn't mean it's necessarily for the better. Incorrect EQ settings can alter the quality of the audio by removing or boosting the wrong frequencies.

It can be used to help clarify dialogue tracks by boosting certain frequencies; it can also remove murky or boomy frequencies and help the overall sound quality of a mix. When you have multiple audio tracks playing simultaneously, EQ can help define one track from another by boosting or cutting particular frequencies.

In the application of boosting or cutting particular frequencies there are also a few controls that determine how the boost or cut will be applied. The first control assigns the key frequency itself; the second is the amount of boost or cut, usually described in decibels; and third is the Q, or width of the boost or cut. If the horizontal line is flat, as shown in Figure 14.4, then no EQ processing is happening. When several frequencies are being changed at one time, they are referred to as bands. Figure 14.4 is an example of a ten-band, graphical EQ device.

There are a number of curves available that will indicate how a boost or cut is applied to the assigned frequency range. A *bell curve* is a very common way to apply EQ to a particular frequency. It is an

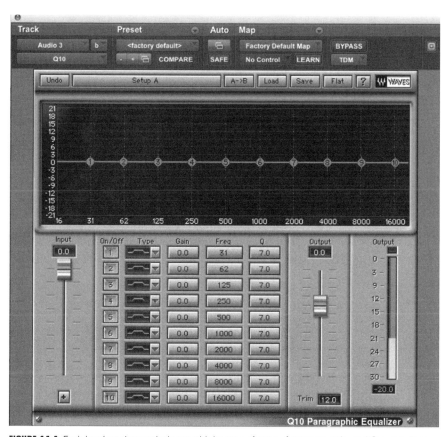

FIGURE 14.4 Each band can be precisely set with its type of curve, frequency, gain, and Q parameters

EQ setting that is shaped like a bell. The Q affects a wide range of frequencies that are near the key frequency. Applying EQ to satisfaction requires a determination of the central frequency to be affected, the size of the Q, and the shape of the curve and the amount of gain that is being cut or boosted. Figure 14.5 is an example of a bell curve.

Another common EQ curve is called a *shelf EQ*. Shelf EQ settings look like a shelf. Various EQ makers implement this differently, and some will apply a slight cut prior to the boost. By the way, these are extreme boosts being applied in these figures to more clearly show the ideas being discussed. Often EQ will be applied at much lower boosts or cuts and at several different frequencies at once. The idea with EQ is generally to do as little as possible to affect the desired change. EQ can easily mangle the recorded audio into something unacceptable. Figure 14.6 is an example of a shelf curve EQ setting.

Another common setting applied with EQ is called a *pass* filter. Pass filters are powerful tools for processing recorded audio. Here are a few examples that might shed light on their particular usage. Perhaps

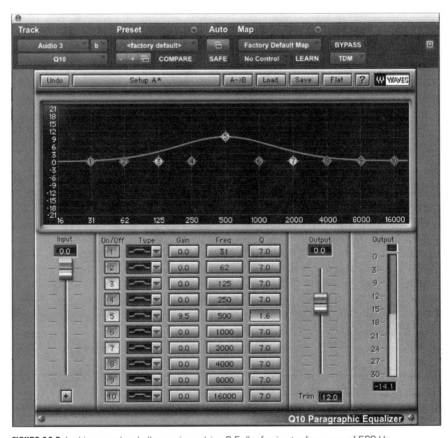

FIGURE 14.5 In this example a bell curve is applying 9.5 db of gain at a frequency of 500 Hz

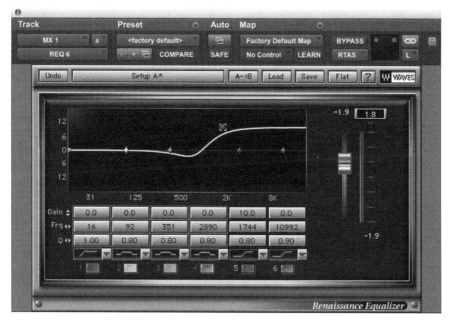

FIGURE 14.6 This example is a shelf curve applying 10 db of gain at a frequency of 1744 Hz

the boom operator had trouble holding the pole and was creating small "boom" sounds during the recording. Often these noises are very low in the frequency range and are difficult to hear without a subwoofer. A high-pass filter may remove all of the noises without affecting the quality of the recording. These filters will remove all of the frequencies at the cut off frequency. Figure 14.7 shows a high-pass and low-pass filter being applied.

Applying both a high-pass filter and a low-pass filter as in Figure 14.7 creates a band of frequencies that will pass through it. The other name for this sort of setting is a *band-pass* EQ, and these are useful in a number of ways. Since band passes limit the frequency range of a recorded signal, they are useful for many things. Many devices such a telephones have a "limited bandwidth," so you can mimic this bandwidth with a band-pass filter.

You may want to try a *notch filter* that can notch out the offending frequency. A notch filter is an EQ setting where the Q is set to a very limited band of frequencies. The idea here is to carve out only the offending frequency and try not to disturb anything else around it. Mix engineers will often "sweep" the notch along that horizontal range of frequencies until the frequency range to reduce or to add is pinpointed. Notches can be very useful in eliminating any type of steady-state noise. Steady is the key idea because if the noise or sound oscillates to other frequencies, then the notch is no longer relevant,

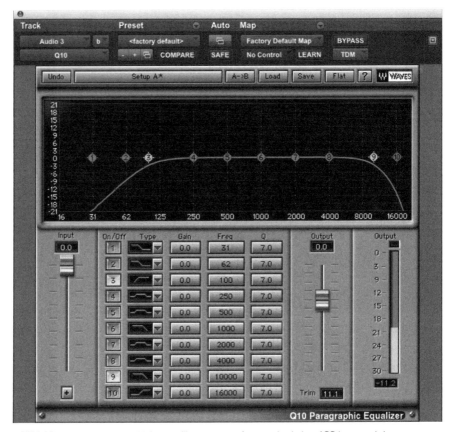

FIGURE 14.7 In this example a high-pass filter removes frequencies below 100 hertz and the low-pass filter removes frequencies above 10,000 hertz

since it is specific to only a narrow range of frequency. Figure 14.8 is an example of a notch filter.

There are no general rules concerning EQ except for one. Typically however, with EQ it is better to make cuts in the signal rather than boosts. By making slight cuts in unwanted frequencies, you will open up all of the tracks in clarity. There can be a tendency of boosting frequencies that in turn leads to more and more boosting. By boosting a particular frequency you are also boosting the gain in general, and that additional gain will have to be reduced somewhere along the line.

Perhaps some of the recordings sound, dull, flat, or a bit "murky," a slight presence boost at 2.5K or 3.5K may help "lift" the voice and a small cut at 300–400 may remove a bit of "boominess."

EQ is an amazing tool with many useful applications and can correct many frequency anomalies. It is not, however, always a solution

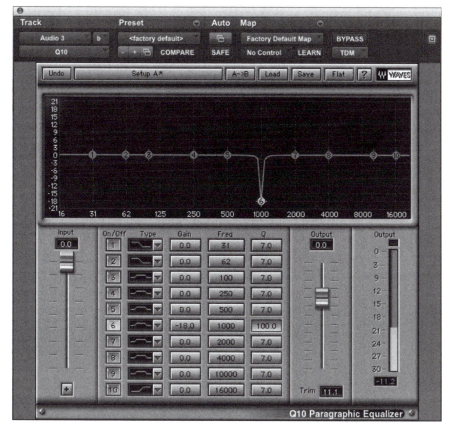

FIGURE 14.8 In this example a notch is removing 18 db of gain with a very tight Q at a frequency of 1000 Hz

for noise problems. It can reduce noise that is in specific frequency bands, but there are "broad band" noises such as air conditioners that cross many frequencies at one time. They usually cannot be notched or pass-filtered out without compromising the quality of the recordings.

Noise Reduction

Noise filters are highly specialized filters that can examine an audio file and remove unwanted aspects from it like noise, hum, and clicks. These devices, which are available as hardware and software can help clean out noisy recordings while maintaining the audio quality of the original recording.

These noise reduction filters are designed to address several key audio problems. *Hum filters* are designed to reduce or eliminate hum in the signal during the recording. *Noise filters* sometimes called *denoisers* are designed to "learn" the noise in the signal and then reduce or eliminate it. Denoisers are designed for broad-band noises. *Click filters* sometimes called *declickers*, are designed to identify clicks in the recording and reduce or eliminate them.

These filters use sophisticated computer technology to analyze digital anomalies in the waveform. For instance, declickers will reduce only the spikes that it sees in the waveform. You can define a threshold that will activate the filter for your particular circumstance.

Spectral analysis is a process that converts a sound wave into an image called a *spectrogram*. This image is an illustration of the sound in a multicolored display. This very advanced form of noise analysis allows you to "repaint" the sound image and reduce or eliminate unwanted sounds. Figure 14.9 is an image of a spectrogram.

Like EQ, noise reduction must be used sparingly and lightly. Often, best results with noise reduction happen with a few light passes rather than one large pass. Noise reduction works by eliminating a part of the signal. It has advanced controls to listen to just the signal being removed. Be aware that "good" parts of the signal could be lost in noise reduction as well as noise. Too much noise reduction also can introduce severe artifacting. It gives the audio a hollow and metallic sort of sound. Be sure to carefully monitor the results so that you are finding the right balance between the signal and the processing.

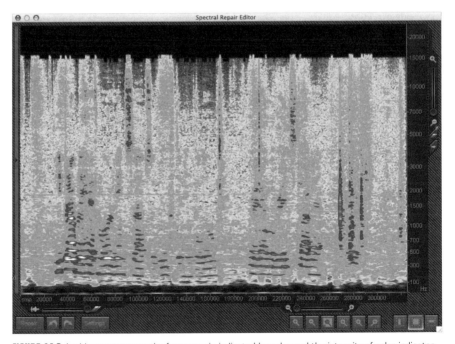

FIGURE 14.9 In this spectrogram the frequency is indicated by color and the intensity of color indicates its amplitude

Special Effects

By using the term *special effects* here I am speaking of devices that audio will be played and processed through rather than sound effects. Effects devices come in many different types. A *delay* unit will cause a repeat of the signal. The amount and intensity of the repetitions is typically user defined.

Reverb devices, as discussed earlier, will add character and dimension to an audio signal by recreating rooms, halls, chambers, and other spaces. Since location audio will have some sort of "room reverberation" in it, reverbs are useful in recreating the space for audio that has been rerecorded such as ADR and Foley.

Reverbs are useful beyond mimicking real spaces. Reverbs can be used in a subjective manner. A proper application of reverb can imply the quality of sound underwater. Or a reverb can be used to have tracks sound very distant, if for instance, a character is feeling ill and the image is fuzzy and they are disoriented. Sometimes a deep and distant reverb is used on audio when a character is remembering sounds from the past. Reverb is a widely used and highly creative tool for sound designers and rerecording mixers.

Some of the other items we've discussed such as EQ can also be used for special effects purposes. For instance, the futz track will essentially be an extreme EQ setting that can limit the band-width of a signal to better mimic a telephone bandwidth. EQ can also be used in these sorts of extreme ways in combination with a delay or a reverb for some of the subjective uses for the story as described above.

Basic Concepts of Mixing

Mixing, like so many other aspects of the filmmaking process, takes time and patience to learn and excel at. You are going to have to mix many projects and listen to them back in various environments to better understand the effect that your filtering and levels produce in different situations. There are also other important considerations such as the mixing space, the equipment used, and the processing applied. These ideas and others explored in the following section are

- Listening
- Mixing Tips
- Other Important Considerations
- Levels, Levels, Levels
- Notes and Changes

Listening

This text began with the idea of developing critical listening skills. Each step of the way, from the location recording to the Foley and ADR recording, from the sound effects to the sound design, your listening skill has been informing your choices. This ever-developing skill, as well as your understanding of the story, the demands and desires of the filmmaker, and your own intuitive instincts guide your decisions in the final mix.

Just as photographers see the detail and the wonder of the world around them, rerecording mixers must hear the detail and the wonder of the world around them, and use that knowledge and experience in their craft. Using the real world of everyday life is an excellent and convenient way to better understand how sound surrounds us in many layers.

However, not all aspects of motion pictures and television represent everyday life. These stories typically present weighty and representative moments, often in extraordinary circumstances. The stories portrayed can have fantastical dimensions, otherworldly dimensions, and even the dimensions of other worlds. These soundscapes are imagined and created for the universe of the story.

With such a rich history, dating back so long and with so many imaginative artists at the helm, film sound is a fascinating and enjoyable research experience. Search the Internet for award-winning films that are noted for their sound and soundtracks. Study these projects at length and use your critical listening skills again. Don't just stick to one genre; try science fiction, thrillers, comedies, and action films. See if there are some sound designers or rerecording mixers whose works you particularly enjoy. Seek out all of their films.

Think of this as research. Use your critical listening skills and don't just get swept up in the story. See if you can better understand how the sound and the mixing are leading you in emotional ways. See if there are subjective moments of sound, such as where the mix emphasizes the ticking of a clock or other intimate sound moments that focus the audience's attention. How does that sort of subjective mixing propel the story ideas in one way or another?

Play those scenes whose sounds impress you most over and over again. Learn how the sound was edited and mixed. Determine if you are hearing Foley or location audio, ADR lines or perhaps some added walla. Dissect these scenes and imagine how the edit looks in a timeline. Imagine how the levels are raised or lowered at various points in the scene. Study from the masters.

Seek out the films of Walter Murch, Randy Thom, Ben Burtt, or Christopher Boyes. Think of the EQ settings that were possibly used. How about the use of reverberation or other effects? Listen to the skillful editing and sound mixing of Murch's *The Conversation*. Listen to the sound design of the animated work of Randy Thom such as *The Polar Express* and compare it with his live-action sound work on *Contact* or on *Castaway*. Listen to the human detail that Ben Burtt creates for *Wall-E* and then compare that with his incredible work on *Munich*. The lessons to be learned from these and other talented sound professionals are as close as the movie theatre or DVD store.

Mixing Tips

Mixing sound is a creative, collaborative endeavor with the filmmaker. The sound mix can define and focus moments in a film to not only better tell the story but also have a deeper emotional impact on the audience.

For instance, there is a scene with a character wearing an armor suit with a helmet. It is a scene of chaos: a bomb has just exploded and there are sirens, people screaming and yelling, and lots of motion. The character is slowly approaching another bomb in an attempt to disarm it. As the scene progresses and the character begins pulling at the wires of the bomb, the mix eliminates all of the elements except for the character's shallow breathing. He peers out at the mayhem and carnage, but all that we, the audience, hear is the breathing.

This focuses us squarely on the task at hand and puts us in the perspective of the character. The mixing process is about defining those moments and using the soundtrack to influence the perceptions and emotions of the audience. These moments will need to be determined with the filmmaker as the mixing commences. They will have been a part of the sound design and editing process, and now the final creative push is in deciding how all of those sound elements blend together to focus the story points and create emotional impact on the audience.

Start the mix with the dialogue track. It is the key track for the overall soundtrack. Add EQ to add clarity to the dialogue tracks and to remove unwanted frequencies. Add reverberation to the ADR and the Foley tracks to better blend them with the original location recordings. Use noise reduction to tame unwanted noise. Finally, use levels and dynamics to create impact and intimacy as the story demands.

Other Important Considerations

There are several factors that can significantly affect the mixing besides the addition of filters and the changing of levels. One of the main influences on how the mix is perceived is the space that the mix is being monitored in. The shape of the room, the items that are in it such as chairs and couches, and the listening angle of the mixer and the client will directly affect the final mix.

Rooms that are not balanced to provide a flat or neutral sound will affect the perception of the audio being played back in that space. The mixer will then make adjustments to alleviate deficiencies that are inherent in the room but may not be inherent in the audio quality itself. Therefore, EQ settings will be made that may adversely affect the final mix when it is reproduced in other settings. If a room has a frequency dip of 2000 Hz for example, the rerecording mixer may add EQ to offset this deficiency. If this is an anomaly of the room, then the EQ setting will sound wrong in other rooms and spaces.

This is a key concept to be understood. Rooms, as we have learned through room tone, are very different from one another. A mixing space should be free of such odd frequency dips and boosts so that the mixer will not be confusing what is heard in the room as an element of the recordings themselves. This is a very common problem when projects are mixed in spaces that are less than ideal.

Another key concept for a good-sounding mix is to monitor the mix through a variety of monitor speakers. At a minimum, have a great pair to act as the main speakers and also monitor the mix through something that would be equivalent to a television set's speakers. Make adjustments on the different speaker sets so that the mix will sound good on both. You will learn a great deal as a budding mixer when playing the mix back on different systems and in different rooms. It will be plainly obvious at that point that further adjustments and refinements will be required to have a mix sound good in a variety of situations.

Another important concept regarding mixing pertains to the monitor level in the space itself. It is also important to listen to the mix at several monitor levels because this too will spotlight other possible problems with the balance and levels. Try to listen to one level through each session. Don't turn the volume up and down as you work but rather work at one level, then come back at a later time and listen a bit lower or higher.

A key concept that often gets ignored is taking breaks. Be sure to take breaks from listening on a regular basis. Ears get used to various frequencies and they can also get tired. Without breaks you will be basing EQ and other choices on improperly heard material. Your ears are your number one resource in sound. Treat them with the respect and the care that they demand and deserve.

Levels, Levels, Levels

As noted, right from the start of production and location audio, levels and gain are a key aspect in mixing. Here it is imperative to not introduce clipping or gain issues with the new mix. In the stacking and playing of multiple layers of sound, it can easily add up to more than the mixing device can handle.

The idea with mixing is to create a strong level that has dynamics so that the mix will alter in intensity and level throughout the piece as the story progresses and changes.

The ideal is to have the final mix play at unity gain and never clip, have good dynamics that matches the dynamics of the story, and have well-blended tracks for a superior sounding soundtrack. If an audience needs to "remix" your program with their remote control, changing the levels to better hear the dialogue or reduce the level of the mix at loud parts, then the mix was not done properly.

When I mix a project, I like to start with the dialogue tracks. I will solo the dialogue tracks to monitor that they blend seamlessly together and that their perspective matches with the shots on-screen. I will also check their overall levels and make sure that they are hot enough to play over competing sources such as sound effects and music. Once I am happy with the dialogue levels I will introduce the other elements of the mix.

Unfortunately, there are no hard-and-fast rules when it comes to levels, be it overall levels or the dynamic range of levels that are proper for a mix. Television mixes that are mastered onto Digibeta tapes will typically be limited to -10 db in the United States. The dynamic range of television programming suffers as a result of this. Mixing film and television is not the same as mixing music, where mixes will typically be set to full scale or peak at 0 db. Remember that this mix will go to other places that may perform more processing on the audio. Give at least a few db of headroom for those other possible processes.

Make it a practice to watch the meters as you mix. You can't depend on the meters alone, but you should not depend on your ears alone either. Find a good balance of verifying levels with the meters and then use your ears to make sure everything sounds great.

Notes and Changes

The final part of the mixing process is playback with the filmmaker making notes and changes. This can be a satisfying and frustrating session. But mostly this is the session where you have to come to terms with the fact that although your contribution has been great, it is still someone else's movie. The filmmaker will have the last call regarding the final levels, the sound effects that are used, and just about any part of the post audio process. This is assuming that you yourself are not the filmmaker.

I mention this because sometimes it is hard to not take a proprietary interest in what you are doing. You certainly will care deeply about the work you've done and probably also have strong feelings and opinions about the work. But at the end of the day, if the filmmaker chooses music over your effects, or decides to go back to the location audio on most of the ADR-recorded lines, there is not much that you can do about it.

You do have a real interest in the project and its outcome, of course, and you should stand up for and fight for things that you feel strongly about. This is just a note of caution, however, since the final choices will most likely rest with someone else. Make your feelings known, but do what is required as a collaborator. This can sometimes be a bit harder than you may imagine.

Summary

If you are at the point of final sound mixing, then you have made it to the end of a very long and complicated road. Sound mixing is where the final choices are made regarding the levels and effects, the music, and the sound design. Sound mixing is where the dialogue gets blended into a cohesive whole and levels and gain are used to spotlight and highlight certain parts of the sonics of the movie.

One of the main elements of rerecording mixing is to take all of the incredible location audio, music, and sound design and create a dynamic, compelling soundtrack. Equally important, however, is to split out the stems of that final mix so that it can be repurposed in a variety of ways. One simple method is using a send and return, bus and aux system to split out the relevant parts of the final mix to individual stems.

While mixing, a number of tools will be deployed. Faders will change gain and levels, and filters such as EQ can reduce troublesome sound issues and add clarity and definition to tracks. Reverberation can be used to help rerecorded tracks blend with the location recordings and can also be used as an effect to create subjective feeling with the sound.

Be sure to keep an eye on your meters as you monitor the mix. The meters will keep your mix within the technical boundaries that have been established for the final mix. It is important to review the mix at various monitor levels as well as through different monitoring systems. It is also important to take breaks and give your ears a respite to better gauge the quality of the mix. Your ears are your final tools to serve you as a rerecording mixer; be sure to treat them well.

Review Questions

Questions like these are likely to appear on exams to test how well you understood and retained the information in this chapter.

1. What is predubbing and why is it useful?
2. What are stems and why would you need them?
3. What are bus sends? What are aux tracks and what is sending and returning?
4. What is EQ and why is it important in rerecording mixing?
5. Why does the room you are mixing in matter?
6. What strategies can you take to better ensure a quality mix?

Discussion/Essay Questions

Your instructor may assign you one or more of the following questions for discussion in class or as the subject of a paper.

1. Describe stem splits and explain a scenario using buses and auxes to create stems from a final mix.
2. Explain a strategy for the mixing session, from working with the client to using mixing tools to outputting a stem mix.

Applying What You've Learned

Research/Lab/Fieldwork Projects

The following lab exercises will give you practice working mixing audio.

1. Route all your dialogue tracks to one track for output.
2. Add reverb to a Foley track to understand its effect.
3. Add EQ to tracks for clarity and experiment with different settings to understand their effect.

NOTE
Students who have ongoing projects may elect to use their own source material, such as video clips, with the instructor's permission.

Resources

The following resources have more information on the topics covered in this chapter.

Bruce Nazarian, MPSE, "Post Audio FAQ's," FilmSound.Org (http://filmsound.org/AudiopostFAQ/audiopostfaq.htm). This is a thorough examination of the post audio process, including mixing. Take particular note of the section detailing Dolby, THX, and DTS encoding and playback technologies.

"Sound for Picture Film/TV," *Mix* magazine (http://mixonline.com/sound4picture/film_tv/). This site gives *Mix* magazine's list of articles that have appeared recently in its pages specifically detailing audio post for film and TV. There are wonderful articles on surround sound mixing as well as ADR and music for film.

CHAPTER 15

OUTPUTTING SOUND AND BACKING UP

OVERVIEW AND LEARNING OBJECTIVES

In this chapter, you will:

- Learn about delivering the mix
- Learn about surround sound
- Discover surround sound encoding and decoding
- Understand the importance of backing up
- Get some final thoughts

Delivering the Mix

You've shot the movie, edited the picture and sound, added sound effects and music, and mixed a great-sounding movie. Now all that's left is to put the new mix onto the final edited master of the project, start sending it out to festivals, and prep for distribution. The ideas discussed in the following section are

- Outputs, Splits, and Stems
- Syncing the Mix to the Edited Picture Master
- Laying the Mix Back to Tape

Outputs, Splits, and Stems

Standard definition television programs will often ask for a series of stems although the master tape of the program may only permit a few tracks of audio to be recorded on it. For instance, a typical standard

277

definition master is a *Digital Betacam* tape. Digital Betacam, also called Digibeta, is a widely used mastering format for material that will be broadcast for television.

The Digibeta format offers four channels of digital audio. As with most recorders, channel 1 is left and channel 2 is right and the remaining two channels 3 and 4 are used for archiving useful stems. One scenario for audio could be: channel 1, left program; channel 2, right program; channel 3, dialogue and narration only; channel 4, mono music and effects.

As discussed earlier, each project will require its own stem outputs. I have had similar scenarios like the one just described except that channels 3 and 4 were instead a left-right pair of M&E. It is good practice to generate more stems than just the four indicated here for instance. Sometimes filmmakers won't understand the need for stems and are only interested in the final mix, be it in stereo or in 5.1 surround sound. Make it a practice to split stems out for them. They may not yet know it yet, but they will likely need it.

The standard, minimum splits that I offer to filmmakers when they do not yet have a firm delivery requirement will break down like this: mix stem, dialogue only stem, music stem, effects stem, music and effects stem. This set of stems will cover their needs in most situations. One word of caution and a reminder about the stem output: The idea with stems is that the individual components, played at unity gain, are an exact recreation of the mix. That being the case, it is important to think about the stems that you've created and possible pitfalls.

For instance, in the delivery scenario described above, if you play the music stem, the effects stem, and the music and effects stem together, then you are adding more than what was the original mix. You need to play back either the M&E stem or the music stem with the effects stem. Playing all of them will not be an accurate reflection of the mix. If you play all of these stems back simultaneously, then you would be playing the M&E track twice, which is not reflective of the final output mix.

Syncing the Mix to the Edited Picture Master

The issue of the final syncing will be dependent on a number of factors, most notably what is the final picture format and what is the final mix format. Some of your mix will be put onto the master, and some of the mix stems may be archived for possible later use.

If you are working exclusively in an NLE like Final Cut Express or Avid Media Composer, then you will probably not have anything to sync. If you've been cutting the audio in the audio timeline of the NLE, then it will simply be a matter of outputting the entire program, both sound and picture, out to a deck.

Another scenario that happens is that a post audio person generates the mix and the final stems are then given to an online editor during the *online* process. Onlining is a video process where the final elements are all put together from the picture edit to do the final mastering on video. Technology is a rapidly changing process for postproduction. It used to be that video files were edited in a lower resolution, to conserve drive space and computer power. This process is known as *off-lining*. Then the online process would reimport all of the original camera tapes at full resolution and regenerate the edit with the original full-quality video. Here the final graphics, *color grading*, and other processes are finalized. Color grading is an artistic and technical process that can change the color values in an image, create better exposure values, and brighten or darken images to set moods. Color grading is also a technical process that sets all of the video values properly before the final output to tape.

If the final mix is being added during the online edit to be output at that time, the online editor will follow the same procedure as when importing the OMF and movie file. The editor will identify and sync the head and tail pops from the mix stems to the newly mastered video edit. He or she will then output the new video and the new audio onto a master tape.

Laying the Mix Back to Tape

Adding the final mix during the online and final video master process can be convenient, and it allows the filmmaker to see and hear the final project in one fell swoop. However, there is another way that the final mix gets married with the master tape, and that is typically done by a post audio facility.

If the final mix and stems were created in a place other than the edit timeline of the picture edit, then the master tape will need to have the audio recorded onto the audio tracks. This process is called audio layback. The DAW that created the final mixes must be electronically synced up with a deck to insert the audio only. Using a protocol called *RS-422*, DAWs can be synced to video decks. RS-422 is a protocol that manufacturers have adopted to connect computers and decks. For video and DAWs, the protocol is used to have decks talk to computers and sync them together. Figure 15.1 is a photo of an RS-422 cable.

In this type of scenario one device is a master and one device is a slave. The timecode is used to sync the various devices together. In a typical professional situation, a DAW such as Pro Tools is locked to a video deck, such as an HDCam, using RS-422. The audio is sent from the DAW, either in analog or digitally into the deck, while replacing the audio track only. Typically the DAW will control the

FIGURE 15.1 RS-422 carries timecode information and sends commands to devices

deck remotely and also arm the audio tracks within the deck to allow for an audio-only recording.

There are also audio-only decks that are used extensively for backups and archival purposes. These are usually eight-track decks that the full mix and splits are laid back to. The most common still in use today is a deck by Tascam called a *DA-88*. A DA-88 deck has eight channels and can use timecode as a syncing protocol. DA-88s use RS-422 to connect between the computer and the deck. Figure 15.2 is a photo of the front of a DA-88 deck.

A DA-88 can also input analog or digital signals. A DA-88 tape will need to be *black and coded* prior to use for audio layback. Black and coding tapes is a process where black video signal, also called black burst, and timecode is laid onto a tape. Then the tape has a standard of reference when it is told what timecode to be at any given point. Without black and coding, the tape will not be able to lock to timecode. Figure 15.3 is a photo of the back of a DA-88.

The DA-88 machine has been a reliable workhorse for many years. Delivery requirements today will still often include a DA-88 stem mix as a line item. Be aware, however, that the machine was last manufactured back in the mid-1990s. It is a reliable technology, but it is also getting a bit old. You may be able to find a used deck at reasonable prices, but be sure that it has digital capabilities. Back then it was a growing trend, today it is a firm reality. Most audio today is

FIGURE 15.2 Although DA-88 tapes continue to be an audio delivery requirement, it is becoming much less common today

FIGURE 15.3 The DA-88 has analog and digital ins and outs as well as word clock, timecode, RS-422 and midi

all digital. Not all of the DA-88 decks were manufactured with digital capabilities.

Surround Sound

Surround sound is a multichannel listening environment for cinema and television that engulfs the audience in sound. Surround sound utilizes many speakers in various configurations surrounding the audience. It is often called five-point-one (5.1), due to a popular surround scheme that uses three front speakers, two rear or surround speakers and one subwoofer that is the "point-one." Typically surround is created in

DAWs, but it can be output using NLEs such as Final Cut Pro, Avid, or Adobe Premiere. The following section will discuss

- What Is Surround Sound?
- Outputting Surround Sound
- Sound Encoding and Decoding

What Is Surround Sound?

Since the beginning of sound for movies there have been a number of attempts and techniques to add multichannel sound to the listening experience. RCA and Bell Labs developed a method in the mid-1930s where they utilized nine channels of audio that were output to nine optical print soundtracks. Although this process had been developed earlier, in 1940 it became known as "Fantasound," when it was used to premiere Walt Disney's "Fantasia" in movie theatres.

Walt Disney wanted better-sounding recordings and playback to accompany "Fantasia." He worked with RCA and several engineers and developed a system where sound would originate as nine optical prints and be remastered onto three optical tracks with a control track that carried metadata. The playback system was elaborate and included dozens and dozens of monitor speakers placed around the auditorium. Ultimately it didn't pan out as a playback standard for film sound, but it was such an impressive audio breakthrough that Walt Disney and RCA won an Academy Award in 1942 for "outstanding contribution to the advancement of the use of sound in motion pictures through the production of Fantasia."

The surround sound that is probably the most commonly available today is *Dolby Digital*. Dolby Digital uses five speakers—left, center, right, left surround, and right surround—for playback, and it includes the low-frequency channel, or LFE, that plays out of the subwoofer. Dolby Digital is built into most DVD players and is the adopted standard for audio as part of the high-definition television specification.

Dolby Digital is widespread, with its decoders built into television sets, DVD players, game consoles, and audio components like amplifiers. You can take advantage of surround-encoded playback with only a stereo output. For instance you could play a Dolby Digital encoded signal from a laptop stereo output. You could then take that output and insert it into a Dolby Digital decoder like an amplifier and it would play back a surround mix.

There are a few other Dolby schemes in wide use today for different applications. Dolby Digital is the standard for television and DVD. Motion pictures can use a process known as *Dolby Printmastering* that creates a special disk that will contain the final mix. Dolby printmastering is for films that will be projected in theatres. There is a special license that is required for this type of Dolby.

Dolby also offers *Dolby E*, an encoding scheme that can take the six channels of audio from a surround mix and encode that onto two channels digitally through AES/EBU cables and connectors. This ingenious encoding scheme allows a digital tape format to carry a number of audio configurations that would include surround, even though it may be limited, such as a Digibeta, to only four channels of digital audio.

In the case of encoding for a Digibeta, you could put the surround mix on channels 1 and 2 and the stereo mix in channels 3 and 4. Or perhaps you may need to include a surround M&E track onto the Digibeta. In that case, you could put the Dolby E surround mix on channels 1 and 2 and the Dolby E surround M&E on channels 3 and 4.

There are several other major surround encoding and playback schemes today. One is a system by Digital Theatre Systems called *DTS*. DTS uses seven monitor speakers and an LFE in its surround system. The other major system is made by Sony and is called Sony Dynamic Digital Sound or *SDDS*. SDDS utilizes eleven monitor speakers and an LFE.

Home theatre systems typically employ a version of DTS or Dolby Digital as a decoding scheme for surround. These systems therefore will be either five or seven surround monitor speakers as well as an LFE. With the advances in disk technology the latest disk called Blu-Ray, has extremely high audio capabilities.

Outputting Surround Sound

Typically, complicated audio mixing that uses surround is moved over to a DAW system for mixing and encoding. DAWs have surround sound capabilities built in as well as a host of surround-specific tools. Most professional audio mixing facilities offer surround mixing and are built to exacting specifications for proper audio playback and monitoring.

Several of the top NLEs also offer surround capabilities. Apple offers some surround sound capabilities in its flagship program Final Cut Pro. As would be expected, the Avid video editing system, also owner of Pro Tools, has surround capabilities as well. Adobe Premiere and Apple's Soundtrack Pro can also be used to output a surround mix. None of this matters much if you only have two speakers, of course!

All of the major DAWs such as Pro Tools, Logic, and Nuendo have surround-mixing capabilities as well as third-party plug-ins that can create Dolby- or DTS-encoded mixes. The Final Cut Pro Suite has a program called Compressor that can take your surround output from Final Cut Pro or Soundtrack Pro and encode the project for Dolby Digital to be used on DVD or Blu-ray high-definition disks.

For outputting multichannel audio in Final Cut Pro you need to go to the Sequence menu. From there you will find the menu item "settings" and it will bring up the settings window. In the settings window click the tab marked "audio outputs." There will be a drop-down menu of presets, one of which will be a surround preset. Load that preset and there you can assign the track output. The tracks can be toggled between stereo pairs or as dual-mono pairs. Figure 15.4 is an image from Final Cut Pro of its surround track assignment.

Now that you've told the sequence that you want to be in a surround mix environment, you can assign the individual tracks in your timeline to the proper output. By right-clicking on the lock icon in the audio timeline of Final Cut Pro, you find an option to alter the output of a given track. Figure 15.5 is an image from Final Cut Pro of the right-click track assignment.

Although these programs do offer some surround routing, unless you have a way to properly monitor your mix you will have to stick to stereo for mixing in most NLEs. Most of us own or have easy access to stereo components in one way or another anyway, which is why most of these programs default as stereo.

Sound Encoding and Decoding

Once you've output your mix, it may still need to be repurposed in other ways. You may need to encode the mix in one of the surround

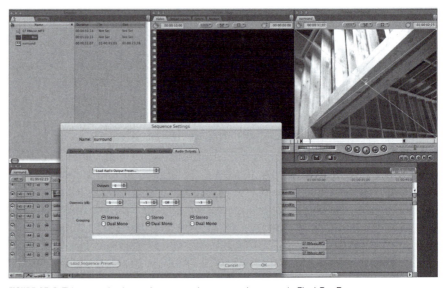

FIGURE 15.4 This example shows the surround output assignments in Final Cut Pro

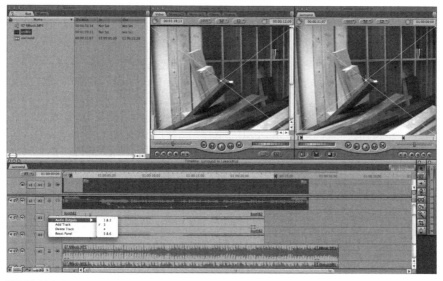

FIGURE 15.5 Right-clicking allows audio assignments in the timeline of Final Cut Pro

schemes already mentioned. For DVD, Dolby Digital encoding is quite common, since its decoder is built into so many of today's entertainment appliances.

Dolby has a whole line of their DVD encoding and decoding audio products now available as software. There was a time when the only way to encode and decode was through their proprietary hardware boxes. This means that most of the Dolby encoding is done faster than real-time. Other programs also license the Dolby technology to support encoding Dolby such as Apple's Compressor, part of the Final Cut Pro Suite of software.

Dolby Digital, also known as *AC-3 encoding*, significantly reduces the mixed audio file sizes. Your audio does not have to be surround to be encoded in AC-3. Stereo audio files can also be encoded in AC-3. AC-3 encoding can reduce the file size to about one-tenth of the original WAV or AIFF mix output. Depending on the media size going onto the DVD, this can be a substantial amount of extra space for the disk.

Whether using Compressor or Dolby's own encoder, be sure to decode the disk and critically check the audio quality. If it is a surround encoding, be sure to listen to it in a different environment than the mixing room to check the quality of the audio. The Dolby Media Tools software bundle allows for immediate decoding of encoded material as well as listening to the various effects that settings can have on the encoded material.

Backing Up

It is essential that after the project is delivered, the sound edit can still be adjusted or changed. A logical scheme must be designed to save the stem outputs and ideally the whole final edit as well. Projects live on long after their initial release. You will need to get back to the mix in case changes are required for a different release or use for the original project. Numerous issues can arise, like the music may need to be changed or perhaps a celebrity will redo the voiceover track. The techniques in this section are

- Backing Up the Stems
- Backing Up the Final Sound Edit

Backing Up the Stems

Backing up the stems should be rather easy. Burn them to a DVD for data archiving. Don't leave stems for an extended period of time on hard drive media. Hard drives will eventually fail, and you will need a better archiving format than hard drives.

Buy quality media when you are archiving your project. Research what the highest-rated currently available media is and use that. You've spent a long time on your project, and you want to ensure, as best as possible, that you are using the most reliable media.

Be sure to have some sort of time reference for the files. A head pop and a tail pop are typically utilized when archiving the final mix stems. Several DAWs will include metadata in their final mix output, such as timecode location. Timecode location can also be added to the metadata of a Dolby encode. After months or even years, it is easy to forget all the nuances of the particular way things were completed. Create a standard that includes a match to the final timecode of the final edited picture master.

Backing Up the Final Sound Edit

The complexity of the backup will depend on your diligence with organization. If you have created a neat series of folders with all of your audio media, then backing up will be as simple as burning a data DVD of those folders. However, as the edit has progressed it may not be quite as organized as it needs to be. You may have dropboxes overfilled and needing some attention.

I highly recommend and cannot stress this strongly enough: *do this organizing now*. There may be little bits of files with cryptic names strewn about on more than one drive, or on more than one media type. Clean up these files and folders now while their importance and meaning is clear. It is quite easy to begin a new project leaving these files unattended. Over time you will forget what all of these things mean and where they should all go. Don't let that happen. It will become increasingly difficult to decipher as time goes on.

If you are using a DAW there may be some additional features to help this process. For instance, Pro Tools has a feature called "save session copy." It can take all of the media that is in the final edit session, no matter if media is spread among different drives and devices, and make a complete, new copy in one place.

If you are doing this as an archival process within Pro Tools, be sure to remove unwanted or unused media from the session first. Anything that gets imported into Pro Tools is considered a part of the session file, whether or not any of the material is actually used in the edit.

Many times, as you edit in Pro Tools, you import sounds and recordings that are eventually not used or are discarded from the timeline as a part of the final edit for whatever reason. Pro Tools has a feature to remove files that are not used in the edit. Once you've removed the unused files from the session, then you can create your new copy of the session. If it is a feature-length project that you've been working on for a while, it is conceivable that there is a lot of media that should be removed. By removing the unused files you can greatly reduce the size of the final archive.

Final Thoughts

Now is the time to enjoy the fruits of your hard labor. Each audio person has a different journey, a different project, different duties and responsibilities, and different experiences. No matter what contribution you made to your particular project, now is the time to celebrate the success of its completion.

We have covered a lot of ground in this text. Each chapter on its own could be a volume or two unto itself. Hopefully, the tools, techniques, and ideas that have been presented here have led you to further exploration and learning. The vast majority of audio professionals will specialize in only one of the many topics covered here. There are professional recordists, who don't mix, professional mixers who don't record, and postproduction audio pros who've never recorded location audio.

In the world of DIY filmmaking it is standard procedure to wear many hats. In the professional world of filmmaking that becomes less true. Learn as much as you can about all aspects of audio. The more a location recordist understands about how their recordings get posted, the better they become. The same can be said for rerecording mixers. A couple of days on-set can be an enlightening experience for someone who mostly works in a sound-controlled, calibrated room.

Now that you've seen the whole process through, you can learn from some mistakes, hone new skills, and venture into the ever-expanding set of digital tools that computers and modern technology give us. Here's to you, working with excellence in all that you do and telling inspiring and compelling stories with your expanding digital filmmaking skills.

Summary

The last part of the post audio process is delivering the final audio tracks mixed to satisfaction and then marrying them back to the final, color-corrected master. There are a number of ways that the mix can be married to the picture, depending on the final delivery format of the master.

Today, motion pictures and television programs are typically mastered to high-definition tape. This will likely be the case for the DIY digital filmmaker. If the mix was prepared separate from the picture edit, then the audio will need to be laid back to the master tape. This can happen either as an audio-only insert recording after the picture has been laid to the master tape or the new mix can be imported by the online editor who will replace the old audio with the new audio and then lay that back to tape.

Surround sound is not only a major element for movies in theatres but also in home audio as well. There are a number of useful surround configurations and encoding schemes for the digital filmmaker. Dolby Digital is probably the most ubiquitous, not only with decoders installed in most televisions and DVD players, but also as a part of the high-definition television specification. Dolby Digital can reduce file sizes significantly while still delivering outstanding audio fidelity.

Once the mix has been married to the final picture and all of the audio stems have been delivered it is imperative to properly archive and store the final mix outputs and also the final edit session. You never know when a filmmaker has either a new creative burst or a pending sale and may need to reedit some or the entire finished project. By having the stems and the edit session readily available, you can be assured that you will have the materials needed if such a situation arises.

Review Questions

Questions like these are likely to appear on exams to test how well you understood and retained the information in this chapter.

1. How does sound get laid back to the final picture?
2. What is RS-422 and why is it important for audio?
3. What is surround sound?
4. What are best practices for archiving the final mix?
5. Why would it be advantageous for a post person to spend time in production? Vice versa?

Discussion/Essay Questions

Your instructor may assign you one or more of the following questions for discussion in class or as the subject of a paper.

1. Describe a typical stem mix and why it is important to have the audio split into various categories.
2. Discuss surround sound on a personal level. How many students have home theatre systems installed? Do you calibrate these systems, do you use these systems on a daily basis and do you monitor and listen to television or DVD with surround sound? Do you find the impact greater than stereo mixes? Why or why not?

Applying What You've Learned

Research/Lab/Fieldwork Projects

The following lab exercises will give you practice working with the final mix outputs and archiving.

1. Generate your final sound mix and sync it to the final picture edit.
2. Import all the stems into the final edited picture timeline.
3. Back up the final mixes in three separate places.

NOTE

Students who have ongoing projects may elect to use their own source material, such as video clips, with the instructor's permission.

Resources

The following resources have more information on the topics covered in this chapter.

Jeff Tyson, "How Movie Sound Works," How Stuff Works (http://www.howstuffworks.com/movie-sound.htm). This article details how analog and digital motion picture audio playback systems work, and it also examines the three major digital movie audio playback systems: Digital Theater Systems (DTS), Dolby Digital, and Sony Dynamic Digital Sound (SDDS).

"QT Movie Exports with Split Track Audio," SuiteTake.com (http://www.suitetake.com/2008/07/13/qt-movie-exports-with-split-track-audio/). This is an excellent article about creating stems with Final Cut Pro and Apple's QuickTime. Be sure to go to SuiteTake's home page as well. There is a lot of valuable information located here.

GLOSSARY

A

AC-3 Encoding: An encoding process created by Dolby Laboratories that significantly reduces audio file sizes while retaining a high-quality signal.

ADR (Automated Dialogue Replacement): The process of rerecording actors' who watch playback of their performances to sync with the picture. ADR replaces production tracks that are noisy or deemed unusable for final mixing. Also known as *looping*.

AES/EBU (Audio Engineering Society/European Broadcast Union Digital Audio Standard): A digital audio protocol that sends and receives digital signal. AES/EBU cables terminate with an XLR connector.

AIFF/AIF (Audio Interchange File Format/Audio Interchange Format): Audio files that are uncompressed and can easily be changed and modified to fit a project's standards without compromising fidelity.

Artifacts: A catchall digital term that indicates a degradation of the original signal.

Audio Controls: A Final Cut Express icon that activates the viewing or hiding of the solo button.

Audio Turnover: The files created by picture editors or their assistants that are needed to start the sound-editing process. All of the media and documentation is turned over to the audio postproduction department.

Audio/Video Settings: A Final Cut Express file menu containing all the settings, presets, and configuration of the audio and video material.

Automation: The process in nonlinear editing of writing processing so it recalls settings and plays them back exactly the same way each time.

Auxiliary Send: A path that allows signal to be split off and routed and sent to various places. Also known as *aux* or *auxes*.

B

B-Roll: The footage used to establish a location, also the additional, non-sync footage that is edited within scenes and interviews.

Back Filling: The process of creating or adding room tone to wherever audio has been removed to make the edit seamless.

Backing Up: The process of saving all the data and the location recordings by transferring it onto another medium such as another hard drive for back up.

Band-Pass: An EQ setting that provides a path for a specific band of frequencies to pass through by limiting the frequency range.

Bed: A background instrumental music track that is played underneath a scene.

Beep Tracks: Tracks that contain three evenly spaced one-frame beeps that cue the talent during an ADR session.

Bell Curve: The bell-shaped EQ (equalizer) setting.

Bins: Special folders inside of nonlinear editing programs used to organize media and files.

Bit Depth: The resolution for the sampling rate in digital audio. The higher the bit depth, the higher the resolution.

Black and Coding: A process where black video signal, also called black burst, and timecode is laid onto a tape. This allows for insert editing on the tape.

Blanket License: A license, available in limitless configurations, that will cover a specific type of programming and that can be drafted to meet any specific needs.

Body Miking: The placement of a hidden wireless microphone on the talent.

Boom Operator: The person who balances and operates the boom pole and positions the shotgun microphone for optimal recordings.

Boom Pole: The long pole that the shotgun microphone is attached to for recording.

Browser: The window on the principal interface of Final Cut Express where all of the imported video clips, audio files, and media are kept.

Bus Send: The path or signal flow of a particular signal. Also known as *bus*.

Burn-in Timecode: The process of superimposing a timecode over the picture file.

BWF (Broadcast WAV Format): A file format created from the WAV file type that has the ability to include metadata such as timecode information.

C

Calibration: The process of using a standard of reference to adjust audio levels uniformly from deck to deck or from medium to medium. Tone is commonly used as the reference for audio in filmmaking.

Canvas: The window on the principal interface of Final Cut Express where you can create, watch, and hear playback of the edit sequence.

Capture: To digitize material.

Clapper: A slate that has a wooden bar across the top that creates a loud clack and is used to sync sound and picture in post when shooting in double-system.

Click Filter: A filter designed to identify the clicks on an audio recording and reduce or eliminate them. Also known as *declicker*.

Circle Takes: Take numbers of recordings that have been circled to indicate that they are the preferred take for that line or recording.

Clip Overlay: The icon in Final Cut Express that allows you to toggle the red lines on and off from viewing.

Clipping: The result when signal is recorded louder than the recording device can support, producing an unpleasant recording that does not retain all the characteristics of the original sound. Also referred to as *distortion*.

Cloth Pass: The mimicking of the sounds of the characters' clothing by Foley artists as they follow action in a given scene.

Color Grading: An artistic and technical process that can change the color values in an image, create better exposure values, and brighten or darken images to set moods. It also verifies that all of the video values are properly set before the final output to tape.

Commercial Music Libraries: Libraries that offer many types of fully produced professional music tracks and license their use at reasonable rates. The music typically can be auditioned online and downloaded for immediate use.

Condenser Microphone: A type of microphone that is sensitive to sound, is low noise in operation, and needs additional power to operate.

Coverage: All the various angles and shots being captured in order to offer a good range of possible edits.

Crossfading: The process of fading an audio clip in while simultaneously fading another audio clip out.

Cutting Sync: Editing an ADR take to match the sync of the location recording.

D

DA-88: A deck by Tascam with eight channels that uses timecode as a syncing protocol, can input analog or digital signals, and uses RS-422 to connect between the computer and the deck.

Decibel (db): A unit of volume measurement in digital audio that indicates how loud things are in the digital world.

Decibel Full Scale (dbfs): A scale of measurement where 0 db is the absolute peak level of the digital audio signal. Measured in the minus range or below the full scale of zero.

Declicker: See *click filter*.

Delay: An audio special effect that causes the signal to repeat with as much intensity as desired.

Deliverables: The necessary material compiled by the producer, such as tapes, film, contracts, scripts, sound reels, signed releases, contracts and agreements etc., that must be delivered in order to distribute the final project.

Denoiser: See *noise filter*.

Digital Audio Workstation (DAW): A computer-based audio recording, editing, and mixing system.

Digital Betacam: A standard and widely used mastering tape format developed by Sony.

Digital Clock: A device that sends sample timing information, called word clock, to each digital device for their precise operation.

Digital to Analog/Analog to Digital (DA/AD): Converter boxes that convert audio from digital to analog and back again, they can be input/output (I/O) devices that can get audio to and from a DAW and come as part of a DAW software/hardware package, usually of a very high quality.

Digitizing: The process of changing the state of media such as audio, video, photos, etc. into a digital file.

Directional: A polar pattern that has a very tight pickup with good side rejection that also picks sound up from the rear.

Distortion: An overload of electrical signal with either too much gain or too much signal for the recording device to handle. Also known as *over-modulation*, *clipping*, *saturation*, or *peaking*.

Dolby Digital: A surround sound system that uses five speakers: left, center, right, left surround, and right surround for playback and includes the low-frequency channel or LFE that plays out of the subwoofer.

Dolby E: An encoding scheme that can take the six channels of audio from a surround mix and encode them onto two channels digitally through AES/EBU cables and connectors.

Dolby Printmastering: A process that creates a special disk that will contain the final mix for films that will be played in sync with film projected in theatres.

Double-System Sound: The process of recording audio on a separate device from the device recording the images. This was the standard process for many years in motion picture film production.

Drones: Powerful sound design or musical elements that are used in many types of projects. Drones are typically low-pitched and played in a continuous manner underneath a scene.

Dry: Describes a sound that contains no additional processing by effects such as reverb, delays, or echoes. Typically, sound effects are recorded as dry as possible to allow the rerecording mixer to add the desired amount of reverb or effects. Also see *Wet*.

DTS (Digital Theatre Systems): A surround encoding and playback scheme that uses seven monitor speakers and an LFE in its surround system.

Dynamic Microphone: Microphones that do not require additional power and are excellent for recording loud sources but are not powerful enough or accurate enough to record properly on-set.

Dynamic Range: The ratio of the lowest (softest) to the highest (loudest) values of sound, measured in decibels. Described by a single number, the larger the number, the better the dynamic range.

E

Embedded OMF: An audio file type that contains all of the metadata and digital audio files in a single file. It will include the entire audio timeline of audio clips, panning, and volume automation, etc., from in point to out point of an NLE.

ENG (Electronic Newsgathering): A mobile production team with a single camera operator in charge of shooting and lighting and a single audio person in charge of microphones, levels, mixing, and recording.

Equalizers (EQ): Audio filters that alter the frequency characteristics of a recorded sound by cutting or boosting frequencies.

Extras: Actors who perform in the backgrounds of scenes and have nothing to do with the characters or the plot.

F

Fader: A controller, typically a slider, that controls the amount of signal being sent from one place to another.

Flash Frame: A pure white frame of video that is edited into black and when played in sequence will "flash."

Flow: The path that the signal is moving through.

Fill: The process of using room tone to cover the spaces in the production tracks to fill moments of unintended true silence or to cover unwanted sounds in the production tracks.

Filters Tab: A Final Cut Express folder that contains all the filters that can be changed or applied to the video or audio content.

Firewire: An advanced protocol computer connector that carries picture and/or audio information and also sends control information to decks or cameras to remotely fast-forward, rewind, set in and out points, and play tapes to digitize them. Firewire does *not* come standard with all computer types.

Fisher Boom: A device used to maneuver the boom remotely with levers and pulleys and is typically operated from a dolly platform.

Foley: The re-creation and rerecording of all of the human sounds in a motion picture or television program.

Foley Artist: A highly skilled performer who mimics the action on-screen and recreates the sounds produced by that action.

Foley Stage: Generally, large rooms that hold many different types of props and also have various surface coverings on the floor, such as concrete, wood, carpet, tile, linoleum, or dirt, to be used for recording Foley for both distance and recording perspectives.

Frame Accurate: Picture editing that accurately matches, frame by frame, and is in sync with the audio tracks.

Frequency Analyzer: A device that examines a recording and displays the characteristics of its frequencies.

Futz Track: A track that contains heavily filtered audio.

G

Gain: The amount of signal that is provided by a microphone amplifier in a mixing board.

Gain Staging: The signal flow moving through different stages of gain.

Guide Track: The final temporary mix that was created by the picture editor before the movie file was exported.

H

Handles: In digital audio and video editing, the media before and after an edit point.

Hard Effects: Sounds that sync to specific action on screen such as a door slam, a knife cut or gunshots.

Hardware Controllers: Devices that look like mixing consoles but offer other features beyond a standard mixing device such as operating DAW software, start and stop, and play and record; they may also include a system for monitoring the sound and accommodate microphone inputs.

HDcam or HDcamSR: A high-resolution digital high-definition master that can play at various frame rates and offer additional audio tracks.

Head Pop: A one-frame audio pop with a corresponding one-frame video image used for syncing purposes. They can be a white flash or the word "start" played two seconds prior to the first frame of picture. Also see *Tail Pop* and *Two-Pop*.

Headroom: The range of audio level from the SOL to the maximum level before clipping.

High Definition: **HD.** Digital television or video with a higher resolution and quality of audio and video than the traditional standard definition.

Hit Points: The significant musical moments in a show's soundtrack that accent the mood of the scene or can pace the scene to its ultimate conclusion.

Hum Filter: A filter designed to reduce or eliminate the hum in a signal during the recording.

Hypercardioid: A polar pattern that has a tight front pickup with good side rejection and a small rear pickup.

I

Impulse Responses: Snapshots of the particular characteristics of a given space. A device will capture the reverb quality of a space when a short, quick sound is created in the space.

Input/Output (I/O): An interface system that allows connection and integration with video and audio decks as well as integrated hardware controller devices.

Inserts: Access points in the mixing console that allow for software or hardware devices to pass between the signal playing from a track into the final mixing track.

ITunes: An audio player developed by Apple with the ability to play and convert audio files.

J

Jam-Sync: The system that calibrates the timecode generated by one device to all of the other devices, such as other cameras or the location audio recorder, so that each is operating with the same timecode.

K

Keyframes: A mechanism for automating parameters in nonlinear editing. Also known as *rubber banding*.

L

Lavaliere: A very small condenser microphone that is well suited for video production recording because of its size, its great flexibility in mounting and hiding, and its excellent sound recording ability.

Leader: A motion picture countdown, timed in seconds, that is used to sync audio and video.

Level: The measurement of a signal's strength.

Limiter: A device built into recorders, cameras, and mixing panels, etc. that limits the recording signal when set to a particular threshold.

Lined Script: A version of the shooting script that has been drawn with vertical lines, notated with the take names of scenes that have been shot in that part of the script.

Linking: The process, in nonlinear editing, of defining the tracks to automate together. Typically two mono files will be linked together to become a stereo pair.

Location Audio: The sound that is recorded on-set during production.

Location Recordist: The main audio person during production that determines the equipment, the crew, and the proper requirements needed for each shot and for each shoot. They will own, rent, or acquire the tools needed to record the audio for the project. They will troubleshoot, interface with the director, work with the actors and director of photography to find optimal microphone placement, and create optimal recordings. Also known as the *location mixer*.

Locked Picture: The final edited picture ready for the audio post to begin.

Lock: An icon in Final Cut Express that sets the tracks in a state that prevents any additional changes to be made.

Loops: Short recordings of music that can play back in an appropriately rhythmic way when placed back to back.

Lossy Compression: The compression process that throws away portions of the signal while retaining quality.

M

Marked Script: A copy of a script being recorded that is marked with the appropriate take numbers next to each scripted line.

Master: A program's final output consisting of the final audio mix married to the final picture.

Master Clock: A clock that serves as the master source of word clock for all of the digital devices linked together. Also known as the *house clock*.

Metadata: The data about data: information about a particular device, recording, or program. An MP3, for example, may include metadata such as the artist name, the song title, and perhaps the album title.

Meters: Measuring devices that display the visual rendering of the levels of signal that are being recorded or played back.

Midi (Musical Instrument Digital Interface): A protocol that sends information to electronic instruments from computers.

Modulation: The changing of keys within a piece of music that can effect its emotional quality.

MP3 (MPEG-1 Audio Layer 3): A lossy compression version of a PCM file (WAV or AIFF).

Music and Effects (M&E) Track: The final mixed track that only contains the mixed effects and the mixed music tracks and is devoid of all dialogue elements.

Music Cue Sheet: The worksheet used by the composer to note down each musical track's title, usage, duration, publisher, and performing rights organization to enforce the royalty payments.

Music Editor: The person in charge of finding music that matches the emotional quality of the scenes who creates a temporary musical score in collaboration with the editor and/or the director. The music editor is also the key liaison between the composer and the post audio team.

Music Placement: The procurement and licensing of a particular song or composition for a television program or a motion picture.

Music Publisher: The administrator of royalty collections, usage agreements, and infringement issues for a composer's music. The publisher also seeks new opportunities for the music to be heard.

Music Supervisor: Professionals whose main task is selecting and licensing music for motion pictures and television. They help select music and negotiate usage licenses, clearance, contracts, and all of the terms relating to music content.

Mute: The feature on a DAW or NLE system that turns off the audio for any one track or recorded file during playback.

N

Noise Filter: A filter designed to "learn" the noise in the signal and then reduce or eliminate it. Also known as a *denoiser*.

Nonlinear Editing: (**NLE**) The editing system that provides random access to all of the media files to be edited without having to fast-forward or rewind as with tapes.

Notch Filter: An EQ setting that sets the Q to a very limited band of frequencies by carving out and removing only the offending frequency.

NTSC (National Television Standards Committee) Television: The television format standard that has a frame rate of 29.97 fps, used in the United States, Japan, South America, and several other countries.

O

Oeuvre: The body of work of a composer.

Off-Line: Describes a process where video files are edited in a lower resolution than the original recordings to conserve drive space and computer power.

Off-Mic: Describes an instance when the sound source is not hitting the microphone element in an ideal way for its particular polar pattern, making the sound muffled, uneven, noisy, or low. Also know as *off-axis*.

Omni-Directional: A microphone polar pattern that picks up sound equally from all sides.

Online: Describes a video process where the final elements are all put together from the off-line picture edit to complete the final mastering on video.

Open Media File (OMF) Interchange Format: An audio file type that is used extensively in audio postproduction for moving audio and from NLEs to DAWs.

P

PAL (Phase Alternating Line) Television: The television format standard with a frame rate of 25 fps that is used in Europe, Scandinavia, Australia, and several other countries.

Panning: The mixing process of moving sound from speaker to speaker for various effects; the movement of sounds across the sound field, often used to follow the action on the screen.

Pass Filter: An EQ filter that removes all of the frequencies at the cutoff frequency.

PCM (Pulse-Code Modulation) Recording: A recording protocol that can create several different audio file formats to be played back on standard equipment.

Performance Rights: The right to perform a composition that was written by a different person.

Phantom Power: The 48-volt current of power that is sent along the microphone cable to operate the electronics inside the condenser microphones.

Pickups: Recordings of extra picture and sound material that is needed to complete an edit.

Plosives: Clips or "pops" on a recording caused by expulsions of air when some consonants, for example *b*, *t*, and most particularly *p*, are spoken into a microphone.

Predubbing: The process of premixing tracks to make the mix more manageable.

Prelapping: The editing technique where you hear the incoming sound of the next scene before the picture appears.

Printmaster: A motion picture film's final output, consisting of the final audio mix married to the final picture.

Production Effects (PFX) Track: An edited audio track that is created during the dialogue edit; the track contains non-dialogue production effects that were recorded on-set in sync with the picture.

Protocols: Required standards for computers to communicate with one another. The connector and the "language" manufactured to interconnect different systems together. Not all protocols require hardware components. One of the most widely used protocols today is the hypertext transfer protocol, also known as *http*.

Pro Tools TDM: A professional DAW used worldwide that can run on Windows or Apple computers.

Proximity Effect: The exaggeration of the low-end frequencies of the voice that make it sound "warmer," "richer," or "fatter."

Polar Patterns: Diagrams that indicate how a particular microphone picks up sound. Some microphones will pick up sound from the front and reject sound coming from the sides, other microphones can pick up sound from all sides. It is important to choose the correct polar pattern to record the sound properly.

Postproduction Supervisor: The crew member in charge of all of the planning, budgeting, and updating in postproduction. This person creates the postproduction schedule, hires and supervises the personnel, and sees the project through to the final edited master; also is typically in charge of all of the deliverables for audio and video.

Pull Up/Pull Down: A mechanical method that is used to reconcile the speed/length differences between footage or programs of different frame rates. Before fast computers made this less of a concern, devices were sped up or slowed down to create the match.

Q

Q: An EQ (equalizer) setting that defines the width of the boost or cut.

QuickTime Media Player (QT): A versatile audio/video player developed by Apple used to view and convert many different types of audio and video files.

R

Rerecording Mixer: The sound crew member responsible for the final mixing of the soundtrack in collaboration with the filmmakers and who is also responsible to output the audio deliverables for a given project. Also known as *postproduction audio mixers*.

Reels: A container that holds film for projection in theatres; film reels typically hold fifteen to twenty minutes worth of film per reel.

Rendering: A process in nonlinear editing that creates special files to allow for real-time playback of many complicated edits, effects, and processes shaping the media of the edit.

Reverb: Reverberation. The effect that results when a sound persists after it is no longer being produced. This occurs when the sound hits objects and walls before returning to the listener.

Room Tone: The sound of the natural ambience of a particular space that is being recorded. Room tone has no talking, no movements, and no sound other than the ambient sound of the space itself. Also referred to as *room noise*.

Royalty-Free Library: An audio library of music or sound effects that assigns the rights to the purchaser of the specific tracks or libraries for life.

RS-422: A protocol that manufacturers have adopted to connect and electronically sync and control audio and video between computers and decks.

S

Safety Take: An additional take of a line to ensure that the line was recorded properly.

Sample Rate: The number of times a digital audio device takes samples of a continuous signal.

Script Supervisor: The production crew member responsible for catching any continuity errors, noting the duration of each take, and logging the action of the take and whether the director indicated a take as good or not good. For the sound department, the script supervisor works with the production sound mixer to make sure that each sound take has a proper slate and that it matches the picture slate.

SDDS (Sony Dynamic Digital Sound): A surround encoding and playback scheme that utilizes eleven monitor speakers and an LFE.

Sends and Returns: The system of sending audio somewhere so it may return to another place.

Sequence Settings: Final Cut Express presets for new sequences determined by the media used in the edit.

Sequencers: Music creation software programs that can playback and record both midi and audio.

Session: In audio postproduction, the editing file type for Pro Tools software. Sessions, in audio, typically refer to any work being done, i.e., a recording session, an editing session, an ADR session, etc.

Shelf EQ: The EQ curve that looks like a shelf.

Shotgun Microphone: A highly directional microphone that has excellent rejection characteristics.

Signal: The actual material/electricity that is moving through microphones either wirelessly or in cables and ends up on a tape or media such as drives or disks.

Signal to Noise Ratio (S/N or SNR): The ratio difference between the signal being recorded versus the noise that is also in the audio or created by the device while recording or playing back the audio.

Slate: The process of verbally stating and recording the scene, take, and other important notes, such as the date, time of day, what is being recorded, or any other valuable information during location audio recording.

Solo: The feature on a DAW or NLE system that allows only one track or recording to play back at a time.

Sound Design: The process of adding sound elements to embellish and heighten the experience of the locked picture edit, creating the sonic world envisioned by the director and by the picture editor.

Sound Designer: A professional sound engineer who is tasked with creating special sound elements such as otherworldly sounds, nonhuman sounds, or other noncompositional sounds and sound effects during the postproduction process.

Sound Tab: A Final Cut Express folder that contains all the mono and stereo audio material.

Sound Utility Person: The general assistant for the sound crew that helps the mixer and the boom operator in whatever way is needed.

Source Buttons: Icons in Final Cut Express that direct the program where to place the media being added to the timeline.

Specifics: The specific props that are being handled for during a Foley recording session.

Spectral Analysis: The process that converts a sound wave into an image called a *spectrogram*.

Spectrogram: An illustration of a sound in a multicolored display created by spectral analysis.

Split Mono: Stereo tracks that have been broken into two separate files instead of one stereo file.

Split Tracks: See *Stems*.

S/PDIF Sony Philips Digital Interface: A connector that looks similar to an RCA connector.

Spotted: The exact timecode where any one particular element is placed.

Spotting Session: A meeting where the sound editor watches the final edit of the picture with the director and editor to discuss the sound in very specific terms.

Stand Alone DAW: A stand-alone *digital audio workstation* that has no additional computer and contains almost everything you need for the DAW in one hardware box.

Standard Definition: The standard of television since it was invented.

Standard Operating Level (SOL): The operating level for a given purpose that in the United States is commonly –20 db, which means there is 20 db of headroom in the level.

Stems: The various elements of a mix that comprise the final mix. Also known as *split tracks* or *splits*.

Supervising Sound Editor: The audio postproduction member who oversees and takes a project through audio post.

Surround Sound: A multichannel listening environment for cinema and television that engulfs the audience in sound by utilizing many speakers in various configurations. Also known as five-point-one (5.1).

Sweeten: To add audio elements to an edit to enhance the soundtrack using sound effects, additional dialogue, or any other additional tracks.

Synchronization Box: A device that syncs other devices, most often video and audio decks, together with the DAW. Also known as a *sync box*.

Synchronization Rights: The right to use, edit, and mix a particular piece of music in sync with a moving image. Also know as *sync rights*.

T

Tabs: Labeled folders in all Final Cut Express windows that organize content.

Talent: An entertainment term that refers to the performers.

Tempo: The speed, denoted by beats per minute (BPM), at which a musical composition is performed.

Temporary Score: An impermanent score created from bits and pieces of already-produced music tracks that serve as the score until it is replaced by the final, composed tracks.

Timecode: The number of frames in film or video depending on the frame rate.

Time Compression Expansion (TC/E): A tool used to shorten or expand time on any particular audio clip without changing the pitch of the audio; it is typically found in DAWs.

Timed Script: A script that has each line of VO script notated with a timing of its duration in the temporary picture edit.

Timeline: The window on the principal interface of Final Cut Express where you place all of the video, audio, and stills and is the main place to complete the bulk of the editing work.

Tone: A 1000-hertz sine wave signal that is used to calibrate gear; an unwavering, occasionally annoying sound.

Track List: The documentation of what audio element is being assigned to what tracks.

Track Names: Numbered labels for the video and audio tracks in Final Cut Express.

True Diversity: A term used to describe wireless microphone systems that include an additional antenna to maximize the connection between the transmitter and the receiver.

Two-Pop: A standard pop in postproduction placed two seconds before the head or at the tail of a project that allows for easy syncing of the movie file and help identifying sync problems.

U

Unity Gain: A term that indicates that the device signal is passing through, a mixing board or a tape recorder, is not adding or in any way changing the gain of the actual signal.

Uncompressed: The state in which an original recording or file has not been changed from the original.

Unprezzing: The process of changing the standard definition file into a high-definition file or converting a stereo mix to a surround mix.

V

Video Tab: A Final Cut Express folder that contains all the video material.

Viewer: The window on the principal interface of Final Cut Express where you can watch or listen to audio and video clips and set inputs and outputs to each clip.

Volume Automation: The feature on nonlinear editing and digital audio workstations that allows changing and saving the volume level of audio clips.

Voice-Over (VO): Spoken narration that reveals concepts and ideas to move the story forward.

VU (Volume Unit) Meter: A classic metering scheme used to measure analog audio signals.

W

Walla: The background murmuring and indistinct words of extras recorded with voice-actors in an ADR session. Walla is useful in many different types of scenes such as restaurant scenes, outdoor scenes, and any scenes where a lot of actors are located.

WAV/WAVE: Waveform Audio Format. Audio files that are uncompressed that can easily be changed and modified to fit a project's standards without compromising fidelity.

Waveform View: A way to view the audio recordings in a timeline with NLEs and DAWs.

Wet: Describes a sound that contains a lot of additional effect, such as reverbs or delays. Also see *Dry*.

Wild Audio: The term used to describe sounds, dialogue, or effects that are generally not in sync with the picture or scripted.

Windows Media Player (WMP): Software, developed by Microsoft Windows, that can play and convert many different types of audio and video files.

Wired Connection: A connection from a microphone attached to a cable that reaches all the way to the mixing board or the recording device.

Wireless Connection: The connection that uses a microphone attached to a transmitter to send the signal out via radio waves wirelessly to a matching receiver that is then hardwired into the mixing board or recording device.

Work-for-Hire: A type of agreement between composers and producers that states that every musical idea, song, or score that the composer creates in regard to the project is owned by the producer or production entity. Work-for-hire agreements are not limited only to work performed by composers, but can apply to any contributing crew member.

Word Clock: The digital clocking information that is sent through cables from device to device.

Worldizing: A term created by Walter Murch designating the technique of amplifying sound elements through speakers in a real-world environment and then recording the resulting playback.

X

X-Track: The extra audio track used by dialogue editors to place audio elements that may or may not be used in the final mix.

XLR: A three-pronged connector, either male or female, that is commonly used for audio purposes, most often for microphone connections.

INDEX

final output preparation, 93
  timecode, 58
25 fps, 41
28 Days Later, 187
29.97 fps, 41
  final output preparation, 93
  timecode, 58, 59
Two-pop, 98, 135

U

Unedited music tracks,
  137–138
Unique locations, 78
Unique sounds, 77–78
Unity gain, 257
Universal Studios, 218
Utility audio assistant, 45

V

Video settings, 111
Video tab, 110
Viewer (Final Cut Express),
  102, 103, 109–111
Vimeo, 245
Vinyl LP, dynamic range, 37
Voice-over (VO), 161
Voice-over recordings, 161–176
  changing things, 169

keeping in time, 173–174
microphone choices/setting
  levels, 163–164
recording cleanup, 174
recording space, 162–163
replacing temporary voice-
  over, 172–173
script marking, 164–165
session, 170–171
technical considerations,
  171–172
timed narration recordings,
  166–169
timed script, 167–168
wild lines, 166
working with talent, 171
Voice-over track, 157
Volume automation, 128
VU meter, 30, 31

W

Wall-E, 4, 204, 271
Walla, 186
Walt Disney, 282
WAV, 92
Waveform, 90
Waveform view, 172
Wet, 209

Wild audio, 74–75
Wild lines, 166, 186
Williams, John, 239
Wind, 52
Windows computers, 126
Windows Media Player
  (WMP), 92
Wired microphone, 23
Wireless microphone, 24–25,
  49–50
Wireless microphone systems,
  24–25
WMP, 92
Work-for-hire agreements, 242
World clock, 127
Worldizing, 4

X

X track, 156
XLR connector, 85
XLR plugs, 30
XLR three-pronged connection,
  23

Y

YouTube, 245

Z

Zero crossing, 39